Occasional papers on scriptural subjects

Benjamin Wills Newton

Nabu Public Domain Reprints:

You are holding a reproduction of an original work published before 1923 that is in the public domain in the United States of America, and possibly other countries. You may freely copy and distribute this work as no entity (individual or corporate) has a copyright on the body of the work. This book may contain prior copyright references, and library stamps (as most of these works were scanned from library copies). These have been scanned and retained as part of the historical artifact.

This book may have occasional imperfections such as missing or blurred pages, poor pictures, errant marks, etc. that were either part of the original artifact, or were introduced by the scanning process. We believe this work is culturally important, and despite the imperfections, have elected to bring it back into print as part of our continuing commitment to the preservation of printed works worldwide. We appreciate your understanding of the imperfections in the preservation process, and hope you enjoy this valuable book.

OCCASIONAL PAPERS

ON

Scriptural Subjects.

BY

BENJAMIN WILLS NEWTON

LONDON
THE SOVEREIGN GRACE ADVENT TESTIMONY
SECRETARY
9 Milnthorpe Road, Chiswick, W.4.
1866.

73237

CONTENTS OF No. IV.

		PAGE
I	Thoughts on Practical Sanctification	1
II.	Jacob's History in Genesis xxix., &c.	18
III.	On the Song of Solomon, from Chapter v. 2 to Chapter vi 3.	30
IV.	On the Song of Solomon, from Chapter vi. 10 to end	39
V.	On Leviticus x.—The Sin of Nadab and Abihu	50
VI.	The Judgments of the Court of Arches, and of the Judicial Committee of the Privy Council, in the Case of the Rev ROWLAND WILLIAMS, D.D, one of the Writers in the Essays and Reviews—Considered	
	Introduction	65
	Section I. Remarks on Dr. Lushington's Judgment	71
	II. On the Judgment pronounced by the Judicial Committee of the Privy Council	91
	Appendix A. Note on Mr Wilson's rejection of the Doctrine of Eternal Punishment	111
	B. Doctrine of the English Reformers on Baptism	117
	C Dr Pusey and his "Eirenicon"	124
	D. The future of Israel ignored by the Modern Maintainers of Catholicity	146
VII.	Salvation by Substitution	149
	Appendix I. Dr. Steane on Imputed Righteousness	172
	II. Clarkson on Imputation	179
	III Extracts from Bishop of Ossory on Justification	184
	IV. Note on the Doctrines of Mr. Irving	188
VIII.	Notes on the Greek of Ephesians i., verse 12 to end	196
IX.	Notes on Psalm lxviii.	217
X.	Notes on Psalm lxxxiv.	236
XI	Postscript.—Note on "Ecce Homo"	253

Thoughts on Practical Sanctification.

NATURALLY, (as has been elsewhere observed) we are criminals in relation to the Courts of God's judgment, and unclean in relation to the Courts of His worship—having, therefore, no title to approach God in peace, much less to serve Him as the priests of His sanctuary: yet the moment we are brought through faith (even though that faith be feeble) into connexion with the one Sacrifice, we are both "justified" and "sanctified," (Rom. v. and Heb. x.)—and that for ever. "Sanctified," says the Apostle, "by the offering of the body of Jesus once:" and again: "by one offering He hath perfected for ever them that are [so] sanctified." By our Substitute's meritorious suffering and obedience in life and in death—means which the wisdom and love of God appointed, God's governmental righteousness has been vindicated, His wrath appeased, and every claim of His holiness *satisfied*. "We owe" (I quote from one of the Puritan writers) "we owe unto God a double debt; first, a debt of obedience; and if that fail, secondly, a debt of punishment. And both these hath Christ freed us from first, by obeying the will of His Father in every thing; and secondly, by suffering whatsoever was due to us for our transgressions."[*] Thus, the double claim of God's holy Law is for ever *satisfied*. Everlasting immunity from wrath and abiding reconciliation and peace with God are the necessary results of this satisfaction. Yet reconciliation and peace are not the only blessings conferred through Christ on the justified. In further attestation to the worthiness and excellency of that eternal Person who obeyed and suffered in the stead of His people, God hath been pleased to admit the justified into a love and favour like to the love and favour that He bears towards His Son. This is sufficiently taught in the memorable words· "Thou hast loved them as thou hast loved Me." Already that love and

---

[*] See Sibbes, "The Church's Riches," Vol. iv. p. 501. Also Archbishop Ussher, "Incarnation of the Son of God," (Works iv. p. 591 and 505)

favour rest upon us; already, as a consequence thereof, life is given unto us in Him risen; and soon we are to be changed into His heavenly likeness in glory, then to have powers communicated to us to know and to serve Him perfectly—all being the result of the imputation of the merits of Him by whose obedience we were "constituted righteous."

The new Covenant of grace, therefore, and all the blessings that are given under it, are founded on the dignity and excellency of that Divine Person who "gave HIMSELF for us." The excellency of the Person of "the Son" is the great central fact, whence all the characteristic blessings of the redeemed, like rays from the centre of light, emanate. Our salvation hath been accomplished by the vicarious obedience and vicarious suffering, in life and in death, of no less a Person than Immanuel. It is He who hath glorified for us God's holy Law by keeping it fully, and by bearing its curse. It is Immanuel who, by the one oblation of Himself once offered, did on the Cross present unto God a full, perfect and sufficient sacrifice, oblation and satisfaction for the sins of all His believing people. On this finished oblation rests our *justification* as described in the fifth of Romans, as well as our *sanctification* as described in the tenth of Hebrews. Both are alike finished and complete; for the work on which they are founded is complete. Our title to draw nigh in peace into the Holiest of all rests now, and will rest for ever, on the righteousness of Another that has been once and for ever sacrificially presented for us. Our title to stand in God's holy presence in everlasting peace is as complete now, whilst we are *not* personally perfect, as it will be in glory, when we *shall* be personally perfect: for that title rests, in time and in eternity, on the same basis—the sacrificial work of our Substitute finished on the Cross. It rests on something altogether external to ourselves—something that is to be viewed altogether apart from any of the results that may be, by God's sovereign grace, wrought, either in us, or upon us, whether at the time when we first believe, or afterwards. The sanctification spoken of in the verse, "sanctified by the offering of the body of Jesus Christ once," is a sanctification that admits neither of increase nor of diminution. Like justification, it is as complete at the first moment of our Christian course as when that course ends in glory. It depends not on any *continuous* work or service even of Christ. It depends solely on the work which He finished once and for ever on the Cross. Our *title* to approach God in peace, whether in the Courts of His judgment or in His Sanctuary, rests, and will for ever rest, not on any change wrought *on* us; not on any righteousness, or holiness, or obedience wrought *in* us, or *by* us; but, solely and altogether, on a righteousness wrought out for us by Immanuel in the days of His flesh. His meritorious obedience for us in life and in death (for He was obedient unto death, even the death of the Cross), forms that righteousness, by the imputation of which we are "constituted righteous" before God. And seeing that they, who have this righteousness imputed unto them, are counted precious according to the preciousness of the righteousness that is imputed to them; and seeing that the preciousness of that righteousness is measured by the infinite value of that eternal Person, whose righteousness it is; it follows, that they, to whom it is imputed, are not only justified, but stand under the value of all the merits of Immanuel for ever and ever. And thus, whilst Imputation is the sole ground of their justification, it is also the sole ground of their subsequent blessing. The redeemed in glory will trace all the blessings, all the joys, all the glories, every gift that God's love and goodness bestows upon them in the ages of eternity, entirely and solely to the imputation of the merits of the Lord their Redeemer; whose merits being infinite, the blessedness is also infinite.

One of the great gifts of God to them whom He is pleased thus to justify is *life*—life suited to His own presence in glory. It is not such life as Adam had when first created, happy and innocent, in Paradise; for that life, though perfect in its kind, and suited to the condition of one who was "of the earth, earthy," was not suited for that glory which "flesh and blood cannot inherit." Therefore, in Christ, who from everlasting was, and unto everlasting shall be, "the living One," ($\dot{o}\ \zeta\omega\nu$ Rev. i.) God hath given to the redeemed, new and heavenly life. At present, this life, as to its fulness, is "hidden with Christ in God," to be communicated to us in all completeness when He returns. In the meanwhile, it is imparted to us measurably here; and therefore, we read of "the new man created according to God in righteousness and true holiness" (Eph. iv. 24): and again, "the new man which is renewed for knowledge after the image of Him that created him" (Col. iii. 10). These words evidently teach, that that which is thus imparted to, and "created in" us, is something entirely *new*; as different from all that pertains to us naturally, as the last Adam, who is heavenly, is different from the first Adam who was earthy. Whilst therefore, the justification and sanctification that come in virtue of the one finished offering on the Cross secure to believers an abiding *title* to draw nigh in peace, even into the Holiest of all; so the creation of "the new man" in them and the superadded and concomitant gift of the Holy Ghost as the Paraclete, to dwell in them, supplies us with an *ability* equally abiding, to draw nigh and to worship and to serve. And thus that other promise of the new Covenant—"I will put my laws into their mind and write them in their hearts," is fulfilled: for wherever "the new man" is, there the laws of God are on the heart written; and "the new man" is wherever faith in Jesus is.

By the creation then of "the new man," and the indwelling of the Holy Spirit, there is implanted in all believers an abiding power of practical sanctification. They *may* indeed greatly repress and hinder that power. They *may* grieve that Holy Spirit "whereby they are sealed unto the day of redemption." Yet still, seeing that it is a power bestowed, because of Christ, under "the everlasting covenant" of grace, it is a gift that is never withdrawn, even from the most unworthy of the family of faith. The development may be greatly hindered, yet the power remains. Nevertheless, though development may be obstructed, it never can, in the case of any true believer, be altogether wanting. There are certain developments that must, more or less markedly, be found in all believers. One of the especial objects of the Epistle of John, is to mark these *necessary* characteristics, in order that they, in whom such characteristics are altogether wanting, might not be recognised (whatever their profession) as really belonging to the fold of Christ. By nature, we are essentially and habitually "doers of evil;" "lovers of the world;" "walkers in darkness;" but when brought to God by means of the gospel of His grace, we become habitually and essentially "doers of good;" "lovers of God;" "walkers in the light:" evidence of this, more or less distinct, being found in our practical ways. Once, we walked in the world's path, and followed it with full purpose of heart: now, we have entered another way—the *narrow* way, and to that way we belong, even though we may stumble in it or walk with halting step. Two practical evidences especially noted in the Scripture as belonging to all true saints, are, first, the having love towards all the family of faith *as such;* secondly, readiness to forgive the trespasses of others *if there be repentance and confession.* They who love not the brotherhood of faith, or who refuse to forgive the trespasses of others, when repented of and acknowledged, do not, we are told, "know God," and are not to be numbered amongst the forgiven. And although, whilst we remain in fallen flesh, we are not delivered from the strugglings of indwelling sin, and are therefore unable to keep with perfectness that holy Law in which, according to "the new man," we delight; we are, nevertheless, enabled so far to resist the law of sin in our members as to prevent its bringing forth its fruits unto death: nay more, we are enabled to render fruit unto God, imperfect indeed, but real—"acceptable to Him through Jesus Christ." Every branch in the true Vine that is altogether fruitless, will not be recognised by the Father as rightfully belonging to the Vine. Such a branch is the symbol of a mere professor. It will finally be "taken away."

Yet, even living branches differ greatly both in the quantity and character of the fruit they bear. It may be scanty and ill-ripened; or more abundant and mature. Fruit has not always its proper beauty and bloom. As in natural, so in spiritual life, there are many things that may hinder development, even where the power of development is. In a new-born babe, there may be the elements of great physical and intellectual strength; but time, nurture, and care, are needed to secure the due development. When first created anew in Christ Jesus, we are neither "fathers," nor "young men" in Him. We are "little children"—babes needing "the unadulterated milk of the Word, that we might grow thereby." Progress is the law of our new condition. That which is justly expected of us is, that we should "grow in grace, and in the knowledge of our God and Saviour"—that we should "grow up into Him in all things which is the Head, even Christ." Growth, increase, advance, are always spoken of in the Scriptures as the right, though not the inseparable characteristics of a Christian condition. The Corinthians and the Hebrews ought not to have halted, or rather retrograded as they did. Yet their retrogression did not take from them that saintship which was given to them, and preserved for them, in and through *Christ*. They were truly sanctified by faith in Jesus, even though their growth and progress in the ways of Christ were stayed. Yet they *ought* to have answered to the desire of God concerning them: they *ought* to have grown. If it had not been the desire of God that all His redeemed people should attain a condition of ripeness and maturity here, (and maturity implies growth) we should not have found the Thessalonians addressed in such words as these: "Now the very God of peace sanctify you wholly, and I pray God your whole spirit, and soul, and body be preserved blameless unto the coming of our Lord Jesus Christ. Faithful is He that calleth you who also will do it."*

"Spirit, soul, and body," are the three constituent parts of man's natural being. Without attempting any vain metaphysical disquisition, intruding into things we know not, it is sufficient to observe that Scripture asserts, and our own consciousness proves the existence of "soul and spirit," as the two constituent parts of our inward nature —distinct, yet so closely connected, that their union, like that of joints and marrow, is used in Scripture to denote a connexion that is virtually inseparable. When the Scripture speaks of "*the spirit* that dwelleth in us lusting unto envy," and tells us that "he who ruleth well *his own spirit* is greater than he that taketh a city," and when the Apostle expresses his desire that the *spirit* of the Thessalonians might be preserved blameless, it is evident, that in these and like passages, (such as 2 Cor. vii.) our own natural spirit is designated; for the

---

* Words in some respect similar to these are found in the Epistle to the Corinthians. "God is faithful by whom ye were called into the fellowship of His Son," &c. In both cases the faithfulness of God to His people is referred to; but the use that is made of that truth, in its application to the respective circumstances of the Corinthians and Thessalonians, is not the same. Nothing perhaps illustrates more forcibly the difference that may exist between true believers in respect of progression in truth and holiness, than the contrast between the practical condition of the saints at Corinth, and those at Thessalonica. The Corinthians, instead of progressing in faith and holiness, had grievously retrograded. They had cost the Apostle many tears. He resolved, under God, to bring them back to the way from which they had wandered; and to this end he reminded himself and them of the grace that had been given them in Christ Jesus, and of the faithfulness that would establish them unto the end "*uncharged* ($ανεγκλητους$) in the day of the Lord Jesus Christ." Observe the word "uncharged." It is a forensic word implying the non-imputation of guilt; denoting, therefore, not practical condition, but judicial standing. The Apostle does not use of the Corinthians the practical word "*blameless*" ($αμεμπτους$). He could not say that they were *blameless*: on the contrary, they were most blameable. All that he said was that the faithfulness of God would preserve them "*uncharged*," that is, free from the imputation of guilt until the end. In the case of the Thessalonians, on the contrary, he expressed his assured conviction that they would be "sanctified completely," and "preserved blameless." "Now may He himself, the God of peace, sanctify you completely; and may in entireness, your spirit, soul and body be preserved blameless at the coming of our Lord Jesus Christ. Faithful is He that calleth you who also will do it."

For further observations on the contrast between $ανεγκλητος$ and $αμεμπτος$ see "Notes on Greek of Romans i." page 110, as advertised at end of this volume.

Holy Spirit, as being God, one with the Father, and the Son, cannot be spoken of as being either "ruled," or "cleansed," or "preserved blameless." Man's natural spirit, like every other part of his original being, has, since the Fall, been brought thoroughly under the mastership and control of indwelling sin. It is morally the servant of that φρονημα σαρκος, that "mind of the flesh which is not subject to the law of God, neither indeed can be." Proud, vain, irritable, restless, often vigorous and energetic, it dwells within us, a living source of misery and sin, ever ready to show its affinity with worldliness and evil, but having no instincts toward holiness—no tendency toward God. Reflection will soon teach us how easily our spirit can be roused to unholy anger, or have its jealous pride awakened—how soon its selfish sensitiveness can be touched—how easily it is attracted and fascinated by the seductiveness of evil—how aided by imagination (than which there is no faculty of the natural heart more dangerous) it ranges throughout the universe, interested in every thing except that which is of God. Even when action is impossible, or by the deliberate resolve of the soul rejected, the spirit can still unholily amuse itself by luxuriating in scenes that fancy paints, or excite itself by desires that are impracticable, or torment itself by regrets that are vain. We speak of a proud spirit, an irritable spirit, a wounded spirit, and the like—expressions that plainly show how conscious we are that there dwells within us something that feels rather than thinks; and by its energy gives an impulse to the soul, as the soul meditates, deliberates, and *resolves*. It is the part of the body to carry such resolve into effect. Thus action is *perfected;* and by the nature of such action, men, who see only outward appearances (for God only knoweth the heart) form their notions of character.

When we are first brought, through the Gospel, into the fold of Christ, we little appreciate either the strength of the evil that is in us, or the strength of the evil that is around us. But as we follow on in the path of faith, experience begins to teach us its lessons. We find ourselves engaged in a warfare in which we have to cope not only with foes without the walls of our citadel, but also with a wily and restless enemy within. The success we hoped for is found, perhaps, but sparingly to attend our efforts, and sometimes attends them not at all and even when successful against the enemy without, we may find ourselves far from successful against the enemy within. Even when the tongue, that member of the body which is so peculiarly the servant of the hasty impulses of our spirit, is duly curbed; and when the soul is carefully watched as to its deliberate purposes or counsels, yet our spirit in its tendency to wander, fret, rebel, and the like, may be very imperfectly controlled. Even right objects may be sought with undue precipitation; and desires not in themselves evil may be indulged under wrong conditions. The longing of the Apostle Paul to visit his nation in Jerusalem, was not in itself a wrong desire; but to resolve on gratifying it contrary to the express direction of the Holy Spirit, was disobedience to God. If his spirit and his tongue had been duly restrained, he would not, on the impulse of the moment, have unwittingly said to the High Priest, "God shall smite thee, thou whited wall;" nor would the disagreement betwixt himself and Barnabas have engendered a contention so sharp as to be called in Scripture παροξυσμος. Nor is it merely a question of resisting the impulses of evil. If the tongue and the other members of our body are to be restrained from evil, it is with the further purpose of their powers being rendered unto God. The lips that are restrained from speaking falsehood and evil may be caused to speak for truth and for God. The soul which, naturally, under the power of sin, cherishes only purposes of evil, may, under the power of God, be made the seat of purposes of good. Our natural spirit, whose vigour and activity may have infused energy into a life of evil, may have its activity "bridled" and so brought under a new control. The natural powers of a believer though still obstructed by the strength of indwelling sin, are no longer under its dominancy. A new and greater power is placed within us, whereby a capacity is given for restraining our evil and for rendering our energies unto God. "His own divine power," says the Apostle, "has been given to us in all things *that pertain to life and godliness*," 2 Peter, i.* Yet *to have* power is not the same thing as to use it. Nor will he who uses it *most*, attain to any thing more than a qualified perfectness; as far removed from the absolute perfectness of Christ, as heaven is distant from earth. Indeed, one of the chief elements in a blameless conversation is habitual self-judgment and confession. He whose spirit, soul, and body, are most preserved in blamelessness, will be most in the habit of recognising and confessing the failures, weaknesses, and short-comings of every passing hour. Absolute perfectness, except in Immanuel, has never been found on earth; and therefore, however great our watchfulness and obedience,

---

* See note on this Passage, in "Occasional Papers," Vol. I., No. I., p. 103

blamelessness (which, be it observed, is not sinlessness) can never be attributed to us here, except our watchfulness and obedience be accompanied by self-judgment, confession, and constant recognition of that blood which cleanseth us from *all* sin. Nowhere is our need of that blood more manifest than when we seek to walk in the paths of light; for nowhere does sin appear more heinous than when detected *there*. And it must, by the honest conscience, be detected there: for, "in many things," says the Apostle, "we all offend." The elements of darkness, therefore, that are in us and in our ways, must, by approach unto the light, become more manifest.

To walk in well-pleasing before God must be the chief present object of every one who is truly wise with the wisdom that cometh from above. Yet there are difficulties to be encountered. With hearts like ours, in a world such as this is, it cannot be easy to maintain a right relation to truth and falsehood, holiness and sin, God and Satan. It is not easy to watch the restless activity of our *spirit;* or to determine aright the resolve of the soul; or to control the actings of the body. We have the sinful *ignorance* of our hearts to contend with as well as their wilfulness. Yet that it is possible to be preserved in blamelessness is evident; otherwise, the Apostle would not have said to the Thessalonians: "faithful is He that calleth you *who also will* do it." There are difficulties; but then we are taught to say unto God, "my Father, thou art the guide of my way." In Him we have to do with One who is gracious, slow to anger and of great kindness—One who is not extreme to mark what is done amiss—One with whom there is forgiveness that He might be feared—One who, in Christ, hath provided for us an Advocate, an Intercessor—a Bishop —a Shepherd and a Friend—One also who worketh in His people, able to do "exceeding abundantly beyond what we ask or think." To Him the Apostle thus commended the Hebrews. "Now the God of peace (that brought again from the dead Him who is the Shepherd of the sheep, the great Shepherd, by the blood of the everlasting Covenant, even our Lord Jesus Christ) make you perfect in every good work, to do His will, working in you that which is well-pleasing in His sight through Jesus Christ, to whom be glory for ever and ever. Amen" It is in passages like these that faith finds her encouragement to press onwards.

In human life, a wise parent seeks to act *objectively* on the heart of the child whom he is training. He draws forth love by showing love; wins confidence by inviting it, and by taking care never to disappoint it. He seeks to awaken his child's interests by setting before him objects of interest: he draws forth and develops his energies by employing them; and acts on his hope by presenting objects of hope. Whilst careful to direct by precept and advice, he seeks also to animate and encourage by promise and reward. So is it in the methods of God. After placing within us the power to worship and to serve Him, He acts *objectively* on our hearts, by setting before us the sure blessings with which His grace has inalienably endowed us in the Son of His love. Take, for example, such a verse as this:— "Now He that stablisheth us with you in Christ, and hath anointed us is God; who hath also sealed us and given the earnest of the Spirit in our hearts." Such are the assurances by which God cheers and encourages the hearts of His people. How could a believer advance in sanctification, if faith and hope and love languished in his soul? And how could they but languish, if God, as a covenant God of grace and promise, had not presented Himself to us, through Christ, as the fixed unchanging object of our confidence and rest? The soul cannot prosper unless the great constituted *objects* which God in His holy Word presents to our faith and hope, are kept habitually before us. Introversion of the soul upon itself will not strengthen; nor when the heart is not acted on objectively, will meditation, or even precept, avail. Exhortation and precept have their place, and a most important place in the school of Christ; but if hortative be *substituted* for declarative ministry—ministry, I mean, declarative of the fulness of God's grace towards His people in Christ, the result, to the true in heart, will be weakness and discouragement—not strength. To direct the souls of God's people to the precepts of the Gospel without due reference to that which His grace has for ever provided in Christ, is as if we were to send forth an army with carefully prepared instructions how to march and where to find the foe, but unprovisioned—no bread provided—no water by the way.

Suppose we find one of our fellow-believers painfully struggling against the sin that dwelleth in us. We may fitly, no doubt, exhort him to continue the struggle. But shall that be all? Shall we not accompany our exhortation with the assurance that he is struggling against an enemy already conquered? Shall we not tell him how God who knoweth thoroughly the heinousness and abomination of indwelling sin ("sin in the flesh," as it is called in Rom. viii. 3) hath already so visited it with judgment in the Person of our sinless Substitute, that not a shadow of its guilt remains to us imputed?

Shall we not remind him that the condition attained for us above the heavens by our risen Head and Representative, is one of perfect freedom, not only from the guilt of sin, but also from its presence—nay more, that it is a condition of life according to the Spirit in all perfectness, and power, and glory; and that this condition, being already ours *representatively*, is soon to be ours *actually*—that it is secured for us under covenant that cannot be broken? Shall we not tell him also how, even here, our "old man"—another name for "sin in the flesh," is so far practically nullified that it never can re-assert its old dominion over us, nor prevail to prevent (however it may obstruct) our acceptably serving God? Exhortation, accompanied by assurances like these, is not the exhortation of direction merely (direction is not all that the soul requires) it is exhortation that brings with it encouragement, comfort, and joy, strengthening us for our pilgrimage and militancy.

Such, accordingly, is the character of all exhortation in the Scriptures. It is founded on the fact that our being called into the path of service here, is a consequence of the blessings already inalienably bestowed on us *in Christ*. The mercies and the gifts freely bestowed in Christ give to us the title and the power to take a position corresponding to those mercies and gifts, here. The heavenly and everlasting blessings given in Christ precede, and are altogether independent of, our service; and therefore, we are asked to serve, not in order that we may attain the blessings, but because we *have* them. "Blessed be the God and Father of our Lord Jesus Christ, who hath blessed us with all spiritual blessings in heavenly places in Christ," are words that may be used, not merely by the advanced believer, but even by the very feeblest in the family of faith. "If," says the Apostle, "one died instead of all, then did the whole die." Believers, therefore, (for of them this passage speaks) are regarded as having in their Representative died. They have passed through judicial death, and God's actings towards them, and their relations to Him are founded on that accomplished fact; so that before they are exhorted to die unto sin daily, it is made known to them that they have already, fully and completely, died to it *in Christ*. So likewise if we are directed to live unto God, it is because we are already alive unto Him in Christ. "In that He died, He died unto sin once, but in that He liveth, He liveth unto God: so do ye reckon yourselves to be dead indeed unto sin, *but alive unto God in Christ Jesus our Lord*" (Rom. vi. 10). If we are exhorted to keep our garments unspotted from the world, it is after we have received the assurance that priestly garments —garments of glory and of beauty are given us as our everlasting heritage in Christ. Thus, by faith, entering into Heaven, and there discerning the blessings already given by God's unchangeable gift in the Son of His love, we then descend, as it were, to our practical place on earth again, comforted and strengthened; even as the priests of Israel of old, after they had entered the sanctuary and had fed on the shew-bread, presented for them on the golden table; and after they had seen the light burning for them and all Israel in the candlestick of gold; and after they had beheld the incense ascending *for* them from the golden altar, came back again to their practical place in Israel, there "to keep knowledge" and "to judge between clean and unclean, holy and unholy"—to "separate the precious from the vile." Grace has taught us to know the true shew-bread presented for us in the heavens; and the true candlestick with its sevenfold light, which, having once shone for us in the earth, does now for ever shine for us in the heavens. All these things we find in Christ —provided by that grace which is made to bear on us abidingly in Him—grace which does not merely come forth and meet us *once* when first, in the scarlet of our sins, we cast ourselves on the blood of expiation, but which abides with us and reigns over us for ever. Grace is that, wherein, says the Apostle, we have been set, or made, by God, to stand. Our advance in practical sanctification, therefore, will greatly depend on the measure in which we recognise the objects which grace sets before us. Take these objects away, and it would be as if the stars were swept from the firmament, and the benighted traveller left to pursue his way in rayless darkness.

Right occupation is another of the means employed by God to promote the practical sanctification of His people. When first brought into the fold of faith, we are necessarily severed from many a former interest. Our relations to good and evil, to the Church and the world, to God and to Satan, are changed. The books, studies, friendships, associations, employments, in which we once delighted, are seen to be too distinctly marked with moral leprosy, for our hearts to find any longer occupancy in them. The commandment, given to all those who feed on the Paschal Lamb, to put away leaven out of their houses, is heard by our consciences; and we soon recognise its need. Nothing, therefore, can be more important than that our energies, if withdrawn from the evil things on which they once spent themselves, should be given to other things sanctioned and approved of God, lest we should pine in languor, or else find ourselves again drawn back towards that Egypt which we have left indeed, but towards which our hearts, as to every natural feeling, still gravitate. Accordingly, God does not lead us into the wilderness without there providing for us new interests—new occupations—new joys. If leavened things are taken away, unleavened things are provided. He is pleased to associate us with Himself in His own interests—the interests of His land—His people, and His Truth. We are at once the congregation and the army of the Lord the character of our service is manifold: our duties various. Israel served in the Temple and in the camp—in the city and in the field · and the offices which they individually filled, were no less various than the places of their service. He, who called them to be His people, appointed the various spheres in which they might serve under Him. We too, have new duties and employments provided for us under God. We have things to seek after, and things to eschew : things to cherish, and things to repress : friends to aid, and foes to resist . strongholds of truth to defend, and strongholds of falsehood to assail. We fight under God not in order to win His favour—that is already and for ever given. In His favour, He has made us His people : in his favour, He has summoned us around His banner, for our honour and for our blessing . that we might share with Truth, its conflicts and its struggles. Experience will soon convince us how the consciousness of being employed for God (however poor or humble our service) will comfort us in hours of downcasting ; and how it will aid us in resisting and controlling even the strongest tendencies of our nature. Thus, too, we learn many lessons. We are taught by our successes, and taught by our failures. We learn what promotes, and what hinders spiritual vigour. It is amidst the realities of warfare that the soldier discovers both his weaknesses and his strength.*

---

* Nor must we forget the incentive to diligence and watchfulness afforded by the promised reward which God's grace (for all is of grace) will bestow in the day of Christ's glory on the *services* of His people, if those services have been wise and well-pleasing in His sight. It is true, indeed, that the highest and most excellent of the blessings that redemption brings, flow exclusively from the vicarious service of Christ for His people, and thus become the common heritage of all the redeemed. That He " loveth us, and freed us from our sins by His own blood, and He made for us a kingdom ; priests unto His God and Father ; " is a verse true equally of all the saved. They will alike " reign in life through One, Jesus Christ"—will be alike changed personally into the likeness of their risen Lord—will alike love

In human life, we well know what diligent attention is bestowed on every thing that is supposed to aid the proper development of our natural vigour. We soon learn to discriminate between that which augments and that which diminishes our strength: and the lessons taught by experience are not readily forgotten. But is the same care bestowed on the nourishment and training of "the new man?" What if believers, forgetful that they need the unadulterated milk of the Word that they might grow thereby, are content to remain partially, if not wrongly, instructed in the Scriptures? What if they neglect to add to their faith and virtue, *knowledge?* What if their minds become furnished with thoughts and doctrines drawn not from the Scriptures but from men? What if by worldly friendships and associations they suffer themselves to be drawn into circumstances where they breathe an atmosphere morally poisoned? What if they refuse to take their stand in the battle-field of Truth, and seek a covert in "large-hearted" neutrality, and wander into the camp of the god of this world, admiring, and perhaps, copying, the manners, and interesting themselves in the interests of those who are strangers and aliens to the Israel of God? Is it not certain that, under such circumstances, the strength of our old corrupt nature will wax giant-like, and the vigour of "the new man" decay? Oh! that God's people would remember that he who wanders to the very extreme verge of the circle of Truth, and there keeps himself in as near contiguity as possible to the darkness beyond, holds both towards evil and towards God a place very different from that of one who retires from those dangerous confines, and seeks to draw nearer and nearer to the light that burns at that circle's centre. "Borderers" are not honoured among men: nor can they receive honour in the Church— I mean, honour from God.

---

as they are loved, and "know as they are known." Nevertheless, there is a reward of service and a praise that will not be the portion of all even of the saved. We read of some who, although recognising and belonging to the one true foundation, do nevertheless embody in their service habits of thought and action that produce results worthless as stubble in the sight of God. Such cannot have their services recognised in the great day. Their "works will be burned"—"they will lose their reward;" whereas, we read of others who will receive a full reward, and have an abundant entrance administered unto them into the everlasting kingdom of their God and Saviour. Thus, whilst there are promises that are absolute and unconditional, and belong to all the redeemed as such, there are other promises made dependent on certain results which may, or may not, be found in believers. The comfort and incentive of both these classes of promises is needed.

One thing essential to an advance in practical sanctification is acquaintance with Holy Scripture, and ready subjection of mind to that which we discern to be therein revealed. If we cherish opinions contrary to the Word of God, if our estimates of all things are not guided thereby, then it is impossible that there should be found in us a growing conformity to the mind of Christ. The cherishing of thoughts unsanctioned by and contrary to Him, constitute an inward disobedience of soul, the consequences of which will be, sooner or later, manifested in corresponding deflections in our outward way. God has revealed that which He has revealed with the avowed object of causing "the man of God" to be "throughly furnished." For the attainment of that end, He has revealed neither too much nor too little. To desire to know more than is written is presumption: to be contented with knowing less, is to be content that darkness should occupy within us a place that should be occupied by light—a place, be it remembered, that is never *unoccupied*; for where light is not, darkness is.

A soul that has formed wrong estimates of the things around it, must have its desires wrongly ordered; and if its desires be wrong, not only its services, but its *prayers*, must be proportionably affected. Our prayers, to be acceptable, must be according to His will: but how can they be according to His will, if they spring from an ignorance which ought to have, and could have, no place in our hearts if we had duly searched His holy Word and sought grace to be subject to that which is there revealed? Christians often deceive themselves into the belief, that if there be sincerity of conviction accompanied by earnest prayer and earnest action, then all is well. But right prayer must be guided by the Holy Spirit; and the Spirit always guides in accordance with the Word that He has written. There may be, as we too well know, both zeal and prayer apart from Truth; and then, how disastrous the results! A vessel may be impelled by mighty power; and there may be a strong hand and resolute will to guide its helm; but what if the chart be unknown or unconsulted? In the arrangements of human life, the consequences of ignorance and presumption are guarded against with jealous care; but in spiritual things, energy unguided by revealed Truth, is often eulogised and admired. Yet, what have we greater reason to dread than the activities of ignorance? When ignorance has been persistently cherished in the near presence of light, how often is it permitted to rush blindly forward and assume the place of knowledge and to act; and then, what is there more obstructive of true holiness —what more ruinous to every thing that should flourish in the Church of God?

Not unfrequently, under the pretence of exalting Christ, "doctrine" is, even by Christians, disparaged and contemned; yet what is "doctrine" except instruction from Christ respecting Himself— instruction respecting the relations in which He has set us towards God, and Himself, and all things? "Doctrine" is the means which God has appointed to convey the right knowledge of Christ to the souls of His people; nor can any thing be more certain than that all knowledge which we may imagine ourselves to have attained in any other way, will prove in the end, illusory and vain. For a saint to suppose that his ways can be sanctified apart from the knowledge of the Word of God, is as if a soldier were to imagine that he could fulfil the duties of his soldiership whilst neglecting the instructions of his Chief; or as if a child should fancy that he could serve and please his father whilst despising the commandments by his father given. Nor must we forget that as darkness is to a weakened eye more welcome than light, so ignorance is congenial to every heart that has enfeebled itself by keeping itself distant from the full light of God's Word. Growth in grace, and growth in Truth, when real, are never treated of, in the Scripture, as opposed conditions. On the contrary, they are always regarded as standing in inseparable connexion, and resulting from the operation of the same Spirit. "Sanctify them through Thy Truth: Thy Word is Truth," are words which plainly show that the knowledge of revealed Truth is a necessary means to sanctification. And again, "If ye abide in me *and my words abide in you*, ye shall ask what ye will, and it shall be done unto you." The "words" of which the Lord here speaks must be taken to include all that His Prophets and Apostles and Himself had spoken, for He was the Author of all. "Desire," said Peter, "the sincere milk of the Word that ye may grow thereby." Peter had not forgotten the parting commandment of His Lord, when He said, "Feed" ($\beta o\sigma\kappa\epsilon$) and "be the shepherd of ($\pi o\iota\mu\alpha\iota\nu\epsilon$) my sheep." The sheep of Christ need to be fed. They need, also, that directive care which it is one chief end of the shepherd's office to supply; and that directive care, as well as the appointed food, reaches them through ministration of the Truth. Apart from it, their souls will be unfed—their steps unguided. "I have no greater joy," said the Apostle John, "than to see my children walking in the Truth."

Are we, then, guided by the light of God's revealed Truth, seeking to maintain a right relation to the evil that is *in* us, watching against it—"bridling it?" Do we seek, also, to stand in a right relation to the evil that is *around* us—that evil which makes the world, religiously and secularly, what it is? Do we seek, by *practical separation*, to bear witness against it? Do we seek, practically, to own and to connect ourselves with the Truth giving our energies to its service; abiding in it? Do we seek to fulfil the duties of our own individual sphere remembering that there is no sphere, however lowly, that does not afford some opportunity for trading with our talent; and that he, who is faithful in little, will be faithful also in much? He, who seeks grace for these things, will find that he is treading the path of true practical sanctification, and advancing in these things which make rich towards God. Advance in such a path may, in the present condition of the Church of God, be attended with peculiar difficulties: yet, they who remember the recompense of the reward, will not be too ready to cry, "a lion is in the way." They will remember Him that is able to encounter for them all lions, and to overcome all enemies—One who is the Shepherd and the Friend as well as the Redeemer of His people.

[To be, D.V. continued.]

Jacob's History in Genesis XXIX., &c.

Abraham and Jacob were alike heirs of the promises of God. For the sake of those promises, which their faith saw afar off and greeted, they "confessed that they were strangers and pilgrims on the earth." Knowing that they were compassed by difficulties and dangers, they looked to God as their refuge. In Him they hoped: in Him they confided. Yet, how different was the manner of their trust.

Abraham was one who *waited* upon God. Although quick and vigorous in action, when action was required, he was careful in his actings *to follow*, not *to go before*, God. From God he sought not only protection and deliverance, but also control and direction. He had learned to say; "my Father, thou art the guide of my way." He mistrusted plans of his own:—schemes of subtilty and deceit his soul abhorred. He looked to God to appoint, and to God to provide; and accordingly, "Jehovah-Jireh" was the name under which he was, in an especial manner, permitted to prove the faithfulness and power and loving-kindness of the Lord. Honour, therefore, and triumph, as well as protective power attended his steps, and he was called "the friend of God."

Far different was the course of Jacob. Although he, too, trod the path of faith, yet, he trod it as one who desired to be, as much as might be, the regulator of his own way. Without ever forgetting God, without ever ceasing to confide in Him, he yet confided also, and that greatly, in his own capacities; and seemed to delight in exalting his own actings into a kind of co-equality with those of God. Without a thought of separating himself from God—without dreaming of prosperity apart from God's favour and blessing, he was yet ever prone to manifest a certain independency of spirit and confidence in his own powers, by acting first, and then expecting God to follow. Fond of plans and subtle contrivances, he not unfrequently made his own way crooked; and then looked to God to rescue him from the difficulties and dangers in which he had involved himself. And although God, in the faithfulness of His love and mercy, abandoned not His servant, yet He caused him to know many sorrows. Straits, difficulties, and trials, accumulated on the path of Jacob—trials, indeed, from which he was from time to time extricated: but the trials of Jacob were, for the most part, not like the trials of Abraham, honourable in themselves and blessed; nor did the manner of the deliverance bring the same honour and glory unto God. So different may be the course of those, who are yet equally children of faith—equally heirs of the kingdom that is to be revealed.

When Abraham was asked whether his son should visit for a season, the land of his forefathers—the land from which he had been called away, Abraham's soul shrank from the very thought. "Beware thou that thou bring not my son thither again . . . . . . only bring not my son thither again," was his twice repeated command. Accordingly, Isaac went not. Abraham's servant was sent. And mark the caution and godly fear with which he fulfilled his mission —how, like his master, he cast himself on God; and watched for tokens of direction from His hand. As he drew near and was about to enter the land to which he journeyed, he said: "O Lord God of my master Abraham, I pray thee, send me good speed this day, and show kindness unto my master Abraham." And when the token which he sought was granted, in Rebekah doing that which he had asked that she might do—"the man, wondering at her, held his peace, to wit whether the Lord had made his journey prosperous or not." And when he found that he had indeed been guided to the house of his master's brethren, " the man bowed down his head and worshipped the Lord. And he said, Blessed be the Lord God of my master Abraham, who hath not left destitute my master of His mercy and His truth: I being in the way, the Lord led me to the house of my master's brethren." And when he found that the object of his mission was attained, "he worshipped the Lord, bowing himself to the earth."

Contrast with this, the course of Jacob. Unbidden by the Lord, and concurring with his mother in devising a method of escape from the danger which their own deceit and subtilty had caused, he quitted, apparently without one misgiving thought, the Land of promise, and went back into the country from which God had separated *him* as well as his fathers. The words of Abraham were remembered not: nor do we read of any act that betokened acknowledgment of God.

He had formed for himself a plan: he had devised for himself a means of escape from a near and threatening danger: and in the execution of this plan, all his thoughts and energies were absorbed. He rushed into the wilderness, and there found himself benighted and alone—and alone he would have remained, if God had not, in faithful mercy, met him and blessed him, and given him that wondrous vision of yet future glory, which Jacob did, after a manner, recognise and welcome; yet so as to show that his thoughts rested on that which *he* proposed to render unto God, far more than on the blessings which God covenanted to bestow *freely* upon him. The nature of those blessings, and their preciousness, it would seem that Jacob neither apprehended, nor endeavoured to apprehend.*

And when he drew near the end of his way and was about to enter into that land from which he and his fathers had been delivered, we might have expected that, at such a moment, he would have peculiarly committed himself unto God. This Abraham's servant had done; although *his* absence from Canaan was caused by no sin, and his visit to the land of the stranger was to be but for a moment—his steps being soon about to be turned Canaan-ward again. But with Jacob it was far otherwise. Dangers, in which he had involved himself, had driven him from Canaan; and a long and sorrowful future awaited him in the land which he had chosen for a refuge; and yet, no supplications, like those of Abraham's servant, are recorded as having passed from his lips. Let it not, however, be supposed that he had either forsaken or forgotten God. Truly he remembered Him, and confided in His mercies; but he greatly confided in himself as well. He highly valued God's help; but he liked to receive it in the way of co-operation, rather than that God's power should manifest itself in the independency of its own sovereign greatness. As he had fought his way through many past difficulties, so he purposed to fight his way again through difficulties yet to come. A heart that relies much on its own resources, and looks to them as the great available means of present succour, will be likely, in the hour of danger, to be occupied mainly with itself; and will find it proportionably difficult to wait on and acknowledge God. Are there none to whom experience has taught this lesson—none who are ready to confess that they resemble Jacob far more than Abraham in their ways?

---

* See "Occasional Papers," Vol. I, No. III., page 16.

Jacob " came unto the land of the people of the east, and he looked and behold, &c." Such are the words which describe the first approach of Jacob to that land which was to be to him, for many years, a land, virtually, of sorrowful captivity. "*He looked*"—that is, he stood and scanned the scene before him; saw what it presented to his view; resolved on the course to be pursued; and acted. It was the *manner*, not the fact, of the look, that gave to it, its character: and we can scarcely be in doubt as to the manner—for how rapid was the action that followed; and there is no mention of God. What can be more contrasted than the mode in which Abraham's servant approached, and that in which Jacob entered, the same land, and the same family? The characteristic circumstances of the one, are utterly wanting in the other. There was no appeal unto God. Jacob went to the shepherds; questioned them; counselled them; found Rachel and Laban; was welcomed; and all seemed to prosper. Yet there was sorrow in store; and in due time the sorrow came. He had found in Laban, a master rather than a friend—a master who was covetous, grasping, subtle, and had little, if any, of the fear of God; for he had in his household, idols. And as Jacob had by subtilty prevailed, so was he now, by subtilty to suffer. Laban's craft deceived him. Seven years Jacob served for Rachel; but when the seven years were ended, Leah, and not Rachel, was given. And when at last Rachel came, strife and sorrow came with her. Servitude under the exacting covetousness of Laban; strife in his own household; the plans and contrivings of jealous rivalry there; toil by day and watching by night in summer heat and in winter cold, and toil unrequited—such were the circumstances that gave to Jacob's life its character in the land which he had chosen for his refuge. And when at last, on the earnest appeal of Jacob, the heart of Laban relented and he consented to give to Jacob the speckled and brown among the flocks, and Jacob began to prosper, prosperity brought with it new sorrows. He had, hitherto, known Laban as an exacting master; he was now to know him as a jealous foe.

The mere fact of Jacob being more prospered than himself (in whatsoever way the prosperity might come) was, no doubt, in itself sufficient to arouse the jealousy of Laban and of his sons. It behoved Jacob to remember this, and to beware of every thing that might tend to invite or stimulate their hatred. It was the purpose of God to prosper Jacob. If therefore he had quietly waited on God, he would surely have received the intended blessing from the silent operation of His hand. There could have been no need for Jacob to scheme, and to devise, and to secure to himself advantage by what Laban must have deemed an act of deceit and fraud. But it was hard for Jacob to be still: hard for him to restrain the inventiveness of his subtilty. He placed striped rods before the stronger of the cattle as they conceived; and so the stronger of the flock became Jacob's, and the weaker Laban's. Can we wonder after this, that the face of Laban was not toward Jacob as before?*

Yet, whatever the action of Jacob, Laban was the oppressor, and Jacob the oppressed. "This twenty years," said Jacob, "have I been with thee; thy ewes and thy she-goats have not cast their young, and the rams of thy flock have I not eaten. That which was torn of beasts I brought not unto thee; I bare the loss of it; of my hand didst thou require it, whether stolen by day, or stolen by night. Thus I was; in the day the drought consumed me, and the frost by night; and my sleep departed from mine eyes. Thus have I been twenty years in thy house; I served thee fourteen years for thy two daughters, and six years for thy cattle: and thou hast changed my wages ten times." (Gen. xxxi. 38.) Rachel also and Leah said: " Is there yet any portion or inheritance for us in our father's house? Are we not counted of him strangers? for he hath sold us, and hath quite devoured also our money." (Gen. xxxi. 14) Their words were not untrue. God marked the oppression, and said to Jacob: " I have seen all that Laban doeth unto thee." (xxxi. 12.) " Return unto thy country, and to thy kindred, and I will deal well with thee." Thus again, in faithful love, God interposed—reminding him of mercies past and of blessings yet to come, and opening up for him a way of present deliverance. Yet Jacob, though protected and comforted, can scarcely be said to have gone forth from the land of his exile in honour. It could not be said of him, that he went not out " in haste, nor by flight." (Is. lii. 12.) On the contrary, "he stole away." " Jacob stole away unawares to Laban the Syrian, in that he told him not that he fled. So he fled with all that he had." (Gen. xxxi. 20.)

---

* It must not be inferred because God permitted or caused the scheme of Jacob to prosper, that therefore He approved it; any more than He approved the plan for deceiving Isaac, though thereby the desired blessing was secured. God, not unfrequently, gives effect to the schemes of His people that He might discipline and chasten them by resulting sorrows—sorrows that would have been avoided, if they had ceased from their own devisings and waited on Him.

He was protected indeed. God checked the pursuit of Laban and restrained his wrath; yet there was little honourable in Jacob's flight. And in his household there was one, and that too the person whom he most dearly loved, on whom rested the guilt of theft and deceit, if not of idolatry. Rachel had stolen her father's gods. Did she fear them? Did she dread lest they should aid her father in his pursuit? Or did she trust in them, and intend to worship them as *her* gods? She could scarcely have taken them with the view of delivering her father from his sin; for, in that case, she would have ground his idols to powder—not hidden them in her tent: nor would a righteous action have sought to screen itself by falsehood. It was too evident that evil deceit and subtilty had not departed from Jacob's house. Jacob, indeed, was guiltless: he knew not of the theft. He knew not that idols were accompanying him on his way. Indeed, just as Laban was eagerly searching out his images, Jacob was preparing to sacrifice unto the Lord. Jacob had failed in many things; but he had not learned to love Laban's idols: his heart had not departed from the living God. Him whom he had worshipped of old, he worshipped still. There was none other in whom he trusted—none other in whom he hoped

Protected then by God, and befriended, though not like Abraham honoured, Jacob returned to the land of his inheritance, there indeed, to experience fresh sorrows, and encounter new dangers. Rebekah he found not. The Scripture, indeed, is silent respecting her death: but, no doubt, she would have been mentioned as Isaac is, if she had lived to welcome the return of her son. Esau however remained, stronger far in power—and it might be, fiercer in wrath, than when Jacob of old fled from his presence: and Esau must be met. Thus, notwithstanding the many years that had intervened, the past came back upon Jacob with all its terror—intensified terror, for Jacob now trembled for others as well as for himself. "I fear him," said he, "lest he will come and smite me, and the mother with the children."

Yet Jacob need not have thus trembled. On the contrary, he had peculiar reason to be strong, and of a good courage. Just before he uttered those words of anguish, God, as if to assure him of his present care, had sent holy angels to meet him. "And when Jacob saw them, he said, This is God's host: and he called the name of that place Mahanaim." Thus then, not only was a heavenly host appointed to watch over Jacob, but he was permitted also to behold them; that so he might be comforted and know the strength provided for him from above. He saw the angels of God, and recognised them as God's host.

It might have been expected, perhaps, that at such a moment, all thought of his own little band—all confidence therein (if indeed he had ever confided in its weakness) would have vanished from the soul of Jacob, and that his eye and his heart would have rested solely on the host of God. But how could Jacob forget himself? Was his own band, that band which his own energies had gathered, to be as nothing? Was it to have no place? If the angels of God were one host, was not *his* band another? So, at least, Jacob seemed to reckon; and therefore, he called the name of that place Mahanaim; i.e. *two* hosts.

But words used by God's people to give expression to their own partial or erring thoughts, are, not unfrequently, in the mercy and grace of God, adopted by Him, to declare His ways and be the exponents of His thoughts—ways which are not as our ways, thoughts which are not as our thoughts. So is it with this word "Mahanaim." It has been adopted by God. It remains to us as a word pregnant with blessed meaning; teaching us of glories in heaven and in earth yet to come, when Jacob's weakness shall give place to Israel's strength, and glory rest upon Immanuel's land. In that day, strengthened with strength from on high, Israel shall become the host of the Lord their God, appointed to serve Him in the earth; but in association with others, more glorious than themselves, even risen saints—who, as being heavenly and glorified, shall serve the Lord in heaven His dwelling place, as well as fulfil the missions entrusted to them in the earth. Thus, there will be two hosts, (Mahanaim) even as there will be two Jerusalems (Jerusalaim)—heavenly and earthly: heaven bestowing, earth receiving; and so linked together in concurrent and harmonious action under God. This is that which shall be seen in the Shulamite in the day of her blessing. Shulamite means the spouse of Solomon; the name bestowed on Israel when married to the great King—the true Solomon. A time is drawing nigh when it shall be said; "Return, return, O Spouse of Solomon; return, return, that we may look upon thee. What will ye see in the Spouse of Solomon? As it were Mahanaim"—i.e. two hosts. Strength in the earth shall be associated with strength and glory in the heavens. This shall be seen in the Shulamite—this shall characterize her in the day of her espousals. Thus then, we learn the true meaning of Mahanaim; a word which, used according to the thoughts of Jacob, must be deemed a word of presumption and folly; for it exalted weakness whilst yet remaining weakness, into the place of strength: but, when used according to the thoughts of God, it becomes a word, true, blessed, and glorious; for it speaks of an hour, when *He* will change weakness into strength; and so give to it that power of co-operation with higher heavenly might, to which Jacob, in the day of his feebleness, seems to have aspired.

But to return to the narrative. The pledge of God's present favour and protection granted in the vision of the heavenly host, afforded to Jacob ground for firmest comfort and hope; for it proved that God was nigh to watch over him and to defend. Yet of this, Jacob seems to have availed himself not at all. After he had uttered the word "Mahanaim," it would almost seem that the thought of Divine protection had vanished from his soul; for the narrative, as it proceeds, is the record of the deepest anxiety and terror. It was a lesson to Jacob; and is a lesson to us—teaching us, that, in the hour of need, comfort and peace will assuredly vanish from the heart, if there be a determined reliance upon our own energies, or a determined leaning on anything of which *we* are supposed to constitute the spring or centre. God will not permit our weakness to be exalted into parity with His strength. He will have weakness viewed as weakness, and strength recognised as strength. Jacob's plan (for it does not appear that he consulted God) was to send messengers to Esau; and when they returned and brought no answer of peace, but only tidings that Esau with an army of four hundred men was coming, Jacob's heart utterly trembled. "Then Jacob was greatly afraid and distressed: and he divided the people that was with him, and the flocks, and herds, and the camels, into two bands; and said, If Esau come to the one company, and smite it, then the other company which is left shall escape."

Few passages in the life of Jacob seem more characteristic than this. He did not forget God. On the contrary, he cried to Him with an exceeding earnest and bitter cry: but before he called on God, he determined what he would do, and did it; even though the plan, on which he fixed, must have seemed to any eye but his own, hopeless: for who could expect that the second of his two feeble bands would escape, if Esau were permitted to sweep the first away? Endangered as Jacob was, could there be any true ground of hope in anything except the direct power of God? Was it not manifest, that if protection were by Him granted, it would be protection full and perfect; but that if not, all Jacob's plannings for the preservation of the second of his bands would be as chaff in the balance and vanity? Yet Jacob seems to have judged otherwise. He appears really to have had a certain hope in this division of his "host" or "band;" for the origin of the word is the same as "Mahanaim." He had now, indeed, constituted for himself "two hosts." When he used the word "Mahanaim," he had reckoned his host as one, and had set it in virtual parity with the host of God; but now, that host of God had vanished from the apprehension of Jacob's soul. It was forgotten. As regarded the apprehensions of Jacob's heart, that host had ceased to exist. His own little band, divided into two, now constituted his "Mahanaim." What were those two? Were they strength or weakness? Could there be a more perfect exhibition of weakness—utter and hopeless? And yet, Jacob's hope lingered there, without, apparently, one thought recurring to his soul respecting the heavenly host which had been sent to meet him. Of Jacob's present "Mahanaim," that angelic host formed no part. What if Jacob's condition had been really in accordance with his own estimate thereof? Could there, in that case, have been any hope? How needful then, to distinguish between the reality of a believer's condition as determined and fixed by God, and that which he himself, in the perplexity or error of his own misguided thoughts, may *think* to be his condition.

In the prayer of Jacob, we find the expression of true humility and of thankfulness to God for His past mercies. There was a reference, also, to God's promise of continued protection; although of this he speaks tremulously—his faith being, evidently, feeble. After his prayer, however, there was more of hopefulness than before. He speaks no more of escaping with the second of his bands after the destruction of the first; but hints at the possibility of deliverance. "He said, I will appease him [Esau] with the present that goeth before me, and afterward I will see his face; peradventure, he will accept of me." We have still, however, to note the characteristic habit of Jacob, in giving prominence to himself. He does not say, I will trust in God to still the wrath of Esau; or even, I trust in God to cause Esau to accept my offering. He said, "*I* will appease"; and made no mention of God. Having formed a new plan—in that plan and its execution his thoughts were for the present absorbed. It had become, as regarded the immediate apprehension of his heart, his present ground of confidence. Yet, he did not, and could not, feel certain of the result. "Peradventure" is the word by which he is obliged to qualify the expression of his hope. "Peradventure he will accept of me." A divided confidence, partly in God, and partly in ourselves, will never bring us beyond "peradventure."

Night came on, and Jacob made his arrangements for resting with his company. But how could a heart full of anxiety and terror rest? It is not every one that can say, "I laid me down and slept; I awaked, for the Lord sustained me; I will not be afraid for ten thousands of the people that set themselves against me round about." Jacob could not say this. He could not rest. He arose that night long before the morning dawned, and sent his wives and children and all that he had, across the river, on the banks of which they had halted. After this, he appears to have returned, and was "left alone."

He was left alone, but not long; for in the form of an angel God met him. And what was the relation in which Jacob set himself to this heavenly visitant, whom, if he recognised not as God, he must have recognised as a messenger that came from God? Did he humble himself? Did he say, what saith my Lord unto his servant? Did he, in any way, take that place which weakness ought to take in the presence of strength? *That* was a place which Jacob had never yet taken; and he took it not now. He would not act as one devoid of strength. On the contrary, he looked upon himself as having strength—strength which he could use. And accordingly, he put it forth against the strength of the angel of God, and they "wrestled."

"Wrestling," it must be remembered, is a word of very definite meaning. It is not used to denote any, or every, development of strength that may be marked by earnestness or perseverance; but it denotes strength measured against strength. It indicates not the relation of an inferior to a superior, (such for example, as is held by a suppliant towards one whom he supplicates) it indicates, on the contrary, a relation of *conflict* in which rival contests with rival—each claiming to have the power of resisting, if not of overthrowing the other. "Wrestling" is the symbol of strength brought into antagonism with strength. Such was the relation which Jacob assumed towards the angel. It had long been his habit to act as if he were possessed of a certain co-equality of power with God. Self-reliance lay, as a canker-worm, at the root of his spiritual healthfulness. His own plans and capabilities occupied a place in his heart that was incompatible with a full and simple reliance on God.

It was needful that he should be taught to cast from him this evil and unholy confidence: and now, the time for the lesson to be given was come. To the very end of the night, Jacob continued to wrestle on. He refused to bend: he persisted in measuring his power against the power of God; and God permitted this long and stubborn display of misdirected strength. But suddenly, just as the morning brake, God touched the sinew in Jacob's thigh. It withered; and in a moment, his power of wrestling was gone. He could wrestle no more. The sinew of his strength was dried up. He halted upon his thigh. It was out of joint. All that he could then do was, to cling to Him who had thus proved Himself able to dry up the springs of his strength: to cling to Him as weakness clings to strength, and to seek His blessing—"I will not let thee go except thou bless me." They were the words, not of the wrestler, but of the enfeebled one casting himself on the grace, and power, and goodness of Another mightier than he; and then, and not till then, the blessing came. His name was changed from Jacob to Israel—"a prince with God." He had seen God's face, and received God's blessing, not in the place where he prevailed in wrestling, but in a place where the sinew of his strength shrank, and the power of wrestling was taken from him for ever. Halting upon his thigh, he crossed the ford of Yabbok—a significant name, for it means "wrestling." He passed that river now, and left it behind him. His back was turned upon it for ever. The morning sun rose upon him in its brightness as he crossed it and left it, halting, but blessed.

It is a scene that reminds us of, and is indeed a pledge of, the coming of that hour when Israel, Jacob's people, after their long night of sorrow and stubborn obduracy shall enter on the day of their blessing. Their stubbornness, indeed, is not as Jacob's, relieved by the counteracting influences of faith. In them, it is unqualified obduracy and rebellion. The evil of Jacob they inherit; but his faith they have not. Nevertheless, a day is coming, when even their hard heart shall be broken. More lowly and contrite even than Jacob, and no longer boasting in the sinew of their own strength, they too, halting on their thigh, shall enter on the day of their new history under the shining of that blessed morning—that morning without clouds, which shall rise upon them in a brightness never to wane. They, too, shall say, we have seen God's face and are preserved. They, too, shall cease for ever from their strugglings against God. They shall wrestle no more, and know why Israel in every age (doing what they understand not) have refused to eat of the sinew that shrank.

Blessed are they who learn the lesson *now;* who feed not on the sinew of their own strength, but lean wholly on God; acting when He bids them act, resting when He bids them rest, following—not directing, their heavenly guide; being in the power of God's blessing, "Israel"—as to themselves, Jacob, the worm.

On the Song of Solomon.

From Chapter v. 2, to Chapter vi. 3.

It has been already observed that the place assigned to her, whose varying experiences are the subject of this Song, was not the City. *There*, man had collocated *his* strength, and stamped the impress of his own name: *that*, therefore, was not the place designed for her, whose distinctive blessing was companionship with her rejected Lord. Like Him she was called "to go without the gate, bearing His reproach." She was to find the place of her rest and her occupation, far away from man's City; in the vineyards or at the sheep-folds; or in some " garden enclosed," where plants of heavenly fragrance could be trained by her for her Lord.

In the previous chapter, we find her in one of her highest positions of honour and blessing. We see her encompassed by plants of pleasant fragrance that had sprung up under the culture of her hand—herself rejoicing in the presence of her Lord, and acknowledged by Him as one that was ministering to His joy. She had asked Him to come into His garden, and He had come and tasted of its honeycomb, and spices, and pleasant fruits. He had commended her, and they had rejoiced together.

But now, how changed the scene! She had forsaken the sheep-fold, and the vineyard, and the garden; she was no longer a sojourner "without the gate;" she had wandered into the City, and found her way into one of its palaces; she had encompassed herself with its delicacies (for she speaks of her fingers dropping with sweet smelling myrrh) and there she had lain down to rest. Her pilgrim-garb was laid aside She was no longer the despised shepherdess, or the keeper of the vineyards, but rather a princess, treading delicately, Kings' Courts. She no longer said, as once she had done; "Tell me, O thou whom my soul loveth, where thou feedest, where thou makest thy flock to rest at noon: for why should I be as one that turneth aside by the flocks of thy companions?" Her companionship with her Lord had ceased; and she sought not to renew it. He still remained unsheltered—"His head filled with dew, and his locks with the drops of the night;" whilst she was resting, or seeking to rest, in the midst of luxuries and refinements which could never have been hers, unless she had abandoned the true place of her service and had ceased to be a sojourner "without the gate."

"I sleep, but my heart waketh." Such was her apology—such the plea by which she would fain have hidden from herself, as well as excused to others, the truth of her condition. But why this difference between her outward circumstances and her inward feelings? Was it needful? Was it right? And could such discrepancy continue? Would the heart long remain wakeful, if the eye and the ear ceased to watch, and the hand to act? And even, if the heart could so watch, what use would there be in such vigilance, if no outward development followed? Who would credit her tale respecting her heart's wakefulness, if all surrounding circumstances contradicted her saying, and proved that her activity had wholly given place to slumber? Yet, false as is the plea, it is one by which believers, have, not unfrequently, deceived themselves; until their slumber has become so deep as to preclude the possibility of arousing them even to a sense of the delusion.

She, however, whose history we are here considering, was not to be allowed to sink into such depth of slumber. Her course was to be arrested. She was speedily to be summoned from her resting place, and brought back to the side of her Lord; for her heart had not yet so lapsed as to be altogether deaf to His voice, or indifferent to its call. Accordingly, when He drew nigh and knocked at the closed door—(the door which herself had closed against Him) as soon as she heard His call, as the call of one who was seeking for Himself shelter from the cold and darkness, and dew of night, she instantly recognised His well-known voice—"It is the voice," said she, "of my beloved that knocketh." Yet she was slow, and even reluctant, to unlock the closed door. "I have put off my coat; how shall I put it on? I have washed my feet; how shall I defile them?" Such were the words with which, at first, she responded to his call. Was it that she was really unwilling to re-assume, for a brief moment, the garment she had put off? Did she really fear that her feet, which she had washed, would be defiled by crossing, for a moment, the chamber of her luxury? Or, did her heart tell her that if her Lord entered that chamber, He would refuse to share with her the shelter she had chosen and would surely summon her from it: and that thus, drawn from her resting place, she too would have to say, that her "head also was filled with dew, and her locks with the drops of the night?" Conscience is quick, under certain circumstances, in anticipating results; though its anticipations are not unfrequently wrong; because though discerning, perhaps, the path of duty and its difficulties, it fails with equal clearness to apprehend the grace and lovingkindness which sustains in that path, and removes or overcomes its difficulties.

Doubtless, she anticipated that she would be called away from her rest; and hence her reluctance. Yet, her folly was not permitted to turn aside the persistency of His grace. He had before knocked: He now sought to *open* the closed door. Her heart was touched; and she arose to unlock it—her "hands dropping with myrrh, and her fingers with sweet smelling myrrh, upon the handles of the lock." Here was the evidence of the luxuriousness of her rest. It was a condition very unlike that of the shepherdess whom the sun had looked upon and blackened; or that of the outcast in the vineyards, despised and spurned by her own mother's children. She opened the door, however; but it was too late. He was gone. "I opened to my beloved; but my beloved had withdrawn himself, and was gone; my soul failed when he spake: I sought him, but I could not find him; I called him, but he gave me no answer." Indeed, He had never designed to enter that chamber, nor to rest where she rested. He had only come there to arouse her. If she desired to find Him, she must thread her way back through the streets of that City into which she never ought to have wandered. She must again go without the gate, and seek Him *there*.

And she *did* seek Him; for her heart was really true to her Lord She returned not to her forbidden rest; but forsaking that goodly chamber, she went forth even at that midnight hour into the dark City, helpless and alone. No voice of love greeted her: no kindly hand sustained, no friendly voice directed her. She was to be chastened, and to know many sorrows ere she again found herself by the side of Him from whom she had wandered. "The watchmen that went about the City found me; they smote me, they wounded me; the keepers of the walls took away my veil from me." Such is her own narrative of her sorrows. The watchmen of man's City, and the keepers of its walls can have no sympathy with any one who is unattracted by that City's glories, and refuses to labour for its interests—having an ear deaf to its melodies, an eye closed to its beauties. "Who is blind but my servant? Or deaf as my messenger that I sent? Who is blind as he that is perfect, and blind as the Lord's servant? Seeing many things, but thou observest not: opening the ears, but he heareth not." Such was the character of the One faithful and true Witness; and such, in measure, is the character of all who remember His example, and follow His steps; for they know that from the days of Cain and of Nimrod to the present hour, unregenerate man under Satan has been lord of the earth, and has stamped upon it the impress of his evil hand. They know too that in this there will be no change, except indeed for advance in rebellion, until the Lord shall be revealed in the brightness of His destroying glory. "Human progress," therefore, is to them, only another name for the advance of unregeneracy to its doom. "Antichrist," "Babylon," "Armageddon," "the wine-press of the wrath of God," "the lake that burneth with fire and brimstone," such are the names that indicate to the eye of faith the end and the goal of all present human progress. The more, therefore, the City of man strengthens itself—the more it illumines itself with brightness, the more the instructed heart trembles; for it knows what "will be in the end thereof." What place then more fearful than that held by those who are the watchmen of man's City—the strengtheners of its greatness—the defenders of its walls.

If that place had been held only by the Nimrods, and Cæsars, and Caiaphases of earth, and their servants; if the world's religiousness had always worn its Pagan or its Jewish garb, and had never assumed the profession of the name of Jesus; if none of Christ's servants had been seduced into the belief that the City of man is being gradually transformed into the City of God, the danger would not be what it at present is. But nominal Christianity has undertaken to sanctify the world's energies. It has encouraged those who give themselves, body and soul, to the advancement and glorification of man's City, and has told them that in so doing they glorify God. It has put the name of Christ upon Christ's enemies, and has striven to identify before the thoughts of men, the City of God and the City of man. And it has wonderfully succeeded. Few recognise that the relation held by the Lord Jesus and His servants the Apostles, towards Caiaphas and Cæsar, and all that morally characterised Jerusalem or Rome, is still the relation in which Truth and its servants stand toward every system, secular or religious, that is formed by the hand, or controlled by the will of unregenerate man. Doubtless, the acknowledgment of this narrows greatly the path of Christ's servants; but is not the way narrow that leadeth unto life? Is the exhortation to "go without the camp, bearing His reproach," limited to any especial time or place? Is it not a commandment addressed to all who own the sanctifying blood of Jesus? "Jesus that He might sanctify the people by His own blood, suffered without the gate. Let us go forth therefore unto Him without the camp, bearing His reproach. For here have we no continuing city, but we seek one to come." Can any words more plainly mark the everlasting difference between the City of God and the City of man? And as the hour of Antichrist draws nigh, this difference becomes, not indeed more real, but more marked, every day.

We cannot wonder that they whose view is bounded by the horizon of earth should greatly glory in man's present progress. The leaders of the world's energies have not laboured in vain. The City of man grows and waxes stronger and stronger every day; and even professed servants of Christ consent to guard it and to become the watchmen of its walls. We can well conceive how, like Nebuchadnezzar of old, they walk about upon its battlements, and look forth upon its greatness and say, "Is not this the City which our hands have formed, and which our skill and wisdom preserve?" Religiously and secularly they glory in it; and woe to the pilgrim stranger that comes across their path and tells them that her Lord whom she worships, is not only distant from, but AGAINST *them* and *it*. We might expect that their wrath would wax hot against her—that they would smite and wound her, for what more hateful in their sight than such thoughts, and ways, and testimonies as hers? But why did she draw nigh them? Did she indeed expect to find in them sympathy, or to obtain from them direction? Did she imagine that *they* could tell her where to find her Lord; or that *they* would be willing to seek Him with her? She may, perhaps, have thought so; for when the people of God with perplexed heart and uneasy conscience find themselves treading a wrong path, surrounded too by the results of their disobedience, it is not often that they view the circumstances around them with calm sobriety of mind. Impulse and excitement, for the most part, rule their steps; and they earn by their own foolishness, chastisement and sorrow. So was it with her.

If, commissioned by her Lord, and coming as from His side, she had met these watchmen and keepers of the City she might have confronted them and triumphed. At any rate, she would have been sustained by His strength. But it was far otherwise now. She appeared before them not only as an alien (that she must ever have been) but as an alien weak, sorrowful, deserted,—and needing, perhaps claiming, help. Were *they* to be the helpers of that which they abominated? They helped her not but they smote her.

In human life, however, they who have power and energy to *act upon* others, are far fewer than those who *are acted on*. Men, for the most part, are the ready subjects of others' influence. Multitudes dwell in man's City who are neither its "watchmen," nor "the keepers of its walls," but its "daughters." Trained under its influences, and unresistingly imbibing from their earliest years its principles, they readily receive from the institutions of society around them an abiding impress. Society prepares the mould, and their characters, like plastic clay, are formed therein. Having little ability, and less desire, to test the principles and practices that prevail around them, they find it far more easy to favour what others favour, than to incur the labour and painfulness of examination. Prosperity, success, numerical increase, popular approbation, and the like, are their tests; and anything that answers thereunto is readily accepted by them as good and true. "Securus judicat orbis terrarum." The universal verdict of society is in their judgment a sufficient warrant for Truth. How can that be wrong which the whole world judges to be right? They know that it is more easy to float with the current than to struggle against it: more pleasant to consort with that which is honoured and dignified, than with that which is outcast and despised. To look too searchingly into any thing is in their estimate the part of folly, rather than of wisdom. They know that as the foot moves most pleasantly when it lightly skims over the ground's surface, so does the heart know least of sorrow when it thinks and feels *superficially*. Carelessly, therefore, they bow down before any thing that educationally they have learned to reverence. When not swayed by habit, they are guided by expediency. Where the multitude leads, they follow. Such is the character of the "daughters of Jerusalem." They are the children of the City of man. It is their parent and their home. They love it—cleave to it—rejoice in it. Nothing is more abhorrent to their hearts than the thought of going without the gate, bearing reproach. If not sensitive to the appeals of Truth, they are very sensitive to ignominy, and dread the scorn of men even more than they covet their approbation. Truth, or such portions of it as admit of being established in a place of dignity and honour they are not unwilling to accept: but *the reproach* of Truth they fear. Is not this the condition of myriads in Christendom now? Floating carelessly on the surface of the stream, they are the sport of every casual influence, and are thus being prepared as a ready prey for that coming hour of delusion, before whose potency none but those who have really the Spirit of Christ will stand. In proportion as the bonds which have hitherto bound human society together are dissolved, and as men become more "like unto fishes of the sea that have no ruler over them," so will they become a more ready prey to the influence of those who will shape the world's moral course at its closing hour, and be swept into that mighty drag-net which will enclose unto perdition.

Yet, even among the daughters of "man's City," grace can, and does find, a remnant. Not unfrequently before, had this pilgrim stranger whom the sun had looked on and blackened, who could speak of the roes and hinds of the field, or of vineyards, or sheepfolds, or of lilies, but knew not the manners of the City, being a stranger to its palaces and its priestly courts—not unfrequently before had this wanderer found herself in the presence of the daughters of Jerusalem. Yet never before had she stood before them as now, in reproach and dishonour, smitten and wounded, and that by the guardians of their City—at a time too when she could no longer say that she was with her Lord, or closely following His footsteps. On the contrary, she had to confess that she had wandered from and lost Him; and she even appealed in the excitement of her harassed heart to *them*, as if *they* could tell her where to find Him whom her soul loved—a vain and foolish appeal, for how could *they* direct her who knew nothing of her Lord or of His ways. Yet such often is the manner of the servants of Christ when they have wandered from the practical place into which He seeks to separate His people. Impulsiveness and excitement give birth to great activities; but there is a want of reflectiveness—a want of sobriety of mind. There is an absence of the calm guidance of Truth; and if this condition of soul continues, if Christ do not quickly bring back to the place where He feeds His separated flock with His own pure Truth, the results are unspeakably sorrowful. What more disastrous than unguided or misguided energy! It is as when soldiers, abandoning their banners and their lawful leaders, rush wildly into the battle-field: or as when a torrent having no channels prepared for its course, spreads desolation where its waters rightly guided would have brought fertility and fruitfulness.

It was, however, otherwise with her whose history we are here considering. Her wandering was not to be prolonged. Her Lord had come and effectually roused her from her evil slumber, and her heart was incapable of rest until she again found herself practically by His side. If she had been content with any thing short of this, she would probably have linked herself in some way to the daughters of Jerusalem, and abjectly submitted to their control, and made the keepers of their walls her masters. When the people of Christ are content to remain in practical distance from their Lord, this commonly becomes their condition—a condition of degradation and debasement. With her, however, it was far otherwise. A secret hand was quickly guiding her back to her place of holy rest, and she was truly willing to follow as it led. Soon, therefore, she ceased from seeking counsel of the daughters of the City, and became to *them* a testifier and a guide. The praises of Him whom her heart loved were in her lips, and that not feignedly. There was fervour in her recital of His excellencies—vigour in her description. It was the utterance of the heart: and although her position was not yet rectified, yet it was *being* rectified. She was not settling down into a place of practical distance from her Lord. Every thought, every expression indicated that her soul was bent on recovering the place which she had lost. Her testimony, therefore, was blessed. It took effect upon the souls of those that heard. And they said at last, "whither is thy beloved gone, O thou fairest among women? whither is thy beloved turned aside? that we may seek Him with thee."

These words are indeed notable. If the daughters of Jerusalem had merely said, we will join thee, or help thee in seeking thy beloved, it might have been nothing more than the expression of a transient feeling which sudden emotion may produce on unstable fickle hearts. But in that case they would not have used the words, "O thou fairest among women." These were indeed strange words to be found in the lips of those who, when they had once before looked on this stranger, had despised her because she had known toil and travail in the vineyard, or at the folds where she had laboured for her Lord, where the sun had scorched her and the storm beaten on her. But now, although she was not only still blackened and worn, but smitten also and wounded, and her heart restless and unhappy, she nevertheless was suddenly addressed by those who had hitherto contemned her, as the "fairest among women." Her blackness had now become comeliness in their sight: her bruises were honourable: her sufferings blessed. The eye of faith was given them. Their estimate of her was changed. They viewed her as she was viewed by Him who had now become their Lord as well as hers; for none but those who have communion of heart with Him can see honour and beauty in those whom man looks on "as the filth of the world and the off-scouring of all things." Wherever the heart's estimate is so altered as to judge *that* to be honour and beauty which before it accounted ignominy and vileness, there must have been a change wrought by the Spirit of the living God. And now grace had accomplished its object. She had been aroused, chastened, taught, and made in sorrow to learn the appointed lesson; yet even in the midst of that sorrow had been so favoured, so blessed, that when she returned to her Lord, she returned to Him with increase. Others had been won to discern His excellencies, and to seek the place in which He loved to dwell. That place she now descried: that place she again found. "My beloved, she said, is gone down into His garden, to the beds of spices, to feed in the gardens, and to gather lilies" These spices and these lilies were not found in the City. They were *without* the gate. There she had before rejoiced in the presence and favour of Him whom her soul loved, and there she rejoiced in Him again: with increased apprehension of the contrast between the rest of the City, and the joys of the garden: with increased consciousness of her need of the mercy and grace of His faithful hand. Once more we find her able to say, "My beloved is mine and I am His. He feedeth among the lilies."

May we learn the lesson. May we fear even to rest in Man's City: much more may we dread to be numbered among its "watchmen." Let us go without the gate, acting *on* Man's City, if we can, so as to gather out of it; but showing ourselves to be not *of* it. If the servants of Christ give themselves over to the world to subserve its purposes and forward its designs, they will find themselves at last like Sampson in the hand of the Philistines—his eyes put out—his Nazarite separation lost—his distinctive strength departed, whilst that which yet remained to him was forced into the service of the stranger—the service of the enemies of the God of Israel.

On the Song of Solomon.

CHAPTER VI. 10, TO END.

THE great object of this Song is, as I have before observed, to mark the place (or rather that which *should* be the place) of the Church, in the midst of the earth's present darkness, whilst her Lord is absent, and herself a pilgrim. The proud City of man and the guardians thereof had no knowledge of her who ventured without the gate, trusting to the guidance of a voice that they knew not. If they thought of her at all, they thought of her only to despise. They understood neither her sorrows nor her joys. Her comeliness, that is to say, her comeliness in the eyes of her heavenly Lord, was in their sight "blackness." What honour in the estimate of the keepers of man's City could attach to one whose blackened visage was scorched by the sun and beaten by the storm; whose home and occupation was at the sheepfold, or in the vineyards, or in the distant valley where flowers and fruits of heavenly preciousness might bloom or ripen, but where nothing was found that was great, or elevated, or ennobling in the estimate of those who desired rather to reign as kings than to go without the Camp bearing the reproach of Truth. Yet *that* was the only place in which she whose joys and sorrows are the subjects of this "Song" could find communion with her Lord. *There* she could rejoice in Him and He in her: but if from that place she wandered, she found not peace, not happiness, but chastisement and sorrow.

But although this "Song" belongs to this present night of suffering, and not to that future hour when Truth shall prosper and be exalted, yet there are in it, interspersed here and there, many allusions to that coming morning of brightness when "the day shall break, and the shadows flee away." Of this the passage before us is an example.

The words "Who is she that LOOKETH FORTH as the morning, fair as the moon, clear as the sun, and terrible as an army with banners?"

are words incapable of being applied to the Church during the present period of its humiliation. The words "LOOKETH FORTH" imply manifestation, and to the Church in the present dispensation no *such* manifestation pertains. Whatever the Church, or any in it, may be in the eyes of Christ, or in the estimate of faith, the time for the declaration of their excellency and preciousness is not yet come. "The world knoweth us not, because it knew Him not." But the moment the day of the coming dispensation dawns, and converted Israel becomes God's witness in the earth, the scene changes. The day of Truth's honour will have come, and Israel as being Truth's witness will of necessity share its exhaltation and triumph. "For Zion's sake will I not hold my peace, and for Jerusalem's sake I will not rest, until the righteousness thereof go forth as brightness, and the salvation thereof as a lamp that burneth And the Gentiles shall see thy righteousness, and all kings thy glory. and thou shalt be called by a new name, which the mouth of the Lord shall name. Thou shalt also be a crown of glory in the hand of the Lord, and a royal diadem in the hand of thy God." Is. lxii. Blessed words, which shall be fulfilled in their season. But they belong not to the present condition of the servants of Truth. To them a far different path has been appointed. It was never intended that *they* should reign as Kings. On the contrary, they were set forth by God as persons appointed to death, who were to be, for Christ's sake, "despised," "reviled," "persecuted," "defamed," "made as the filth of the world and the off-scouring of all things." (1 Cor. iv. 9., &c.) Such was the path trodden by the Apostles. It was no self-chosen course. Their sufferings were not earned by haughtiness, or self-will, or fanatical peculiarities. They resulted from simple, straightforward humble adherence to Christ and to His Truth: and therefore their sufferings were blessed. But with the Apostles, we may almost say that *such* sufferings ceased. St. Paul intimated that it would be so, when he said, "I think that God hath set forth us the Apostles *last*, as persons appointed to death." St. Paul marked with sorrow the disposition that prevailed in those around him, to reign rather than to suffer; to be *within* rather than *without* the Camp Throughout the last eighteen hundred years, few have even desired the place which the pilgrim-stranger in this Song is described as holding. They have sought after the Throne far more than "the Valley:" influence has been purchased by the sacrifice of Truth: and the practical power of Christianity has in proportion waned.

Yet, however Christ would have rejoiced in seeing His people treading patiently the path of holy separation, it is not, and cannot be, pleasing in His sight that falsehood and iniquity should prevail, or that His people should be despised and His Truth rejected. His wisdom and grace may cause Him for a season to acquiesce in this, but it is His purpose finally that Righteousness and Truth and the servants thereof should flourish in the earth and triumph. Even then, if His Church throughout this dispensation had kept her proper place of faithful separateness, He still would have looked forward to and welcomed the approach of that hour when the place of suffering will be exchanged for one of honour, and when she who is appointed to be His new witness in the earth shall "look forth in brightness, fair as the moon, clear as the sun, and terrible as an army with banners."

But, seeing that the people of God have greatly failed in keeping their proper place of separateness, and have become weak in the day of conflict, we find in this an added reason why the coming day of Israel's return unto the Lord should be looked forward to, as a relief against the oppressive sense of the earth's present fruitlessness. Fruitfulness, if found any where, would be found in "the valley;" the place, that is, of retired humble separateness, where alone fruits ripen meet for the Lord—where alone "the vines flourish and the pomegranates bud." Such "valleys" cannot be found every where; nor can we create them for ourselves when and where we please. Many indeed have sought to do this. We love to choose for ourselves the spots we cultivate, and to determine for ourselves the character and limits of our separation. But "the valley" of true fruitfulness cannot thus be gained. It is a place unto which the wisdom, and Truth, and Spirit of Christ can alone guide. In seeking it the understanding and conscience must be exercised as well as the heart. There must be ability to discern Truth, and grace to follow it when discerned; otherwise, the true "valley" of blessing at the foot of the mountains of Bether (separation) will not be reached. It would be too much to say that it has been reached by *none;* for it is spoken of as a place not unknown to her whose history is set before us in this "Song." Yet her companions were few. She is evidently spoken of as one singularly isolated and alone. Few accompanied her to "the valley;" few joined her in watching over the vines and pomegranates that were there; and the consequence was paucity of fruit. I do not indeed say that this paucity was caused solely by the fewness of those that shared her labours. There might also have been languor in her own discouraged hand; or the blighting noxious influences of earth might have been permitted to destroy. All these causes may have concurrently operated to produce the result plainly indicated in the words that follow: "I went down into the garden of nuts to see the fruits of the valley, and to see whether the vine flourished, and the pomegranates budded. Or ever I was aware, (i e. suddenly) my soul set me on the chariots of my willing people." The Lord visited the valley. He does not indeed say that He found *no* fruit; but evidently He found not that which satisfied His desires, and therefore His heart turned to the future. "Suddenly my soul set me on the chariots of my willing people." His soul looked onward to the day of Israel's strength when they shall be willing in the day of His power, in the beauties of holiness from the womb of the morning—the first birth, that is, of the millennial day, when they "shall blossom and bud, and fill the face of the world with fruit."

And can *we* (feeble and limited as our apprehensions are) can even *we* contemplate the present condition of Christianity and not feel a certain comfort and relief in turning from it to that future hour when Truth shall no longer be successfully resisted by its enemies, or find its interests betrayed by the weakness and unfaithfulness of its friends? The history of Christendom throughout, from the day the Apostles died on to the present hour, has been a sorrowful and evil history. The professing Gentile Church has not continued in God's goodness, and therefore, like a diseased and cankered branch, it is to be cut off from the olive tree of blessing. The reaction against the ritualistic abominations of Christendom that took place at the time of the Reformation, was an intervention of God's goodness, for which His true people praise Him and will praise Him for ever and ever: yet Protestantism, even in the days of its early vigour, was content to spare not a few of the fetters which Ritualism and Superstition had forged, and was tempted to forge other bonds which have fatally bound those who wear them to the thrones and potentates of earth, and not unfrequently made the true saints of God like so many Jehoshaphats following in the train of Ahab. There is indeed still some true Protestantism, and we thank God for it; but for the most part the Protestanism of the present hour is nominal merely. Some so-called Protestants, deceiving and deceived, are rushing back to the vile idolatries and superstitions of Rome: others are plunging into the black darkness of Neologian Infidelity; whilst another part look calmly on with Gallio-like indifference, careless about every thing save that which bears upon their interests in earth—being worshippers of "human-progress," and not unfrequently of Mammon.

At various periods in the history of Protestantism attempts have been made by many to emancipate themselves from restraints that have borne injuriously on their consciences; nor have such efforts been unprospered when the Word of God has been really adhered to as the Guide. Liberty is precious; but true holy liberty can only be gained by close subjection to the *revealed* will of God as declared in Holy Scripture.

None but the servants of Truth are really free. If not cleaving to the Truth, we are sure to be in servitude to some form of delusive error that human selfishness under Satan has constructed for the advancement of its own ends: and thus man—not God, will be our Master. The present is a moment of great activity among many Christians who have set themselves free, as they say, from the restraint of human systems, that they may serve the Lord with unfettered hand. But what is more dangerous than a hand that has struck off former fetters, but refuses to submit itself to the restraining guidance of Truth? Nor is subjection to Truth the work of a moment. It is not easy for such as we, with all our ignorance and all our prejudices, to read and interpret the Word of God with calm sobriety of mind. Nor is it easy in such a day as this to cleave to the faith once delivered to the saints. It is far easier to talk smooth things about love, "large-heartedness" and the like, and to join in the prevailing cry against Creeds and Confessions and "old orthodox Theology," and all "stereotyped" form of doctrine; as if the Holy Spirit disowned precision, and clearness, and fixedness, and delighted in vagueness, mystification, and change. The Apostle thought otherwise when he said, "We use great plainness of speech;" and when he exhorted Timothy to remember "the form of sound words," and to keep through the Holy Ghost that precious deposit of Truth which had been committed to him. Order, surely, and not confusion, should characterize the assemblies and arrangements of God's people; but this cannot be unless the Word of God be rigorously applied as the test of all doctrine and all practice, and unless teachers qualified by God's own Spirit be recognised as the appointed means by which His people are to be fed with the food that is needful to their growth. If such teachers sent of God be not sought after and owned; if all the Lord's people are supposed to be occasionally, if not abidingly, "prophets;" if circumstances connected with wealth, birth, or worldly standing, are deemed to give fitness for control, or presidency, or prominence in the Church of God—what then can be expected except confusion, error, and finally, heretical departure from the faith? In Cromwell's camp it was said that there were none to be taught, because all were teachers. "It was said of Athens that you might walk through her streets, and more readily find gods than men: it might be said of the latter years of the Commonwealth that there were almost as many sects as worshippers." This description is true, and we well know the terribleness of the reaction that followed. An hour of liberty after bondage is the very time when the closest guidance of God's Truth is needed; and *that* cannot be received by His people collectively except through His Word, unfolded by persons whom He has, by His Spirit, qualified. If the saints of God individually were instructed in Holy Scripture and loved it, they would soon be able to discern who were, and who were not, fitted to be Guides. They would be able to discern the ruin of the walls of Truth, and might be perhaps privileged to aid in their restoration. But in default of such knowledge, their condition must be as that of the blind or the deaf, whose wisdom, while they so continue, is to be quiet and sit still. Nehemiah welcomed the co-operation of all who were *able* to labour with him for the restoration of the walls of Jerusalem. But a necessary qualification in those who so laboured was, that they should be capable of distinguishing between "rubbish" and "stones;" or at any rate, that they should be willing to submit to the guidance of those who were able to make the needed distinction. Of this we may be very sure, that Truth alone can guide to the true "valley" of separation, or give vigour and fruitfulness to that which is planted there.

The relations, past, present, and to come of the earth, and all things in it, whether of men individually, or of nations corporately, or of Rulers, or of Israel, or of the Church, both professing and true—the relations in which all these stand to God and God to them, is abundantly revealed in Scripture: and the right knowledge of these relations is the knowledge of Truth. Yet how little is the apprehension of these things either possessed or sought after! The various lessons taught by the different dispensations that have been or are yet to be, are not learned. Even the difference between a paradisiacal earth that did *not* groan, and a fallen earth that *does* groan, is feebly recognised; and Christians (even true Christians) marvel when they are told that they are as branches or twigs, few and little, that grow on a cankered bough—a bough destined to be broken off in judgment, although in them (the twigs) God's grace has preserved life, and sap, and fruitfulness which He will not fail to acknowledge both now and in the day of glory. Few, however, understand the lesson. They know not what the branch is, nor the canker, nor the coming excision, nor that which is to follow thereon. "Ah Lord God! they say of me, Doth he not speak parables?" were the words of the Prophet of old. The Prophets and Apostles would still say so if they could visit earth and witness the manner in which their testimonies respecting the future are received.

But how altered the scene when the veil shall at last be rent from the heart of Israel. Not only shall the light of Truth break upon their souls with a fulness and power which we Gentiles have not known, but their hearts shall be prepared not only to welcome the light, but to retain and to use it with a faithfulness and vigour that will not languish, but be maintained continuously. "The Redeemer shall come to Zion, and unto them that turn from transgression in Jacob, saith the Lord. As for me, this is my covenant with them, saith the Lord; my Spirit that is upon thee, and my words which I have put in thy mouth, shall not depart out of thy mouth, nor out of the mouth of thy seed, nor out of the mouth of thy seed's seed, saith the Lord, from henceforth and for ever." Is. lix. 20. "I will betroth thee unto me for ever; yea, I will betroth thee unto me in righteousness, and in judgment, and in lovingkindness, and in mercies. I will even betroth thee unto me in faithfulness: and thou shalt know the Lord." Hosea ii. 19. "The remnant of Israel shall not do iniquity, nor speak lies; neither shall a deceitful tongue be found in their mouth: for they shall feed and lie down, and none shall make them afraid." Zeph. iii. 13. Their soul shall be as the soul of a weaned child. Ps. cxxxi. They shall lean wholly on the Lord their God, and therefore shall be as Mount Zion which cannot be removed, but abideth for ever. Ps. cxxv. It shall be said of them, "Behold, how good and how pleasant it is for brethren to dwell together in unity." Ps. cxxxiii. Thus shall they be indeed a prepared people, fitted to have communion with the thoughts and intentions of the Lord—fitted under Him as priests to instruct, and as kings to govern all nations. They shall be "a kingdom of priests." "Men shall call them priests of our Lord, and ministers of our God. All that see them shall acknowledge then that they are the seed that the Lord has blessed."

Well therefore can we understand the reason of the call to the Shulamite (i.e. to the Bride of Solomon) to return. "Return, return, O Shulamite; return, return, that we may look upon thee." Not till the true Solomon shall appear and establish His glory in the earth, and call the daughter of Zion back to His love, and teach her to call Him Ishi (my husband) and betroth her unto Him for ever in faithfulness, and lovingkindness, and in mercy—not till then, shall the darkness that now broods over the nations depart, nor Truth have in the earth any better witness to its power than such as is supplied by the checked and hindered fruitfulness of that valley, which, even if it were rightly fruitful, would still find its fruitfulness despised. However faithfully and successfully the pilgrim-stranger might have laboured, she and her labours would still have been by men contemned.

But it shall be otherwise with the Shulamite. In her shall be seen grace and glory. The standing that she will take in earth will be one of manifested strength and glorious power. In her shall be seen Mahanaim—*two* hosts.

"Mahanaim" was a word used by Jacob when on his return with his little band from the land of his exile, the angels of God met him. And when Jacob saw them he said, "This is God's host: and he called the name of that place Mahanaim"—i.e. "two hosts." Jacob, as I have elsewhere observed,* was ever wont to magnify his own strength, and to exalt it into virtual co-equality with the strength of God. We might indeed have supposed that in beholding the might and majesty of the Host of God, Jacob would have forgotten his own little company: but he did not; for it was not the habit of Jacob to forget himself, nor any thing connected with himself. He could not forget the band which he for so many years had laboured to gather; nor consent that it should stand in any other place than one of acknowledged association with the Host of Heaven. Hence the word, "Mahanaim."

Yet expressions which God may permit or cause His servants to use, may conceal beneath them a meaning which they who use them apprehend not. So was it with the word, "Mahanaim." It em-

---

See "History of Jacob," p.p. 25, 26.

bodies a truth for which heaven and earth, in ages yet to come, will praise and magnify the God of Jacob for ever. For an hour is coming when Israel, after having been "brought very low," shall suddenly be strengthened by the Lord of Hosts their God, "when I have bent Judah for me, filled the bow with Ephraim, and raised up thy sons, O Zion, against thy sons, O Greece, and made thee as the sword of a mighty man. And the Lord shall be seen over them, and his arrow shall go forth as the lightning: and the Lord God shall blow the trumpet, and shall go with whirlwinds of the south." Zech. ix. 13. "And thou, O tower of the flock, the strong hold of the daughter of Zion, unto thee shall it come, even the first dominion; the kingdom shall come to the daughter of Jerusalem . . . . . for I will make thine horn iron and thy hoofs brass: and thou shalt beat in pieces many people: and I will consecrate their gain unto the Lord, and their substance unto the Lord of the whole earth." Micah iv 8, 13. See also Micah vii. 16. These, and many other like passages, supply abundant evidence as to Israel being made the host of the Lord *in the earth*. Yet not in dissociation from the hosts that are above. "Thither cause thy mighty ones to come down, O Lord," are words used in relation to the time of Israel's deliverance. "The Lord, my God shall come, and all the saints with thee" "The house of David shall be as God, as the angel of the Lord before them." "The Lord shall be seen over them." The strength and glory of the host of heaven shall thus be connected with the strength of Israel in the earth; so that duplication of might, heavenly and earthly, shall mark the condition of the Bride of Solomon in the day of her espousals —a condition well answering to the expression which Jacob ignorantly, yet prophetically used, when he uttered the word, "Mahanaim."

From the prominence given in this passage to the Shulamite and her glory, it might almost seem as if the pilgrim-stranger, who up to that moment had been the peculiar object of the Lord's solicitude and love, were forgotten: but it was far otherwise. A glory was to be hers greater and more perfect than that which the Shulamite was *then* to inherit: I speak not now of her final destiny. She who had so long sojourned in the earth as an outcast-wanderer, was now to share her Lord's unearthly glory above the heavens. Many times during the course of her pilgrimage she had been addressed as one to whom honour and glory pertained. Although never said to "*look forth*" as the morning (for that would have implied manifestation) yet she is described as being in her Lord's estimate comparable to one who moved in solemn state and majesty in the train of a triumphant monarch: (see chap. i.) and again: "Thou art beautiful, O my love, as Tirzah, comely as Jerusalem, terrible as an army with banners"—anticipative words descriptive of a glory that she deserved, and which in due time she would receive. And now that time had come She was to be numbered with that heavenly host, whose presence was to give to the Shulamite, one of the chief and most distinctive characteristics of her glory. She was to constitute part of that heavenly host that was appointed to watch over the Shulamite from above, and to minister to her from that heavenly City into which flesh and blood cannot enter. She was now to join her Lord on those mountains of Bether (separation) to which on former occasions she had bid Him return until the morning should break, and the shadows flee away, and the time be come for her to share His heavenly separation. And now that time had drawn nigh. She was soon to join her Lord on the mountains of His separation, and to become His associate in that distant glory

But what was her practical condition when thus called away unto her heavenly home? Was it one of weakness, or of strength? In another part of this "Song" we find the answer. She is described as coming up out of the wilderness as one faint and weary, leaning on the arm of her Beloved. The leaning was indeed a token of weakness: but the arm on which she leaned was almighty, and therein she had everlasting strength.

She leaned, evidently, as one very conscious that she was weak · very conscious that she was cast as a burden on the sufficiency of His faithful arm. There was no disposition to feed on the sinew of her own strength. No mention is made by her of past experiences either of sorrow, or of joy. There had been times when she had spoken of her "gardens" and her "pomegranates," her "milk" and her "spices," and when she had asked her Lord to come and view *with* her the scene of her labour and of their common joy. There had been times when, filled with the comfort of His love, she had besought the daughters of Jerusalem not to arouse Him as He rested with her in her lowly habitation. But it was otherwise now. Now that the termination of her wilderness-sojourn had really come, and new scenes were opening before her, her soul turned not to the thought of that which she had ministered unto the Lord: she thought only of that which she needed to be ministered to her. She made no mention of *her* ministrations. The sheep-folds, the vineyards, the garden, the valley, all her labours, all her joys, and all her sorrows connected therewith, were as things of the past. To *them* she looked not for the sustainment and comfort that she needed then. She knew that her need could be met by one thing only, even by love, full, faithful, free, almighty; and she knew where to look for that love. "Set me as a seal upon thine heart, as a seal upon thine arm," was her language; for thy heart is faithful, and thine arm almighty. If I were to mistrust thy love—if I were to question its faithfulness, how then would the love I bear to thee become to me the source of anguish unspeakable, for "jealousy is cruel as the grave: the coals thereof are coals of fire, which hath a most vehement flame." But I mistrust not thy love: wholly I lean on it. I know that it is love faithful and true—love that "many waters cannot quench, neither can the floods drown it." It is love, too, that is free as well as faithful, flowing spontaneously from the depths of its own fulness; for how can love be purchased? "If a man would give all the substance of his house for love, it would utterly be contemned." On such love she leaned: by such love she was sustained. *So* she left the wilderness: *so* she entered into her rest.

On Leviticus X.—The sin of Nadab and Abihu.

In the previous chapters of this book God had determined, in much detail, the order and method of the service appointed for His own holy Tabernacle. Of all the characteristics of that Tabernacle, none was more distinctive than the presence there of the perpetual fire on the Burnt offering altar. "The fire upon the altar shall be burning in it; it shall not be put out: and the priest shall burn wood on it every morning, and lay the burnt offering in order upon it; and he shall burn thereon the fat of the peace offerings. The fire shall ever be burning upon the altar; it shall never go out." Lev. vi. 12. This perpetual fire thus burning on the altar was the symbol appointed by God as the expression of His holiness in its relation to His people. Fire, taken simply by itself, is the symbol of the searching consuming power of holiness. Fire burns up dross: it consumes stubble: it searches into all things: it elicits fragrance where fragrance is, and consumes corruption where corruption is found. Here, however, the symbol is not fire merely, but fire burning on the Burnt offering altar—the expression not of holiness only, but of holiness appeased, placated, satisfied. For it had fed on sacrifice— sacrifice appointed of God. Thereon the fire of the altar had fed gratefully, and was *satisfied*. It was, therefore, fire that Israel could approach in peace. It welcomed their offerings and their gifts. The coal taken from that altar could touch the unclean lips of the sinner, and it could be said, "Lo, this hath touched thy lips; and thine iniquity is taken away, and thy sin purged." Is. vi. 7. Whilst holiness, as holiness, must burn destructively against every thing that is unclean or sinful, propitiated holiness—holiness *satisfied* by sacrifice, becomes the power of deliverance and blessing. Such was the lesson taught at the Burnt offering altar. It was the place of holiness, but the place of peace also, because of propitiation by means of sacrifice.

Accordingly, it was the appointment of the Lord that Aaron and the priestly family should use no fire in His Tabernacle, save that which burned on the Burnt offering altar. But this commandment was no sooner given than it was disobeyed. No sooner had Israel been placed under the sweet-smelling savour of the offered and accepted sacrifice, and *so* received God's blessing, than some among them turned the very privilege thus accorded them of approaching God in peace, into an occasion of transgression and deadly sin. "Nadab and Abihu, the sons of Aaron, took either of them his censer, and put fire therein, and put incense thereon, and offered strange fire before the Lord, which he commanded them not." They substituted for the fire of the altar other fire—fire that had *not* fed on sacrifice—unpropitiated fire, as if they, sinners, could, apart from sacrifice and bloodshedding, meet and have communion with the purity and holiness of God. This was, in truth, the meaning of their deed. They altered the symbol by which God had declared the ground of His relation in peace to His people. They virtually said that they would worship an unpropitiated God. The result was that fire went out from the Lord, and devoured them, and they died before the Lord.

Unless we knew the blinding power of sin, and the subtilty of the great deceiver, we should scarcely conceive it possible for the heart of man to sink into such a condition of fatuity as to imagine that it has ability and right to judge the ways of God. Who but God is competent to determine the claims of His own holiness? "His ways are not as our ways, nor His thoughts as our thoughts." Surely if there be any thing in which it behoves man to bow implicitly and unreservedly to God, it is when God reveals any thing respecting Himself and the way by which man—sinful man, can appear as an accepted worshipper in His presence. Are sinners to determine in what manner it is meet for God to exercise His love, and in what manner it is fitting for them to receive it? Yet that school of neologian infidelity that is now spreading 'around us pretend to be able to do this. Amidst all their disagreements (and their disagreements, notwithstanding "the verifying faculty" of which they boast, are infinite) they all, with the exception of such as deny the personal existence of a Supreme Being, admit that men are not quite independent of God and of His love. They allow that we do in many things need the exercise of God's love towards us; but they agree in saying that for God to display His love in saving us through the vicarious penal sufferings and obedience of a Substitute, is a thing unworthy of God and injurious to the dignity of man. *That* method of love, consequently, they reject: and in rejecting it, they reject the only kind of love that can reach man unto salvation.

Such was the character of the sin of Nadab and Abihu. They well knew that God was not wont, arbitrarily and groundlessly, to appoint what He appointed. Their consciences must have told them that each of His ordinances involved in them some sacred principle of Truth, of which *He* understood the value, even though *they* might fail to discern it. Audaciously to impugn His wisdom and contravene His commandment was, therefore, rebellion; and rebellion is as the sin of witchcraft—great, that is, as the sin of turning to unclean spirits for aid, and avowedly abandoning the living God. Yet Truth taught partially through types and shadows, brings not with it the same responsibility as attaches to the knowledge of those who live in the noon-tide light of revelation. God had not at that time spoken to us by His Son. The Holy Ghost had not at that time been sent down from heaven to unfold the reasons for the suffering and death of the Holy One. But now the one expiatory sacrifice, typified and predicted of old, has been offered. It has been preached also. The method of God's mercy has been explained; and multitudes have professed it to be their hope. Yet with the lip only, for they continue not in their confession. They abide not in that which they have professedly acknowledged as truth. As soon as some modern Nadab or Abihu crosses their path, substituting for the relations of God in redemption other relations in which the vicarious punishment of a Sin-bearer, wounded for the transgressions and bruised for the iniquities of His people, is ignored, they listen. They discern not, or (if they discern) they reject not the falsehood. They give ear to the smooth syren sounds and are taken in the snare. These are "the withdrawers," the non-abiders in Christ (see Heb x., and 1 John ii.) against whom the Apostles warn us. "They went out from us because they were not of us; for if they had been of us, they would no doubt have continued with us, but they went out that they might be made manifest that they were not all of us." As the day of Antichrist draws nigh, we shall behold myriads upon myriads treading this path. Multitudes, even in this favoured land, under the influence of that neologian or pantheistic infidelity of which Maurice, Jowett, Stanley, Kingsley, and their friends are the present upholders, have not only entered this path, but are pursuing and following it out to its very extremes. It is a path surely leading to perdition: for if the one true sacrifice as preached by the Apostles of Jesus be rejected, there remains no more sacrifice for sins. God has no other sacrifice in reserve. "There remaineth only a fearful looking for of judgment and fiery indignation that shall devour the adversaries."

Yet Satan is able to assume the garb of an angel of light. Where light from God has shone brightly, he is unable to deceive by darkness only. He finds it needful, therefore, to invest his servants with garments that bear some resemblance to the garments of the sanctuary, and to cause them to use incomplete, partial truth. Truth severed from the connexions with which God has associated it in His Word, answers the purpose of the Deceiver well. Accordingly, many of the modern teachers of Infidelity speak much of the goodness and beneficence of the character of God. They speak of His "fatherhood" towards men as His "offspring;" and of the love which, as the Father of His creatures, He exercises towards them all. Many of them are earnest, energetic, and zealous, not merely in spreading what they assume to be Truth, but also in deeds of philanthropy and mercy. They seek to relieve human woe, and to hush the groan of creation. They inveigh (and often justly) against many of the arrangements which human selfishness and pride have enforced not only in the world, but in the Church. They would reform and rectify society by new principles which (they say) the long-despised voice, not indeed of revelation, but of man's inner consciousness teaches. As Absalom in the day of David's weakness and age, pointed to the evils which David's rule had failed to overcome, and boasted of the new prosperity which his principles would give to Israel, so these teachers, refusing to distinguish between Truth and Truth's corruptions, and ascribing to Truth itself the consequences of the sin of its professed servants, delight in pointing the finger of scorn at the past history of Christianity, and ask whether Creeds and Bible Christianity have brought to men true prosperity and peace. Therefore, say they, let Creeds perish. Let the Bible be deposed from the supremacy into which the folly of some have sought to exalt it. Instead thereof, let the inner voice of humanity speak, and then there shall be prosperity. The mind of man, according to them, has an innate heavenly power of judging all things, and therefore can extract from the Bible, as from all other things, all that is worthy of being extracted, and can reject the dross. Being thus competent to guide itself it is independent of external legislation. It needs not written, much less stereotyped law. Such is their doctrine. Of what avail then is their devotedness—devotedness to a deadly system like this? What avails it that they speak smooth things respecting the "fatherhood" of God and the like? It is true that there is a sense in which God is their Father. But does he not say, "If I be a father, where is mine honour?" And can we honour God if we reject His Word—that Word of which He saith that He hath magnified it above all His name?

We deny not that man by creation has a right to speak of God as a Father. Thus Adam is called "the son of God," and the Apostle when speaking of the vile and idolatrous, yet intellectual Athenians, speaks of them as "the offspring of God." We admit this natural relation of man to God: nor do we desire to depreciate it as if nothing worth. Great graciousness, and longsuffering, and kindness, and love, are manifested by God towards men as men. He is "kind to the unthankful and evil." He does them good in that He sends them rain from heaven and fruitful seasons filling their hearts with food and gladness. He maintains before their consciences by the witness of the works that He hath made, a perpetual testimony to "His eternal power and Godhead." He grants to them providential mercies also, and sends among them the light of His Truth. All these things are mercies—mercies unspeakable, for which men ought to magnify and praise His name. But do they praise Him, or own Him, or worship Him? No. Conscience testifies—facts testify—Scripture testifies, that all these mercies are either despised, or else misused and perverted. Man by the very use of the mercies that are vouchsafed to him as a creature, aggravates his guilt, and proves that he is altogether dead in trespasses and sin. He proves that what he really needs is not light but *life*. He needs both ability and will to walk in light, and he needs also pardon. And this pardon and this life are in the Gospel provided: but provided in *Another*; and that other a sin-bearer, and therefore, a wrath-bearer—One who satisfieth the claims of God's governmental holiness by vicarious suffering and vicarious obedience in life and in death. But this is the very truth which the boasted verifying faculty repudiates; and in repudiating it, rejects the testimony of the Holy Ghost, and rejects salvation. Professedly magnifying God's fatherhood by creation, it scorns His fatherhood in redemption. Yet under the first fatherhood we perish because of our sin. His fatherhood in redemption alone brings salvation. They who attempt to worship God apart from the appeasement provided in the blood of the one great Sacrifice, repeat the sin of Nadab and Abihu; and must, except they repent, perish everlastingly. It is indeed a sin that brings with it in its train many others: but it is in itself a deliberate rejection of the one way of God's salvation All who say that they can meet God's unpropitiated holiness, must reject as useless the propitiation provided in Christ. They scorn the word that saith of Him *as the sacrifice*, "Look unto Him, and be ye saved, all ye ends of the earth."

Aaron's anguish was great when he beheld the hand of God thus stretched out destructively against his house. Yet, terrible as was the blow, it stayed the progress of the evil. It prevented fresh transgression on the part of those who had sinned, and preserved others from being drawn into the same abyss. But it is otherwise now. Judgment, whilst threatened merely, men despise: and thus evil becomes not only extended in scope but intensified in character. Can any one deny this, who with the Bible in his hand views what is now passing in the midst of Protestant Christendom? In viewing the scene around us, we have far greater reason to weep than either Aaron or Jeremiah. In the place where there has been most light, most privilege, most blessing, and where God still waits to be gracious, "lawlessness"—libertinism of soul is advancing most.

There is still indeed, even as there ever has been in every past dispensation, a remnant according to the election of grace; and among them there are *some*, though they may perhaps be but a few, who are beginning to read aright the lesson of this present hour. There are some who weep. For such the instruction and comfort of this chapter is especially intended. It is true indeed that the place held by Aaron and his sons, as typically bearing the iniquity of the congregation before the Lord, finds no counterpart in any office or service committed to any among the servants of Christ. In this Aaron and his household were types only of One—even of Him who once bore and for ever put away the sins of all His believing people. All their sins having been put away by His one finished offering (Heb. x.) there remains no need, no possibility of offering for sin again: for how could any thing be offered with a view of putting away that which is already gone? But there were other services connected with the Tabernacle beside those which had for their object the making atonement for sin; and in many of those services the people of Christ find the foreshadowing of relations which they at present hold towards God. For they too are priests: they too belong to the sanctuary of God, and find an altar there at which they feed. It is theirs also to offer the sacrifices of praise and thanksgiving, and to watch over and guard God's holy truths, and to learn with their lips to keep wisdom, and to put a difference between "holy and unholy, clean and unclean." The people of God (unless indeed their inward eye becomes enfeebled or darkened) well know the value and the honour of such services, and the blessedness of abiding stedfastly in them. And they are commanded to abide in them. No sorrow, no sense of discouragement,—not even the presence of apostasy in the very circle within which they stand is to daunt them, or to cause them to forget that the consecration of their God is upon their heads. Aaron and his sons that were left, were not to uncover their heads—that would have indicated that they renounced the service of their God, for the covered head was a token of professed subjection to Him whom they served: nor were they to rend their garments, for that would have been a virtual abandonment of the priestly office in which they had been called to serve. Therefore, however great may be the increase of evil and of sorrow (and they will increase greatly as the latter day comes on) the people of God have to take heed that none of these things move them or tempt them to retire from that Tabernacle and service to which God has called them, and to which, through His grace they belong, and shall belong for ever. They who shall surely be found in the Courts of His glory above, should be by nothing driven from the Courts of His service here.

They who reject the one way of approach unto God's covenant mercies through the one sacrifice once and for ever offered, are accustomed to speak much of looking through nature up to nature's God, and of worshipping in nature's temple the great beneficent Father of His creatures. Ignorant of the manner in which the Fall has affected creation physically, and themselves morally, they think to open up for themselves in the world's wide sphere, springs unnumbered of satisfying joy,—of training for themselves many a pleasant plant, many a fruitful vineyard, whose grapes shall fill their cups with the wine of gladness. The present is peculiarly a moment when men are looking forward to the earth's future with bright anticipation; expectant of the hour when the vineyards they are planting so busily shall yield their fruit. And fruit they *will* yield. But as is the vine, so also shall be the fruit. "Their vine is of the vine of Sodom and of the fields of Gomorrah: their grapes are grapes of gall, their clusters are bitter: their wine is the poison of dragons and the cruel venom of asps." Such grapes, such wine, the children of faith, the priests of God's sanctuary, must never touch.

I do not indeed say that the believer finds in earth no "wine" of which he may taste. On the contrary, we read of those who are dear to us in the flesh as well as in the Spirit. We know that God has supplied to us, and that richly, things for enjoyment—$εις$ $απολαυσιν$. We do not say, "Touch not, taste not, handle not," but we welcome the gifts of God's goodness, and take them as Jonathan took the honey in the wood (1 Sam. xiv. 24) and give God thanks, saying "the earth is the Lord's and the fulness thereof." Yet, however numerous the springs of holy joy thus supplied within the sphere of nature, it is not to that sphere that the child of faith turns when he seeks strength for the service of the sanctuary. He knows that that which strengthens for earth is far different from that which strengthens for heaven, and that the purest cup of earthly joy brings with it danger, for it may be immoderately, or else unseasonably, drank. At the best it has no tendency to quicken those sensibilities to things "unseen," which it is one of the chief objects of the instruction of the sanctuary to develop; because on their right development holy discrimination between good and evil depends. They consequently "who know the plague of their own heart," and how it is the tendency of our flesh to misuse or to pervert the best natural gifts of God's goodness, find little difficulty in apprehending the reason of the commandment given unto Aaron, "Do not drink wine nor strong drink, thou, nor thy sons with thee, when ye go into the Tabernacle of the congregation, lest ye die: it shall be a statute for ever throughout your generations. And that ye may put difference between holy and unholy, and between unclean and clean; and that ye may teach the children of Israel all the statutes which the Lord hath spoken unto them by the hand of Moses."

Amongst all the relations that we hold in earth there are none— none of our joys, or interests, or occupations, or services, of which we can say that from *them*, or the remembrance of them, we can derive strength for entrance into the sanctuary to meet the light, and holiness, and purity that are there. It belongs only to God, and to Him acting in the power of redemption, to provide that which is able to strengthen for His own holy presence. In calling His people near to serve Him in His sanctuary, He strengthens them not with the wine of earth, but with food from His own altar; and that food was

H

SACRIFICE. "Take," said Moses, "the meat-offering that remaineth of the offerings of the Lord made by fire, and eat it without leaven beside the altar: for it is most holy: . . . . . And the wave-breast and heave-shoulder shall ye eat in a clean place &c."

The meat-offering was the type of the pure unleavened character of Christ presented for us on the altar of the Cross—"an offering made by fire of a sweet savour unto the Lord." There is nothing that the believer more acutely feels in seeking to serve in the sanctuary, than the imperfectness inseparably connected with all those developments of thought and feeling that constitute what we call "character." However much the believer may long after perfectness, he well knows that there is nothing that he can bring (to use the typical language of this chapter) to the altar of God where that pure and holy and searching fire burneth, and say, "in these thoughts and in these services—indeed in all that I think and do, there is nothing, O God, in which the holy fire of thine altar will find any thing contrary to its own holiness." He cannot say, "Behold, O Lord, the shoulder of my strength: its strength is perfect, and it hath been, is being, and ever shall be, used only for Thee. It hath shrunk from no burden; it hath laboured and wearied not; all that it behoved it to bear, it hath borne, and that with a perfectness that hath in nothing fallen short of Thine own." He cannot lay bare his heart before the Lord and say, "Behold it, O Lord. Inspect my heart in all its tendencies, and Thou wilt find only that which is pure and holy as Thyself." Where amongst the sons of men is "the breast" that can thus be "waived" before the Lord, or where that shoulder of strength which can thus be presented and the inspection of His holiness challenged? Yet such a "shoulder" and such a "breast" must be found somewhere; or else the servants of God would be provided with no food whereby they could be strengthened to serve Him in the Sanctuary. Accordingly, God, in the abounding of His mercy and grace, hath provided it—provided it in Immanuel. In the strength of His vicarious service, in the presentation of His inward perfectness, in the offering of His perfect character, we find the antitypes to the heave-shoulder, and wave-breast, and unleavened meat-offering on which God commanded the priests of His Sanctuary to feed. All this perfectness has been presented for us, once and for ever; on our one altar, the Cross. God provided it in order to meet the claims of His own holiness, and also to supply unto us food: that we might not pine as those who have no perfectness of strength, no perfectness of inward being, no perfectness of character, but that we might be able to say, that we have all provided for us in Another, even in Him who hath served and offered *in our stead*. This is food indeed: better than any wine that can in any wise be extracted out of the circumstances of this fallen earth.

But there were injunctions also respecting the place and manner in which the meat-offering was to be fed on. It was to be eaten " without leaven " in close proximity to the altar. Being, as I have already said, a type of the pure unleavened character of Christ, no leaven was to be mingled with it when offered on the altar of God: nor, after it had been offered, was it to be fed upon *with* leaven.

No one who really knows the Truth of God could for a moment tolerate the thought that there was a shadow of imperfectness either in *the nature* or in *the character* of Christ. He was at once " without blemish " ($αμωμος$) and " without spot " ($ασπιλος$).* In Him heavenliness was seen, manifested and sustained in all patient perfectness in the midst of the sorrows and corruptions of earth. Nor are God's people altogether unconscious of the blessedness of the great truth, that the Holy One has presented unto God for them the value of His own character in all its tried and developed excellency. They know what it is to strengthen themselves by feeding on this food; and that too, " near the altar "—that is to say, at the place where the claim of God's holiness and the manner in which that claim has been satisfied by the pure unleavened offering is brought to remembrance. It is a place so holy that even the very best of our services must appear as " leaven " there—how much more all that springs from our worldliness or evil. The command therefore not to conjoin with the meat-offering, when we feed on it, " leaven," is, in effect, a commandment to conjoin with it nothing. Its excellency is an isolated excellency. We are to feed on it alone—eschewing evil, eschewing ourselves, and every thing that emanates from ourselves.

We must not however forget that food even when provided and set before us is not necessarily fed on. Of this we have a memorable example in Aaron himself. He, together with his sons, as having to bear *typically* the sins of those whom they represented, were especially

---

* See the difference between these words considered in " Notes on the Greek of the First Chapter of Romans," page 110, as advertised at end of this volume.

commanded to feed on the Sin-offering whenever its blood had not been brought into the holy place. By feeding thereon he was to be made strong to bear (typically of course, not really) the iniquities of the congregation, and it was, moreover, a eucharistic act—an act of thankful and happy recognition of the mercy received by himself and by all whom as Priest he represented, in that the sin for which the offering had been presented was, by means of such offering, expiated and forgiven. If he fed not on it in the appointed manner, his priestly work was not accomplished. He would, as Priest, fail in attaining the appointed end. And he *did* fail. The sorrow that had fallen on him and on his house was, he said, so heavy, that he had no strength to perform the appointed service. A heart that sorrow hath crushed cannot be as if it were uncrushed. This was Aaron's condition, and Moses saw it was so and acquiesced; for Moses had no power to remove the cause of the shortcoming by turning Aaron's weakness into strength.

Aaron had "infirmity" (Heb. vii. 28); and it was meet that he should exhibit it. It was meet that he should stand in emphatic contrast with that Holy One in all whose services and relations before God and before man, we find, not failure or weakness, but steadfastness and strength. Needing no sacrifice for Himself, but coming to be a Priest for others, He found Himself at the moment when He was about to perform His great priestly act of offering Himself up as the one sacrifice for sin, surrounded by circumstances which would have dismayed and shaken the constancy of any heart excepting His. Christ was not devoid of feeling. His very holiness gave acuteness to all His sensibilities: and His appreciations of every thing were perfect because His soul was in perfect communion with God. His grief was not unreal when, at the close of His ministry He had to say, "Israel is not gathered" (Is. xlix. 5), and when He wept over Jerusalem; or when, beholding apostasy manifested in the midst of the few whom He had gathered around Himself, He said, "he that eateth bread with me hath lifted up his heel against me;" or when He heard Peter denying Him with cursing and oaths; or when He beheld all His disciples forsake Him and flee. The ruin seemed irrevocable and complete; and this too was the moment when He was about to meet that baptism of suffering wherewith He was to be baptised—where our apprehensions fail to follow Him. Here were sorrows indeed: sorrows that would have overwhelmed hopelessly and for ever, any one excepting Him who was appointed to bear them and to overcome.

But He was the Rock; and as a Rock He stood. Psalms were in His lips even on the Cross. No depth of suffering took from Him His ability to praise and to give thanks. Out of the depths His cry ascended; and it was a cry of confidence and love towards Him whom He was glorifying in the fires. Aaron quailed under calamity, and his Priesthood failed; but Jesus overcame, and His priesthood abideth for ever. "The law maketh men high priests which have infirmity; but the word of the oath, which was since the law, maketh the Son, who is consecrated for evermore." According to the power of that perfect offering once and for ever made, He ever liveth to make intercession for His people, "nor shall He fail nor be discouraged until He hath set judgment in the earth, and the isles shall wait for His law."

Of all the servants of Christ, there probably have been none who so well understood what it was to strengthen himself for his service by feeding on the Sin-offering as St. Paul. He had, indeed, no typical place to sustain like that of Aaron in foreshadowing Christ. Christ had come: Christ had completed the great work of redemption: and it was St. Paul's joy to search into and apprehend that which Christ had wrought for His people. He knew that the one, once-offered, finished sacrifice had placed its protective power over all God's believing people for ever and ever; that their inheritance was love, and not judgment; and that almighty grace reigned over them for evermore. It was his consciousness of this that enabled him amidst all discouragements, whether present or foreseen, to serve with a hope that never languished, and a vigour that never was impaired. At Corinth and in Galatia, he knew much anguish and many tears; yet in neither place did he quail before the storm. He strengthened himself in the remembrance that the saints of God are loved with an everlasting love, and blessed with blessings that no circumstances can alienate; and therefore if they wandered, he laboured for their restoration; and though they might cease to love him, he continued to love and to serve them still. "Though the more abundantly I love you the less I be loved." And afterwards at the close of his course, when the Church, because of the creeping in of wicked men and seducers, was beginning to cease from being the witness of Truth, and was entering on that disastrous course of evil which has since made Christendom what it is, how did St. Paul, though bitterly mourning over the present evil and prophetically cognisant of that which was to come, uphold the fainting hands of Timothy; beseeching him still to labour and to serve. What though perilous times were to come—what though other saints of God were to turn away from him, as those in Asia had; did not the "firm foundation" that God had laid remain that which it ever was? Did not the Lord know them who were His? Had the love in which the people of God were called, changed? Might not Timothy still strengthen himself in the grace that was in Christ Jesus and remember that God had not given him "the spirit of timidity ($\delta\epsilon\iota\lambda\iota\alpha s$), but of love, and of power, and of soundness of mind?" And though the Church might have become as "a large house" in which vessels unto dishonour were mingled up with vessels that were unto honour, yet this only afforded the servant of God fresh opportunity for holy discrimination that he might purge himself of the one, and gather around himself the other. The abounding of falsehood only made it the more needful for him to hold fast "the form of sound words," and to keep by the Holy Ghost that dwelt in him the precious deposit of Truth committed to his charge. This St. Paul did, and this he exhorted Timothy to do. "The bow" of the Apostle "abode in strength." The holy energy of his spirit did not give way under all the pressure that was allowed to bear down upon him during the concluding years of his ministry. The grace that had strengthened him at the beginning continued to strengthen him at the close, and gave him habitually to know and to appreciate the preciousness of that Sin-offering which was still the same whether it sheltered the children of the kingdom in the hour of their united strength, or during the prolonged season of their disunion, scattering, and weakness. He looked for and received the continued supply of the spirit of Christ (Philippians i. 19) and was able during the darkest period of his course to say, "I am strong as to all things through Christ that strengtheneth me."

As to ourselves, we are now, in all probability entering on the last phase but one of the lengthened reign of evil. The old age of iniquity is being reached. Men more advanced in disobedience than Nadab and Abihu are triumphing in the prosperity of their schemes; and professing Protestantism is being divided between the mummeries and idolatries of ecclesiastical corruption, or else is giving itself over to the licentiousness of infidel speculation. Yet few even of Christ's people recognise these things, or care to give heed to the warnings of Scripture touching the latter days. They either ignore altogether the rising evil, and speak hopefully and boastfully of progress in good; or else say that the clouds, though they may seem to threaten, will soon disperse and vanish before the increasing power of the light of Truth. Others again, whilst owning the approach of a coming struggle with the powers of darkness, tell us with all confidence (though Scripture positively teaches the reverse) that the saints of God are to be taken from the earth before the hour of Truth's last conflict comes, and would have us believe that it is a blessing to be deprived of the honour of fighting in that last great battle field where soldiership for Christ is most needed, and triumph is most glorious. They count it no honour to be numbered among the faithful few who will at that time "overcome because of the blood of the Lamb and the word of their testimony, and will not love their lives unto the death." (Rev. xii. 11.)

To see such obstinate determination not to bow to Holy Scripture at a moment when there ought to be the closest adhesion to its testimonies, is bitterly discouraging: for all hope of union in the Truth (the only union which is really in the Spirit) is hereby frustrated. Yet on this very account it is the more needful that we should strengthen ourselves by feeding on the Sin-offering and hold fast our confession. This chapter of apostasy and sorrow does not nullify the blessing with which the preceding chapter concludes. There we see all Israel congregated and placed under the protection of accepted sacrifice. Moses and Aaron, the King and Priest conjointly, spread forth their hands and blessed them. Fire from heaven came down and consumed the sacrifice. It was Heaven's attestation to its excellency. The people saw and shouted, and fell on their faces. It was indeed a transitory scene; but it was typical. It was a type appointed of God, and therefore a pledge from Him of that yet future hour when Israel, humble but rejoicing, shall stand in manifested and everlasting acceptance under the excellency of the one true Sacrifice and receive the blessing of the true Priest and King, the great Melchisedek—whom to foreshadow it was needful that Moses and Aaron should unite their offices. Then too around Melchisedek in His glory, shall stand, raised and glorified likewise, a priestly family—even all who from Abel downward have suffered the reproach of Christ and of His Truth. They shall be strengthened according to His glory then, and "follow Him whithersoever He goeth," and enter with Him the heavenly Sanctuary to reign and to serve under Him and with Him, "made Kings and Priests unto God."

But whilst for *these* blessings we wait until the day of glory dawns, we have also blessings in possession; for all the *spiritual* blessings of Israel in the day of their acceptance we forestal. Already has our great Melchisedek placed us under the everlasting protection of the one finished and accepted sacrifice. Already has He spread forth His hands towards us and blessed us. It was His last act on earth as He ascended into the heavens. Already to us has come, and that for ever, "the acceptable time, and the day of salvation." Heaven is opened over our heads in peace and in complacency, never to be closed again. Such are the present mercies in which we are called to rejoice with "joy unspeakable," yet chastened, because of our knowledge of ourselves and of the circumstances around us; that so our confidence might be combined with reverence and godly fear; that we might "cleanse ourselves from all filthiness of the flesh and spirit, perfecting holiness in the fear of God." That which strengthens unto this end is holy strength that cometh from God.

Introduction.

The Judgments of the Court of Arches, and of the Judicial Committee of the Privy Council, in the case of the REV. ROWLAND WILLIAMS, D.D., *one of the writers in the Essays and Reviews—Considered.*

THERE are two ways in which Holy Scripture may be degraded from the place assigned to it by God. It may be directly charged with falsehood; or else, its truthfulness being admitted, it may, nevertheless, be deprived of its supremacy by the exaltation of other writings, or of Tradition, or of Decrees, into co-equal authority with it.

It scarcely need be said that the mere acknowledgment of the authority of Scripture is not sufficient to constitute a true Christian. Personal faith—personal reliance of soul on the blood of expiation alone brings into the fold of Jesus. Yet it should be remembered, that the denial of the supreme authority of Scripture in either of the ways mentioned, involves, *ipso facto*, in the guilt of direct rebellion against the government of God. God, as the great Ruler of the Universe, has sent into the world His written Word abundantly attested by adequate evidence; and He requires that its authority should be recognised by all who have that evidence presented to them. It is evidence too strong (if honestly examined) to be rejected by any, except those who wilfully blind themselves to its force. As then, the subject of an earthly monarch would be deemed a rebel if he deliberately refused to own the authority of ALL his sovereign's laws; or, if he exalted into co-equality with them other pretended laws which his king had *not* sanctioned, so, he who rejects that Book which God has sent into the world as the one authoritative exponent of His will (either by charging it with falsehood, or by exalting anything else into co-equality therewith) does thereby constitute himself a rebel against the Divine government. He commits a breach of the most important of the natural relations in which man, as a creature, stands before God.

A revived apprehension of the honour and reverence due to God's Holy Word gave to the Protestant Reformation its chief impulse. The Reformers in contending with the Papists argued for the sole authority of Holy Scripture. In contending for its *sole* authority it is superfluous to say that they contended for its truthfulness. The assertion of the supreme authority of Scripture formed the very keystone of the Protestant arch. Protestantism rejected the blasphemous dogma of Neology, that the inspiration of the writers of Scripture differed not in kind from the so-called inspiration of Milton, or Luther, or any ordinary Christian; and they equally rejected the no less blasphemous doctrine of the Romanist that " there is a divine voice *immutably and infallibly* guiding the Church at this hour."*
The Romanist affirms that a verifying and legislative faculty resides in what he is pleased to denominate the Catholic Church. The Neologian contends that such a faculty dwells in mankind generally, whereby each man is made the regulator of his own way. If the one system be Scylla, the other is Charybdis. Both equally destroy, and that for ever.

The government of England, at the time of the Reformation, apprehended the momentous importance of this question. Solemnly and formally, they acknowledge Holy Scripture as coming truly from God, and as containing, and alone containing, the authoritative revelation of His will.

As a consequence of this national recognition of the Scripture, great and peculiar mercies have been vouchsafed to our Land. Will any one deny this who reviews the history of this country for the last three hundred years, and contrasts it with that of other countries (France, Italy, Spain) where the Scripture has not been similarly recognised or disseminated?

But how different is England's governmental relation to the Bible now!

A few years ago, Neologian Teachers, openly impugning the truthfulness of Holy Scripture, suddenly appeared in the established Church. The Government of England were not unacquainted with the history of Neology in Germany and elsewhere. They knew what havoc it had wrought in foreign lands; how it had doubted, and questioned, and subtilised, and analysed, until it had made Truth a

---

* See Dr. Manning as approvingly quoted by Dr. Pusey. Eirenicon, p. 9.

phantom, and left humanity like a ruined wreck to drift rudderless on the dark ocean of sceptical uncertainty. I am "rolling rudderless," said Coleridge in 1807, "the wreck of what I once was." "Wretched, helpless, hopeless," was his description of himself seven years later. Coleridge had drunk deep of Germanism; and on him primarily rests the responsibility of introducing it into this country. Coleridge's personal history was well known in England; and did of itself supply a sufficient warning.

But no warnings have been heeded. On the contrary, Neology has, in the persons of some of its chief teachers, been by the government of England smiled on, honoured, dignified. Witness the positions held by such men as Mr. Jowett, and Dr. Stanley, and Kingsley. See the efficient aid rendered to the system by the Bishop of London. Have the government, in appointing such men to places of honour and influence, acted in accordance with the desires of the people of England, or have they run counter to them? The people of this country are wont to speak loudly enough when they deem any of their political rights or their commercial interests to be endangered. "Public opinion" in England claims to be supreme; and certainly its voice, when uttered, is no weak one. Oftentimes it has shown itself sufficiently strong to compel even the most resolute governments to pause, and not unfrequently to retrace their steps. But, in the present case, public opinion has made no such effort. It has looked on with Gallio-like indifference, and by its silence, sanctioned.

The selection for high office of persons like Jowett, Stanley, and Kingsley, was a sufficiently ominous act. But it has been quickly followed by another. The Crown has since been appealed to judicially. The Bishop of Salisbury demanded that certain passages contained in an essay of Dr. Rowland Williams, and published in a volume entitled "Essays and Reviews" should be condemned as contrary to "the Articles and Formularies of the Established Church." The following is the condensed form of accusation. "We article and object to you, the said Reverend Rowland Williams, that the manifest tendency, scope, object, and design of the whole essay is to inculcate a disbelief in the Divine inspiration and authority of the Holy Scriptures contained in the Old and New Testament; to reduce the said Holy Scriptures to the level of a mere human composition, such as the writings of Luther and of Milton; to deny that the Old Testament contains prophecies or predictions of Our Saviour and other persons and events; to deny that the Prophets, speaking under the special inspiration of the Holy Spirit, foretold human events; to deny altogether or greatly discredit the truth and genuineness of the historical portions of the Old Testament and the truth and genuineness of certain parts of the New Testament, and the truth and reality of the miracles recorded as facts in the Old and New Testaments; to deny or interpret by a meaning at variance with that of the Church the doctrines of original sin, of infant baptism, of justification by faith, of atonement and propitiation by the death of our Saviour, and of the incarnation of our Saviour. And this was and is true, and we article and object as before."

The Cause was heard in two Courts: first, before Dr. Lushington, the Dean of the Court of Arches; and secondly, on appeal, before the "Judicial Committee of the Privy Council;" which Court, to use the words of Dr. Lushington, is "the highest Court that exercises Ecclesiastical Jurisdiction in this realm." The result has been that Dr. Williams has been acquitted on *every* charge; and thus a licence to teach Neologian infidelity in the high places of the Establishment, as unrestrictedly as the most ardent votary of infidelity need desire, has been granted. Evidence of this, and of the manner in which the appointed tests were either altered or evaded so as to insure acquittal, will be found in the following pages. Yet "public opinion" slumbers on with an indifference that seems to betoken judicial infatuation.

If it be admitted that the national and governmental recognition of the supremacy of Holy Scripture has, from the reign of Edward VI. till now, brought upon this country great and peculiar blessings, can we suppose that a governmental act by which the Bible has been dishonoured and degraded should be acquiesced in by the nation at large, without bringing down upon our land great and peculiar judgments? A plague has already been sent among our herds; our flocks also appear to be threatened, and other judgments seem to impend. Surely mere general confession will not avail to meet the emergency of the present hour. A specific sin has been nationally committed: a sin of the deepest dye, and it is needful that it should be specifically confessed and repented of.

I have no expectation that the following statements will have any effect upon what is called the public mind. Few, probably, will care to read them; and if even they should be read, they will be read to be despised. Yet I deem it a duty to endeavour to make my fellow country-men acquainted with facts which many, I fear, have very

INTRODUCTION.

inadequately, if at all, apprehended. I deem it also a duty to offer an individual protest (however feeble and ineffectual) against a judgment which has certainly been based on a principle of "non-natural" interpretation hitherto unknown in our Judicial Courts. I feel too, a melancholy satisfaction in recurring to the past and in vindicating the Reformers from the unjust imputation of having omitted to maintain in the Articles and Formularies, by them sanctioned, the absolute truthfulness of Holy Scripture, and the great and essential doctrine of the transference to believers of the merits of Christ their Saviour.

The Church of God too—the true Church ought to consider these things, and to see in them "signs of the times"—signs that loudly call on them to arouse themselves, and to take up a very different position from that which they are at present occupying in the great battle-field of falsehood and truth. If we would uphold the Bible, we must obey the Bible. We must shun compromise and Jehoshaphat-like alliances with the enemies of God. We must be willing to separate between the precious and the vile, and not suffer ourselves to be deluded by the notion that we are not individually responsible for acts done *officially*, or obedience rendered *officially*.

There are some who acknowledge that a great sin has been committed, and that evil is at present progressing fearfully; but yet they comfort themselves with the thought that there will be a re-action, and that the Truth will yet prevail. Eventually, indeed, Truth *will* prevail: but *not* in the present dispensation. The Scripture declares that in the present dispensation (and *that* it is with which we are now concerned) Truth will *not* prevail. On the contrary, "evil men and seducers will wax worse and worse," and Antichrist will close the scene.

Others have said that this Judgment of the Privy Council, fearful as it is, is yet but one Judgment on one specific case, and does not necessarily determine future Judgments on future cases. But it has been determined by high legal authority* that the principle enunciated in this Judgment will certainly not be departed from in any future case that can be brought within the same category. The *same* statements, therefore, as those made by Dr. Williams, may with impunity be spread through the length and breadth of our land by

---

* See case submitted to Sir Roundell Palmer and Sir Hugh Cairns by Dr. Pusey.

ministers authorised, paid, and dignified, by the nation. No Neologist need desire to exceed the limits that have been allowed to Dr. Williams and Mr. Wilson. The passages quoted from their Essays and presented for adjudication, contain the very pith and marrow of Neology. An advanced Neologian may well satisfy himself with a far narrower limit, and yet spread the dogmas of Neology to his heart's content Of this we may be very sure, that the tests that have been relaxed for the purposes of this Judgment, will never again be applied in their proper stringency. In future cases (should they arise) we shall see them yet further relaxed. The temper of the hour hates stringency, and loves relaxation; and Governors are looked upon as mere functionaries set to represent the mind of society. Nor are we concerned with hypothetical speculations about the future. A national sin *has been* committed. Courts exercising the judicial authority of the Crown in this realm have pronounced judgments, by means of which Clergymen of the Established Church who have imputed falsehood to the Word of God are permitted to retain their ministerial positions, with liberty to teach for the future what they have taught in the past. The Laws of England, or, at any rate, the administrators of those laws have refused to restrain the governmentally authorised religious Teachers of England from assailing the truthfulness of the Word of the living God. The Scripture, therefore, has been by this act, nationally dishonoured. The question is whether this great transgression shall be repented of, and its consequences obviated, before it is too late.

Remarks on Dr. Lushington's Judgment.

"THE CHIEF QUESTION TO BE TREATED OF IN THE PRESENT CASE IS ONE OF MOMENTOUS IMPORTANCE TO THE CLERGY AND THE LAITY. IT IS NO LESS THAN THE QUESTION OF THE AUTHORITY (TO USE THE BEST TERM I CAN) TO BE ASCRIBED BY THE CLERGY TO THE BIBLE."

SUCH are the words by which Dr. Lushington himself prefaces his judgment; and they are most true. It is indeed a question of "*momentous importance*" to us all, whether the Clergy of the Protestant Establishment in this realm shall, henceforward, have a legalised right to dishonour and degrade "God's word written" by attributing to it *falsehood*.

One might have supposed that when a Protestant Ecclesiastical Judge found himself able to state the question thus, he would have regarded it as a question which, tried by any of the standards of the Protestant Reformation, admitted of no debate. For if there was one doctrine which all the Protestant Churches that trace their origin to the Reformation, accepted without qualification and without reserve, it was the doctrine of the supreme and exclusive authority of Scripture. The Bible, the whole Bible, and the Bible only, was declared to be the one standard by which all statements were to be tested—all principles tried. This doctrine was the very key-stone of the Protestant arch. It was the great subject of the Reformers' conflict with Rome. Rome exalted the Apocrypha, Tradition and Decrees, into co-equality with the Scripture; whilst the Reformers contended that the Scripture only was the Word of God, and therefore alone authoritative.

"The Church of Rome," says Bishop Burnet, "and we do both
"agree that the Scriptures are of Divine inspiration. Those of that
"communion acknowledge that every thing contained in the Scripture

"is true and comes from God; but they add to this that the Books of "the New Testament were occasionally written and not with the "design of making them the full Rule of faith, but many things were "delivered orally by the Apostles, which if they are faithfully trans- "mitted to us, are to be received by us with the same submission and "respect that we pay to their writings: and they also believe that "these traditions are conveyed down infallibly to us, and that to "distinguish betwixt true and false doctrines and traditions there "must be an infallible authority lodged by Christ with His Church. "We on the contrary, affirm that the Scriptures are a complete rule "of faith, and that the whole Christian religion is contained in them, "and nowhere else."* *Burnet on Sixth Article.*

Conflicting with Rome on a subject so vitally important as this, the Reformers well weighed the opinions they advanced. The autho-

---

* When the Roman Catholic speaks of Scripture, he does not mean thereby the Hebrew and Greek of the Old and New Testaments, but the Vulgate Latin Edition, or the Douay and Rhemish *translations*, embracing also *the Apocrypha*. This is his Bible, and this, *together with tradition*, constitutes his rule of faith, or what he calls the revealed or inspired Word of God. Thus the writers of the Trent Catechism say :—"All the doctrines of Christianity are derived from the Word of God, *which includes Scripture and Tradition*." Again· "If we would have the whole rule of Christian faith and practice, we must not be content with those Scriptures which Timothy knew from his infancy, that is, with the Old Testament alone, nor yet with the New Testament, without taking along with it the Traditions of the Apostles and the interpretation of the Church, to which the Apostles delivered both the book and the true meaning of it" (See Note of the Roman Catholic version on 2 Tim. iii. 16) Again, we read in Milner's "End of Controversy," Letter x. p. 53 ·—"The Catholic Rule of Faith is not merely the written word of God, but the whole word of God both written and unwritten; in other words, Scripture and Tradition, and these propounded and explained by the Catholic Church. This implies that we have a twofold rule or law, and that we have an interpreter or judge to explain it, and to decide upon it in all doubtful points." Thus Scripture, the Apocrypha, Tradition written and unwritten, and all as interpreted by the Church or Clergy, form the Word of God, or the rule of faith, according to the Church of Rome. See Elliott's "*Delineation of Roman Catholicism*," *p 8, sold at 66, Paternoster Row*

Now, I say, it is an act of direct rebellion against God to establish *two* or *many* rules of faith, when God has established only *one* and this the Roman Church has deliberately and avowedly done. It stands therefore in as distinct a place of rebellion against the Legislation of God as Neology does. The doctrine of continuous inspiration as held by Dr. Williams, is not more false (though its form be different) from that held by Dr. Manning and Dr. Pusey. Contrast with the statements just given, those of the Reformers —"In Holy Scripture is *fully*

rity, and *exclusive* authority, of Scripture on every subject of which it treats, was made by them the very foundation of the system they were constructing. They refused to admit, in any sense, the continuousness of authoritative inspiration such as that which was possessed by the Prophets and Apostles. They maintained that *such* inspiration did with the Apostles cease; and that at their death the Canon of Scripture closed. In the xx. and xxi. Articles the English Reformers expressly refuse to acknowledge *as authoritative* either the decrees of any Church or Churches, or of General Councils. They refused to ascribe to them such a presence of the Holy Ghost as would, if it had been granted, have rendered their decrees equal in authority with Scripture. By thus denying the continuousness of that kind of inspiration that was vouchsafed to the writers of Holy Scripture, the Reformers *essentially* differed both from the Papists and from the Neologians, who both assert the continuousness of such inspiration—the Papist, in order that he may give infallibility to Popes and Councils—the Neologian, in order that he may drag down Apostles and Prophets to the standing of other men, and place Milton and Shakespeare on the same level with Paul or John. The very foundation doctrine, therefore, of every Protestant Confession framed at the Reformation, was in direct antagonism to the system both of the Papist and the Neologian.

The following extracts sufficiently show the tone in which the early English Reformers thought and wrote respecting Holy Scripture.—
" We receive and embrace all the canonical Scriptures both of the Old
" and New Testament; giving thanks to our God, who hath raised up
" unto us that light which we might ever have before our eyes, lest
" either by the subtilty of men, or by the snare of the devil, we should
" be carried away to errors or lies. Also we confess that these be the
" heavenly voices, whereby God hath opened unto us His will . . . .
" that they be the foundations of the Prophets and Apostles where-
" upon is built the Church of God: *that they be the very sure and*

---

contained what we ought to do, and what to eschew, what to believe, what to love, and what to look for at God's hands at length." *Homily* i. See also *Hom*. xxviii. 2.

So likewise *Nowell's Catechism*, p. 3. Question.—Dost thou then affirm that all things necessary *to godliness* and salvation are contained in the written word of God? Answer.—Yea for it were a point of intolerable ungodliness and madness, to think either that God had left an imperfect doctrine, or that man were able to make that perfect, which God left imperfect.

"*infallible rule whereby may be tried whether the Church do swerve or err,* "*and whereunto all ecclesiastical doctrine ought to be called to account;* "and that against these Scriptures neither law, nor any custom ought "to be heard; no, though Paul himself, nor an angel from heaven "should come and teach the contrary." Gal. i. 8. *Confession of England—Art. ix. in Jewell's Apology.**

So likewise in the Homilies (the doctrines of which are made binding on all the Clergy by Article xxxv.) we read:

"The ordinary way to attain this knowledge (the knowledge of God "and of ourselves) is with diligence to hear and read the Holy "Scriptures. *For the whole Scriptures,* saith St. Paul, were given by "inspiration of God. And shall we Christian men think to learn the "knowledge of God and of ourselves in any earthly man's work or "writing sooner or better than in the Holy Scriptures, written by in-"spiration of the Holy Ghost? The Scriptures were not brought "unto us by the will of man, but holy men of God, as witnesseth "St. Peter, spake as they were moved by the Holy Spirit of God." *Homily xxii. Part* I.

In the Collect for the second Sunday in Advent we find these words: "Blessed Lord, who hast caused ALL Holy Scriptures to be

---

* "Bishop Jewell's Apology is recognised in Canon xxx. of the Canons of 1603 as the Apology of The Church of England, and is quoted by Hooker (Eccle. Pol ii. 6.) under the name of 'The English Apology.' Collier states that it was approved by the Queen and set forth with the consent of the Bishops. (Eccl. Hist. ii. 479.) And Bishop Jewell himself, in his 'Reply to Harding,' says, that he had the conscience of the English Clergy, and that the book had the Queen's license. It was first published in 1562, the very same year as our present Articles; and 'by Queen Elizabeth, King James, King Charles, and four successive Archbishops, the Apology was ordered to be read and chained up in all Parish Churches throughout England and Wales.' [Watt, under the name Jewell.] And of this work, and Nowell's Catechism, Bishop Randolph thus speaks in the Preface to his 'Enchiridion.' 'My choice has been principally directed to such works as had the sanction of public authority, and which may, therefore, *be relied on as containing the final and decided opinions of our Reformers, approved of in the general by the Church at large.* . . . . . Of this kind, that is, thus publicly received, were Jewell's Apology and Nowell's Catechism, the former of which is said to have been published with the consent of the Bishops, and was *always understood to speak the sense of the whole Church,* in whose name it is written, the latter had the *express sanction of Convocation.* . . . . . Both these works were publicly received and allowed." *Dean Goode on the Eucharist. Vol. ii., p.* 727. *Note.*

written for our learning," &c. Now there can be no doubt as to what writings are included under the title "Holy Scriptures," for they are expressly enumerated in the sixth Article. To the acceptance of that Article, as well as to the use of the aforesaid prayer, every Clergyman binds himself by oath. He *must* use this prayer, and therein he solemnly addresses God as One who has "*caused to be written*" all the books declared to be Holy Scripture in the sixth Article. And inasmuch as it cannot be supposed that God who is "holy" would have "*caused* to be written" that which is *false*, it follows that the use of this prayer is a solemn acknowledgment on the part of every Clergyman that *all* that is written in the Old and New Testament is *true*.

In the Ordination Service, the Deacon on being asked, " Do you unfeignedly believe all the Canonical Scriptures of the Old and New Testament ? " is required to answer, " I do believe them."

I repeat then, that in the whole compass of human history there is no fact more surely established than this—that the Reformers held *all* the books of the Old and New Testaments to come from the direct inspiration of God, and therefore to be infallibly true and authoritative, and alone authoritative. and this their judgment respecting Holy Scripture they have unequivocally expressed in the Articles, and Formularies by them authorized.

Bearing these things in mind, we should deem it unaccountable, if we did not know the tendency of the times, that an Ecclesiastical Judge in England, whose office would seem to require that he should interpret the Articles and Formularies literally and in strict accordance with the intention of their framers, should from the judgment-seat declare, that when the Deacon in reply to the question, " Do you unfeignedly believe ALL the Canonical Scriptures of the Old and New Testament ? " answers, " I do believe them "—this reply is to be understood to mean that he believes that " the Holy Scripture contains every thing necessary to salvation, and to that extent they have the *direct* sanction of the Almighty." *Dr. Lushington's Judgment, page* 16.

Now, inasmuch as the words, " I do believe them," refer not to any particular subject treated of in the Scriptures, but to the Scriptures *as a whole* (the question being, " Do you believe ALL the Canonical Scriptures of the Old and New Testament ? "—such Canonical Scriptures being in the sixth Article enumerated) it is evident that this question is by Dr. Lushington altered, and that it should be put thus: "Do you unfeignedly believe that the Scriptures contain every thing necessary to salvation, and that *to that extent* they have the direct sanction of the Almighty?" But this is quite another question. It is not the question asked in the Prayer Book; nor could its being answered in the affirmative, in any way satisfy the demand of those who prescribed it. Dr. Lushington, therefore, in altering the question has assumed the place of Legislator instead of Judge. I speak not of his motives: but he has certainly not administered the law as it stands. The question in the Ordination Service is most definite and precise. Indeed, it would be impossible to devise a test more definite. The Reformers deemed it sufficient (and so it is) to guard one of the most important avenues of truth. But by the alteration of Dr. Lushington the test is nullified: the barrier is removed, and the avenue left unguarded. We see the consequences of this in the present judgment.

And this decision of Dr. Lushington appears the more extraordinary when we test it by principles that he has himself laid down in the 16th page of his judgment. He there says when referring to the sixth Article; "it becomes then of the last importance to ascertain "what is meant by 'Holy Scripture,' and by that which 'containeth "all things necessary to salvation.' The Article declares that Holy "Scripture is contained in the Canonical Books enumerated, and in "the New Testament. But that is no explanation of what is meant "by 'Holy Scripture,' or by the word 'Canonical.' I am not at all "surprised at this silence, because I apprehend *that the meaning of* "*both expressions was fully understood at the time, and that explanation* "*was deemed wholly unnecessary.** I think that the expression 'Holy "Scripture' well understood by all, meant Scripture contradis-"tinguished from all other writings, and that the adjective 'Holy' "denoted Divine origin. I think that the meaning of the word "'Canonical' clearly appears upon the face of the Article itself, "namely, Books whose authority was never doubted in the Church; "and by 'authority,' I mean Divine authority, for there is no other "authority which by possibility could cause them to contain all "things necessary for salvation. This doctrine is, moreover, dis-"tinctly stated in the Twentieth Article, which declares that 'it is "not lawful for the Church to ordain anything that is contrary to

---

* The italics are mine.

" God's Word written, neither may it so expound one place of Scrip-
" ture, that it be repugnant to another.' The expressions, 'God's
" Word written,' and 'Scripture,' are in this Article plainly iden-
" tical." *Judgment, p.* 16, 17.

It seems marvellous that Dr. Lushington should have enunciated these principles, so true and excellent, and yet have pronounced the judgment that he has. For if the Articles whenever they use the word "Scripture" mean thereby '*God's Word written;*' and if by 'Holy' they mean '*of Divine origin,*' and if by 'Canonical' they mean of '*Divine authority,*' how can Dr. Lushington imagine that he represents the Articles (which as a Judge he was bound to do) when he declares himself satisfied with the profession of a *bonâ fide* belief that the Holy Scriptures "contain everything necessary to salvation, and that, *to that extent* they have the *direct* sanction of the Almighty?" Why, according to Dr Lushington's own admission, the Articles do by their use of the words 'Holy,' and 'Canonical,' and 'God's Word written,' declare that the *whole* of the sacred writings have the direct sanction of the Almighty, and are put forth by His authority. How can that which is by Him written, and promulgated by His authority, have His sanction to a limited extent only? We may safely affirm, therefore, that if the question in the Ordination service had been taken literally as it stands, and if Dr. Lushington had adhered to his own definitions of 'Holy' 'Canonical,' &c., his sentence on every point on which he has acquitted Dr. Williams, would have been reversed.

Let us now consider the statements presented to Dr Lushington for judgment, but which he refused to condemn. Dr. Williams, in his Essay, refers with approval to Coleridge, as throwing "secular prognos-tication altogether out of the idea of Prophecy;" that is to say, the Old Testament Prophets, according to Dr Williams, predicted, pro-perly speaking, no future events, and therefore were in no proper sense Prophets at all This, of course, sets aside all "*Messianic* Prophecy," that is, all prediction respecting the personal history of our Lord con-sequently, it is competent according to the present Judgment, for any Minister of the Church of England to deny that there is any pre-diction in the Old Testament either respecting the birth, suffering, death, resurrection, or coming again of our Lord. And yet the New Testament over and over again affirms that these things were foretold in the Old Testament, and quotes numberless passages in proof there-of. Think, for example, of Christ's conversation with the disciples going to Emmaus. "Beginning at Moses and all the prophets, He expounded unto them in all the Scriptures the things concerning Himself." *Luke xxiv.* 27. If Dr. Williams' assertion be accepted, we must say either that Luke has ascribed to our Lord words which He did not utter; or that He who is our God and Saviour, spake that which is untrue. Our Lord is stated in Luke to have affirmed that there is "Messianic Prophecy,"—that is, "prediction as to the appearing and history of Himself in the Old Testament." Dr. Williams affirms that there is *not*.

That such liberty of charging falsehood on our blessed Lord, or on Scripture, is accorded by the present Judgment, is manifest from the following words of Dr. Lushington. "*Now, admitting that Dr. Williams* has, in the extracts just read, denied Messianic Prophecy . . . . . I cannot say that the Articles have been impugned in this particular." *Judgment, p.* 21 * Observe, we are permitted to assume that Dr. Williams has denied the existence of "Messianic Prophecy," and yet he is not, if tried by the Articles and Formularies to be condemned; so that now any Clergyman may, if he so please, assert that predictions which Christ and His Apostles affirm to exist in the Old Testament do *not* exist, and may thereby stamp the whole of the *New* Testament with falsehood, and yet such a clergyman may be esteemed legally guiltless. His mouth cannot be stopped.

Now admitting for the moment that the Articles are as silent as Dr. Lushington supposes, and admitting also for argument sake that an ecclesiastical Judge must not be asked to interpret Scripture doctrinally, yet surely we may ask him to refer to Scripture on a question of *fact*. We refer to no question of doctrine when we ask attention to the fact that the following historic statement is found in the Gospel of John "They" (the soldiers) said, therefore, among themselves, Let us not rend it, but cast lots for it, whose it shall be: that the scripture might be fulfilled, which saith, They parted my raiment among them, and for my vesture they did cast lots." *John xix.* 24. Now it is a fact that in these and like instances (see note

---

* The words of Dr. Lushington are: "Now admitting that Dr. Williams, in the extracts just read, has denied 'Messianic Prophecy,' I cannot find in the Articles of Religion quoted, namely, the sixth and seventh, any direct mention of 'Messianic Prophecy,' or undoubted reference to it, although it is possible that with regard to the seventh Article, others may be of a different opinion. The Court then cannot say that the Articles have been infringed in this particular." *Judgment, p.* 21.

subjoined)* the New Testament writers do assert that the Old Testa-

PROPHECY.	FULFILMENT.
*" It was not he that hated me that did magnify himself against me; then *I would have hid myself from him* . but it was thou, a man mine equal, *my guide*, and mine own familiar friend." Ps. lv. 12, 13.	" And Judas also, which betrayed Him, *knew the place* . for Jesus ofttimes resorted thither with His disciples." John xviii. 2.
" And I said unto them, If ye think good, give me my price; . . . . . so they *weighed* for my price thirty pieces of silver." Zech. xi. 12.	" What will ye give me, and I will deliver him unto you ? And they *covenanted with* him for thirty pieces of silver." Matt. xxvi. 15.
" And the Lord said unto me, Cast it unto the potter a goodly price that I was priced at of them And I took the thirty pieces of silver, and cast them to the potter, in *the house of the Lord*." Zech. xi. 13.	" Then Judas . . . . . brought again the thirty pieces of silver . . . and . cast them down *in the temple* . . . . And the chief priests took the silver pieces . . . . . and bought with them the potter's field." Matt. xxvii. 3—7.
" They shall smite the judge of Israel with a rod upon the cheek." Micah v. 1	" They took the reed . . . . and smote Him on the head." Matt. xxvii. 34.
" They gave me also gall for my meat; and in my thirst they gave me vinegar to drink." Ps. lxix. 21.	" They gave Him vinegar to drink mingled with gall . and when He had tasted thereof, He would not drink." Matt. xxvii. 34.
" My God, my God, why hast thou forsaken me ? " Ps. xxii. 1.	" Jesus cried with a loud voice, saying, My God, my God, why hast thou forsaken me ? " Matt. xxvii. 46.
" I hid not my face from shame and spitting " Is. l. 6.	" Then they spit upon Him." Matt. xxvii. 46.
" They pierced my hands and my feet " Ps. xxii. 16.	" They crucified Him." John xix. 18.
" Ye shall not break a bone thereof." Ex. xii. 46. " He keepeth all his bones : not one of them is broken." Ps. xxxiv 20.	" These things were done, that the scripture should be fulfilled. A bone of Him shall not be broken " John xix. 36.
" He was numbered with the transgressors." Is. liii. 12.	" They crucified Him, and the malefactors, one on the right hand, and the other on the left." Luke xxiii. 33.
" They part my garments among them." Ps. xxii. 18.	" Then the soldiers . . . . . took His garments, and made four parts, to every soldier a part." John xix. 23
" They cast lots upon my vesture." Ps. xxii. 18.	" Now the coat was without seam, woven from the top throughout. They said therefore among themselves Let us not rend it, but cast lots for it, whose it shall be." John xix. 23, 24.

ment Prophets did predict certain events that were fulfilled in Christ: and it is equally plain (Dr Lushington *permits it to be so assumed*) that Dr. Williams affirms that no such events were predicted. Consequently, he asserts that the New Testament writers stated what was *not* true; whereby he contradicts those Articles which declare the New Testament to be true, inasmuch as they declare it to be "God's Word written," "Holy" and "Canonical;" that is, says Dr. Lushington, "of Divine authority." Articles which declare the New Testament to be this, must condemn a person who affirms that the declarations of the New Testament are false.

But further: I maintain that the Articles do expressly affirm the existence of "Messianic prophecy," for in the seventh Article we read, "The Old Testament is not contrary to the New; for both in the "Old and New Testament everlasting life is offered to Mankind by "Christ, (or *through* Christ, *per* Christum, see Latin Article) who is the "only Mediator between God and Man, being both God and Man. "Wherefore they are not to be heard, which feign that the old "Fathers did look only for transitory promises?" *Art. vii.*

Now this Article speaks of an offer of eternal life through Christ, and of "promises" also of eternal blessings through Him being made in the Old Testament before Christ came. Therefore the Article affirms that there was prediction respecting Christ, and the blessings to come through Him, in the Old Testament. In other words, it affirms the existence of "Messianic Prophecy"—the very thing which Dr. Williams denies, and which any Clergyman may now deny with impunity.

Again, any clergyman is allowed under the present judgment to distinguish '*the man Daniel*' from '*the Book of Daniel*,' and may affirm that the Book was not written by Daniel, but by some other person who lived hundreds of years afterwards in the reign of Antiochus Epiphanes, and falsely ascribed his book to the true Daniel. And yet the Gospels of Matthew and Mark* tell us that Christ our God and Saviour—the God of truth, declared that Daniel *was* the author of the Book that bears his name: and Daniel, over and over again, declares it of himself. Nevertheless, a Clergyman may, on a question of fact like this, impute falsehood to the Gospels and to the Book of Daniel, and yet be held not to offend against the Article

---

* See Matt. xxiv. and Mark xiii.

which declares that this book is "Holy," i.e. of Divine origin; and "Canonical," i e. of "Divine Authority;" and a part of "God's Word written." Did the framers of the Articles imagine that God could be the Author of falsehood? They certainly did not know that a book could be pronounced false and canonical at the same time.

A clergyman may further sneer at the notion of the personality of Jonah, and declare the narrative respecting the whale to be a "*late legend founded on misconception,*" and so accuse our Lord, or else the Gospel of Matthew, of falsehood; for in that Gospel it is said that the Lord referred to the so-called "legend," asserted its truth, and applied it to Himself. See Matt. xii. 40. If such latitude of teaching be allowed in the case of Daniel and of Jonah, like liberty must of course be accorded in the case of the other Prophets and all other parts of Scripture.

Dr. Lushington, in his Judgment, draws no distinction between denying the genuineness of a book *whose authorship is determined by the Scripture*, and respecting the authorship of a book when the Scripture is silent concerning it.* Respecting the authorship of "The Acts," or the "Epistle to the Hebrews," I am at liberty to enquire, for the Scripture does not authoritatively determine the authorship of those Books; but as respects the Book of Daniel and the second Epistle of Peter the case is different, for the authorship of the Book of Daniel is determined by itself, and also by the words of our Lord as recorded in Matthew and Mark: and the authorship of the second Epistle of Peter is determined by itself in the first verse of the first chapter; and seeing that it would be absurd to suppose that the Articles would accept as "Canonical," books that either assign to themselves, or claim for others, a false origin, it is manifest that Dr. Williams in asserting the untruthfulness of Daniel and of the

---

* Thus Dr. Lushington says "I must therefore conclude that Dr. Williams has denied the genuineness of the second Epistle of Peter. If I were to condemn on this statement I must hold that the denying a book to be genuine necessarily implies a denial of its canonicity, &c." *See Judgment p. 23.*

Most unquestionably the denying a book to be genuine (i.e. written by him whose name it bears) does necessarily imply a denial of its canonicity, *if, as in the present case, the book expressly mentions its author.* The Epistle commences "Simon Peter, a servant and an Apostle, &c " If the Epistle was not written by Peter, it commences with a deliberate falsehood. Dr. Williams in asserting that it was *not* written by Peter charges it with falsehood, and thereby denies its canonicity, and contradicts the Article.

Gospels of Matthew and Mark in reference to Daniel, and in asserting the untruthfulness of the second Epistle of Peter in ascribing to itself a false origin, does thereby deny that these books are "Canonical" in the sense in which that word is admitted by Dr. Lushington to be used in the sixth Article.

Moreover, a Clergyman is now permitted to affirm that words which are allowed by all (for there is no question about variation of reading) to be recorded in the Gospels as spoken by our Lord Himself were not so spoken by Him. It is to be held lawful that a Clergyman should, if he please, comment thus:

"The verse [John iii. 13] that 'no man hath ascended up to "Heaven, but He that came down,' is intelligible as a free comment "near the end of the first century, but has no meaning in our Lord's "mouth at the time when the Ascension had not been heard of." *Williams as quoted in p. 22 of Judgment.*

Thus, without any pretence of manuscript variation or interpolation, Dr. Williams asserts, simply because it pleases him so to assert, that words which St. John declares to have been solemnly spoken by our Lord were not so spoken at all: his reason for this assertion evidently being that he will not accord to the Lord, any more than to the Prophets, the power of prediction.

Dr. Lushington in his judgment remarks:

"If I understand this passage correctly, the meaning is, that these "words were never uttered by our Saviour at the time, or on the "occasion indicated, but were added at a period subsequent to His "death. This certainly is a specimen of very bold criticism; but how "is it a contravention of the sixth Article, or the declaration of "belief?" *Judgment p. 22.*

I reply that it contravenes the Articles, because it ascribes a deliberate falsehood to St. John's Gospel; and a book that contains falsehoods or mistakes cannot be said to be "Canonical," or "Holy," in the sense in which it is admitted by Dr. Lushington that the Articles use those expressions.

Again; the writings of Moses—writings which were expressly quoted by our Lord as of Divine authority, and recognised by Him as a part of that Scripture which He said "cannot be broken," may now be spoken of by any Clergyman as containing "half-ideal, half-traditional notices of the beginnings of our race." The words of Dr. Williams are: "In the half-ideal, half-traditional notice of the "beginnings of our race compiled in Genesis, we are bid [that is by

Bunsen] notice the "combination of documents and the recurrence of barely consistent genealogies." *Judgment p.* 13.

This sentence was presented to Dr. Lushington for judgment, but he declined to say that it was in contrariety to the Articles, although the Articles declare the Books of Moses to be "Canonical," that is, says Dr. Lushington, of "Divine authority;" and "holy," that is, says Dr. Lushington, "of Divine origin," and therefore to be used together with the rest of God's Word written as a test of all other writings whatsoever. Could writings that contain "half-ideal," "half-traditional notices" be at the same time authoritative tests of Truth?

A Clergyman may also maintain that the statements of Holy Scripture as to historical facts, such as the Deluge, may be understood in a figurative or non-natural sense. On this point Dr. Lushington observes:

"My first enquiry must be, what is the offence imputed to Dr. "Williams. It is this, that Dr. Williams maintains that the state- "ments of Holy Scripture as to historical facts may be read and "understood in a wholly figurative and in a non-natural sense, and it "is alleged that so to do is an offence against the sixth and seventh "Articles of religion and the Deacon's declaration of belief. *Now,* "*assuming that Dr. Williams has done all that he has been charged with,* "where am I to find in the sixth and seventh Articles any words "constituting such an interpretation of Scripture an offence?" *Judgment p.* 24.

Observe, we are permitted to assume that Dr. Williams does maintain that the statements of Holy Scripture as to historical facts may be "read and understood in a wholly figurative and in a *non-natural sense;*" and yet though it be admitted that he has done this, we are told from the judgment-seat that he cannot, according to the Articles and Formularies of the Church of England, be condemned. But when the Deacon is asked, "*Do you unfeignedly believe all the Canonical Scriptures of the Old and New Testament?*" and is required to answer, "*I do believe them,*"—does Dr. Lushington really think that they who originally appointed that such demands should be made and such an answer given, would have been satisfied with the reply, "*I believe them in a wholly figurative and in a non-natural sense?*" And if Dr. Lushington believes that such an answer would not only not have satisfied, but that it would have been indignantly rejected, was he not bound in applying the tests before him, to have had respect to the intention of the framers of those tests, and to adhere rigidly to their exact and literal meaning? If in the application of tests no regard is to be had either to the natural meaning of words, or to the *animus imponentis*, what rule is left to guide us? Is the determination of the meaning to be abandoned to the caprice of each individual judge who may, whenever he pleases, adopt the "non-natural" principle? If so, is it not better that we should dispense both with tests and judges?

In another passage Dr. Williams sneers at what he is pleased to call, "the Augustinian notion of a curse inherited by infants." Now although I admit that there is a want of fulness in the ninth Article (and therefore the Article was revised by the Westminster Assembly in 1643)* yet it is very evident that the ninth Article as it stands, speaks, and rightly speaks, of an inherited corruption of nature which we derive from our first parent; and it is equally evident that Dr. Williams rejects the thought of "inherited" evil in any way. He would equally object to the doctrine of the guilt of Adam's first transgression being imputed, and to the doctrine that we are born with corrupt natures because of Adam. However, in this case, perhaps, the want of precision in the ninth Article unamended, may, in some degree, account for the acquittal that has been pronounced. A door, nevertheless, is thus opened for every Clergyman who may desire it, to speak disparagingly or contemptuously of that great foundation doctrine of our holy faith of which the ninth Article treats.

In another passage Dr. Williams writes as follows: "Thus the "incarnation becomes with our author as purely spiritual as it was "with St. Paul: the Son of David by birth is the Son of God by the "Spirit of holiness."

These words were alleged (and rightly) by the Bishop of Salisbury to be "a denial of the second Article of Religion, and a maintaining that the Son of God did not take upon Himself man's nature in the womb of the blessed Virgin."

Dr. Lushington, however, has refused to admit this. He observes thus: "To deny the truth of the second Article of Religion would be "one of the most serious Ecclesiastical offences; but the more serious "the charge, the more strict should be the proof."

"Assuming, for the sake of the argument, that Dr. Williams here

---

* The Article as revised by the Westminster Assembly stands thus: "Original sin standeth not in the following of Adam, as the Pelagians do vainly talk; but together with his first sin imputed, it is the fault and corruption of the nature of every man that naturally is propagated from Adam, &c."

"avows as his own, the doctrine which he expressly attributes to
"Baron Bunsen, there is a grave objection to the admission of this
"Article (of charge) The *prima facie* meaning of the passage im-
"pugned is, that Baron Bunsen entertained the same opinion of the
"incarnation as St. Paul; and if this were all—if it were a mere
"general statement of this kind—it would not be possible for me to
"condemn it; for no one would seriously contend that what St. Paul
"really wrote is contrary to the doctrine taught by the Church in
"the second Article of Religion. But the question is whether Dr.
"Williams does or does not improperly ascribe to St. Paul particular
"opinions on the incarnation, and allow them to be his own."

"Now Dr. Williams refers the reader in a note to certain verses in
"the Epistle to the Romans as containing the views which in his
"Essay he ascribes to St. Paul. These are Rom. i. 1, 4 "

"Paul, an apostle of Jesus Christ, called to be an apostle, separated
"unto the gospel of God (which He had promised afore by His
"prophets in the Holy Scriptures) concerning His Son Jesus Christ
"our Lord, which was made of the seed of David according to the
"flesh; and declared to be the Son of God with power, according to
"the spirit of holiness by the resurrection from the dead."

"Compare with these verses, the words in the text of the Essay, viz:
'Thus the incarnation becomes with our author as purely spiritual
"as it was with St. Paul; the Son of David by birth is the Son of
"God by the Spirit of holiness,—' seems to me not an unfair quota-
"tion, or rather expression of what St. Paul wrote, with one excep-
"tion; the exception is the omission of the concluding words, 'by
"the resurrection from the dead.' It is by no means clear that
"there was the least intention to reject or even to exclude these
"words. The omission of part when the whole is designated, does
"not in any degree prove that the words were intentionally omitted,
"much less omitted with a guilty intention. I must also, in can-
"dour, add that the omission of these words does not seem to me
"truly to affect the meaning of the sentence. The beginning of the
"fourth verse imports that Jesus Christ was declared to be the Son
"of God; and the remainder states the manner in which that decla-
"ration was made. True it is that, with reference to the power con-
"ferred, mention is made of the greatest of all proofs, the resurrection
"from the dead: but that, though the greatest of all proofs, is only
"one amongst very many others, that Jesus Christ was declared to
"be the Son of God."

"I am of opinion that the omission of the reference to the re-"surrection does not appear to be necessarily either intentional "or culpable; and I must reject the Article (of accusation). *Judg-*"*ment p.* 26.

Such is the decision of Dr. Lushington: and an extraordinary decision it is. He thinks that the words of the Essay are not an unfair expression of what St. Paul wrote, with one exception,—the reference to the resurrection, of which exception, however, he makes nothing. Yet what can be more material?

But before we turn to that point, we have to ask what the words, "*purely spiritual,*" as applied to the Incarnation, mean? Dr. Williams, adopting the views of Bunsen, speaks of the Incarnation of our God and Saviour as " purely spiritual!" Now what do these words mean? They must mean, either that the Son of God when He was pleased to become incarnate did *not* take a true body of flesh but a spiritual body, which would be heresy: or they must mean that the Saviour was at His birth the Son of David, and nothing more; and that He is the Son of God by possession of, and by moral conformation unto, that Holy Spirit wherewith He was anointed. This last I apprehend to be the meaning expressed by Dr. Williams in the words—" the Son of David by birth is the Son of God by the Spirit of holiness." Thus the pre-existence and Deity of our Lord as the eternal Son of the Father, and His miraculous generation and birth of Mary (on which ground also He is called " the Son of God " —see Luke i. 35) are denied. Is not this heresy? Does not such a statement contravene the second Article, and every other Article and Creed that treats of the doctrine of the Trinity or of the Incarnation?

And now as respects the quotation from the Epistle to the Romans, Dr. Lushington thinks that the words of the Essay are not an unfair expression of what St. Paul wrote; with one exception—the reference to the resurrection. In turning to the passage referred to, we find two contrasted clauses, the first of which speaks of Christ " being made, or having become ($\gamma\epsilon\nu o\mu\epsilon\nu o\varsigma$) of the seed of David according to the flesh." Here, as is admitted by all, the Incarnation is spoken of; but is it spoken of as "*purely spiritual?*" The next clause speaks not of Christ being made or becoming anything by Incarnation (that is the subject of the first clause) but it speaks of Christ being " declared the Son of God *in power* by resurrection from the dead." The first clause tells us of the step that brought the Son of God from heaven to earth: the second tells us of that other step out of death which has brought Him into resurrection-power and glory—a power and glory that is not according to the flesh (κατα σαρκα) but according to the Spirit of holiness (κατα πνευμα ἁγιωσυνης). Yet although these two clauses are thus markedly contrasted, I am asked to admit that it is no improper use of Scripture to apply to the Incarnation of our Lord that second clause which avowedly, and in the way of contrast, points to His present resurrection-condition in power and glory. We cannot wonder, therefore, that the words by "the resurrection from the dead," should be by Dr. Williams omitted, because if they are introduced they would render an application of the clause to the Incarnation impossible. Accordingly, although they are the emphatic words of the clause they are omitted —and what is more, other words of the clause are altered: for ὁρισθεις (*declared* or rather *defined as by a separating limit*) is quietly treated as if it were ων or γενομενος (who became); and the words "*according to* (κατα) the Spirit of holiness," are quietly changed into "*by* the Spirit of holiness," which would have required εν, or δια with the genitive. If confusion like this be permitted and deemed immaterial, darkness must of course accumulate, and what transgressor may not escape under the covert of thick darkness. I do not accuse Dr. Lushington of making this comment with a view of intentionally darkening—he is evidently himself perplexed. But the result as regards the Truth is the same.

In another passage presented to Dr. Lushington for judgment occur these words:

"Again on the side of external criticism, we find the evidences of "our Canonical books, and of the patristic authors nearest to them, "are sufficient to prove illustration in outward act of principles per- "petually true; but not adequate to guarantee narratives inherently "incredible, or precepts evidently wrong." *Dr. Williams as quoted, p.* 19 *of Judgment.*

On this passage Dr. Lushington pronounces judgment as follows:

"The passage goes on to speak of the necessity of our assuming in "ourselves a verifying faculty. What is the true meaning of these "words? I apprehend it must mean this: that the Clergy (for I "speak of these only) are at liberty to reject parts of Scripture upon "their own opinion that the narrative is 'inherently incredible;' to "disregard precepts in Holy Writ because they think them 'evi- "dently wrong' Whatever I may think as to the danger of the "liberty so claimed, still if the liberty do not extend to the impugn-

"ing of the Articles of Religion or the Formularies, the matter is
"beyond my cognizance. To determine, upon the sentence quoted,
"that Dr. Williams has claimed the right to carry his criticism to
"the length of impugning the Articles or the Formularies, would, I
"conceive, be to affix a meaning upon this sentence which it does
"not necessarily bear." *Judgment p.* 19.

Thus, then, a Clergyman is now permitted to teach that he and other men (for the Essay does not restrict the statement to Clergymen) have a "verifying faculty not unlike the discretion which a mathematician would use in weighing a treatise on geometry, or the liberty which a musician would reserve in reporting a law of harmony," and that by this innate faculty he can test the truth of the Scriptures: and further, that the Scriptures need to be thus tested, for that they contain "narratives inherently incredible," and "precepts evidently wrong."

Now when the English Reformers pronounced certain books to be "canonical," and to be "the Word of God," and to be "Holy," and to have been "caused to be written" by God "for our learning," and that all other writings and statements are to be tested thereby, is it not manifest that such declarations respecting Holy Scripture *were intended* to preclude and *do* preclude, every one who accepts them, from saying, either that he has "a verifying faculty" whereby to judge Scripture, or that such a verifying faculty is needed because the Scripture contains "narratives inherently incredible," and "precepts evidently wrong?" There cannot be two co-equal tests. Scripture and the "verifying faculty" cannot together reign. He who declares his allegiance to the one must renounce the other. Dr. Williams makes the supposed "verifying faculty" supreme. How then can he be at one with Articles that uncompromisingly declare the supremacy of Scripture? Dr. Williams further asserts that the Bible is in many things false—that it contains "narratives inherently incredible," and "precepts evidently wrong," and yet he is supposed to be at one with Articles that declare Scripture to be the alone authoritative test of doctrine. Furthermore, do not the Articles and Formularies pronounce God to be "*holy*," and the Scripture to be "holy?" And is falsehood compatible with "holiness?" It must be, if a book that contains "narratives inherently incredible," and "precepts evidently wrong," is yet pronounced to be "*holy*," and to be "caused to be written" by a "*holy* God."

The liberty granted to neologian teaching in some of its worst forms, by the judgment of Dr. Lushington is so wide, that we are obliged to regard the condemnation pronounced by him on three of the statements of Dr. Williams as of little moment. On three points, however, Dr. Williams was condemned as having contravened the Articles:

I. Because he has characterized without qualification the Bible to be an "expression of devout reason."

II. Because he has defined "*propitiation*" in a sense that contravenes the Articles.

III. Because he has contravened the Articles in the definition he has given of "*justification*," and in speaking of "merit by transfer" as "a fiction."

For error on these all-important and vital points he was condemned—to what? To deprivation of his office and benefice *for one year*, and to the costs of the suit! At the end of the one year he was to be allowed, *without recantation*, to resume his office. Against this sentence permission of appeal was granted and exercised. The cause was carried to the Judicial Committee of the Privy Council. Dr. Lushington's judgment was reversed; and thus even the feeble and imperfect barrier against Neology which Dr. Lushington's Judgment had left, has been overthrown. In what manner, will be seen from the next section.*

---

* Dr. Lushington's reasons for not requiring a recantation are curious enough. He says

"I will candidly state that, if I suspend Dr. Williams, as unquestionably I "shall, I do think there would be something very objectionable in continuing that "suspension until Dr. Williams recants, and so by means of the deprivation of "income, and of exclusion from his living, force a recantation which may in "reality not come from the heart, but be made merely for the sake of recovering "those advantages and privileges which a recantation only could give. I have a "great objection to make any Decree, or pass any Sentence, which would place any "Clergyman of this Church under that temptation, to make a false recantation of "his error.

"The sentence I shall pronounce is this,—and it is in the hope that it will be "sufficient to warn Dr. Williams, with his ability and learning, of the error he has "committed, so that when he carefully considers all the proceedings, it may pro- "duce all the beneficial effect that can be obtained."

It is very evident that if this principle be admitted, no declarations of belief, involving if not made the loss of privileges, should be required of any; for no doubt such declarations when required are temptations to untruthfulness. Nevertheless, men do not deem it uncharitable or unwise to require from one another declarations in things affecting the security of their own institutions, national and social. It is only in the things of God that we find this wondrous considerateness and breadth of charity!

SECTION II.

On the Judgment pronounced by the Judicial Committee of the Privy Council.

LAMENTABLE as the consequences of Dr. Lushington's judgment are, and wide as is the door thereby opened to soul-destroying error, yet that judgment did exempt the Scripture from *part* of the degradation prepared for it; for Dr. Lushington forbad that the Scripture should be called " an expression of devout reason ; " or that it should be termed " the written voice of the congregation." He forbad also that the guidance of the Divine Spirit vouchsafed to the writers of Holy Scripture should be spoken of as identical with that which was granted to Luther, or Milton, or to other ordinary Christians. This Judgment, however, has by the Court of Appeal been reversed.

Commenting on the passage in which Dr. Williams had spoken of the Bible as " an expression of devout reason," Dr. Lushington had remarked as follows:

"These are words which Dr. Williams puts into the mouth of " Baron Bunsen. Dr. Williams does not reprobate the opinions so " expressed. I think looking at the whole of the Essay, he approves " and adopts them. This passage, if I correctly understand it, asserts " an affirmative proposition, that the Bible is an expression of devout " reason. Now is such a proposition in conflict with the Articles of " Religion cited, namely, the sixth, seventh and twentieth?—for I " disclaim referring to the passages of Scripture also pleaded."

"The sixth Article declares that 'Holy Scripture containeth all " things necessary for salvation.' I have held that these words " necessarily imply the proposition that the Scriptures so far as the " salvation of man is concerned, have been written by the inter-

"position of the almighty power of God. With every desire to put
"upon Dr. Williams's words a construction reconcileable with the
"Article, I must hold that to characterize without qualification the
"Bible as an expression of devout reason, is inconsistent with the
"doctrine that it was written by the interposition of God; which
"doctrine I have said, is an indispensable part of the sixth Article.
"It appears to me, that if the Bible in matters essential to salvation
"be declared to have emanated from Divine power, all suppositions
"inconsistent with that declaration are necessarily excluded. If it
"be God's Word written, as said in the twentieth Article, it is not
"the expression of devout reason. Devout reason belongs to the acts
"and doings of man and not to the works of the Almighty." *Judgment of Dr. Lushington, p.* 19.

On the statement that the Bible was "the written voice of the congregation," Dr. Lushington observed thus:

"So far as my knowledge extends, there is not to be found in
"the Articles or in the Formularies a single syllable consistent with
"the assertion that the Bible is the written voice of the congre-
"gation. The doctrine of the Church of England is expressed in
"the twentieth Article, that the Bible is the 'written Word of God.'
". . . . . . I hold the comparison with Luther and Milton to be
"erroneous; erroneous because the doctrine of the Church, in the
"Articles of Religion cited is, that the sacred writers wrote from the
"influence of a supernatural power to effect a given object, clearly
"distinct from the ordinary operation of God's omnipotence on the
"minds of men in its ordinary course."

"I am of opinion that the second and fourth passages above
"quoted, according to the only construction I can put upon them,
"are not to be reconciled with the Articles of Religion cited. I
"hold that the sixth and seventh Articles of Religion impose the
"obligation of acknowledging that the Bible, in matters essential to
"salvation, is the written Word of God; [It is abundantly evident
that the Articles and Formularies (see Collect for Second Sunday in
Advent) and not merely those parts of Scripture that refer to matters
essential to salvation declare ALL Scripture to be written by inspiration of God] "that it was written by the interposition of the Al-
"mighty, supernaturally brought to operate. I hold that to declare
"the Bible to be an expression of devout reason—to be the written
"voice of the congregation, is a violation of the sixth and seventh
"Articles of Religion, I think such positions are substantially incon-

"sistent with the all-important doctrine imposed by law, that the "Bible is God's Word written." *Dr. Lushington's Judgment*, p. 19.

On page 17 of Judgment Dr. Lushington observes:

"It has been said that the Church has not in these Articles or else"where defined inspiration. It is no part of my duty to define it, and "I shall not attempt to do so; but I must put a construction upon "the Articles, and I hold that in the phrases 'God's Word written,' "and 'the Holy Scripture containeth all things necessary to salva"tion,' is necessarily implied the doctrine that in all matters neces"sary for salvation, the Holy Scriptures emanated from the extra"ordinary and preternatural interposition of the Almighty—the "special mode and limit unknown to man. It is true that all good "gifts spring from the same source—from the power and will of the "Almighty—but the gifts of genius or of mental power, even in a "greater degree than is common, the gifts of any faculty of mind or "body in unusual excellence, the existence of these qualities in the "highest perfection overleaps not the ordinary course of human affairs, "and is plainly to be distinguished from the special interposition of "God, which is necessarily implied in these Articles as the cause and "origin of the Scriptures. I must hold, therefore, that any Clergy"man who advisedly maintains, whether in direct or indirect language, "that the Holy Scriptures proceed from the same mental powers as "have produced other works, or vice versâ, even with the qualifica"tion that these powers in the one case and in the other differ in "degree, impairs the Divine authority of Holy Scripture, does in fact "maintain that the Bible is not God's Word written, but is the work "of man, and thereby contravenes the sixth and twentieth Articles of "Religion."

What can be more just than this decision? But does not the same course of reasoning that leads to this conclusion necessitate our saying also that the Articles condemn any Clergyman who charges untruthfulness upon any part of that Bible which the Articles pronounced to be *as a whole* "Holy" (that is ." of Divine origin") and "Canonical" (that is " of Divine authority")? The Articles avowedly apply the terms "Holy" and "Canonical" to ALL the Books of the Old and New Testaments, whereby the truthfulness of those Books is asserted as to *all* the subjects of which they treat: for it would be absurd to say that any book or collection of books that were sometimes true, and at other times false, could be pronounced as a whole "Holy" and "Canonical." Let Dr. Lushington's just and necessary definitions be adhered to faithfully, [see page 76 of preceding paper] and Dr. Williams would stand condemned on almost every point on which he was charged. It might not indeed have been competent for the Court of Appeal to rectify such parts of Dr. Lushington's Judgment as were not formally presented to them; yet they might have confirmed his sentence on the points presented, have sanctioned the principles on which that sentence was founded, and expressed their regret that those principles had not in every case been consistently applied. But the Court of Appeal did no such thing. They were otherwise minded. So far from wishing to extend the scope of Dr. Lushington's sentence of condemnation, they determined to quench it altogether.

Their Judgment is one of the most extraordinary that the annals of judicature supply. In reading it one cannot but be surprized that the definitions and arguments of Dr. Lushington should be passed over, virtually unnoticed. If his arguments are capable of refutation, why are they not refuted? Supreme Courts in setting aside the decisions of inferior tribunals, are commonly accustomed to show the fallacy of the arguments by which those decisions have been sustained. If Dr. Lushington's definition of the sense in which the Articles use "Holy" and "Canonical" be wrong, let it be *proved* to be wrong. Let just and accurate definitions be established. Let every false argument be exposed; and let other arguments plain, lucid, and irrefutable be given. No amount of vigilance, or care, or labour can be too great for a cause like this, for its importance transcends conception. The argument that Dr. Lushington has founded on the meaning of the word "devout," seems to a plain mind, to be conclusive of the point at issue. Why has not that argument been refuted?

Let us again consider that argument, bearing in mind that the Court of Appeal lay down as one of their principles, that the "plain grammatical" meaning of words must be taken. Now what is the plain grammatical meaning of "devout?" It indicates, and can only indicate the relation of an inferior to a superior. Therefore it is a word incapable of application to God; for God neither renders, nor owes *devotion* to any. He is the one supreme and only wise God. Consequently, he who affirms that Scripture is the expression of "*devout reason*," does thereby ascribe it to a source other than God. This is a "*conclusion directly involved*" in Dr. Williams' assertion, and for conclusions "*directly involved*," the Court allows that he is responsible. That which "devout reason" expresses is one thing, and that which God speaks is another: and the Articles affirm the Scripture to be "God's Word written," and therefore not the utterance of "devout reason." Such was Dr. Lushington's argument! Has it been answered? No: for it is unanswerable.

The English Reformers were not faultless; but certainly they were neither fanatics nor enthusiasts. They were wont to demand evidence for that which they accredited. When, for example, Rome claimed authority for the Apocryphal Books and for Tradition, they tested the claim, and rejected it. They deemed it madness to say with the Romanist that Popes or Councils could speak or judge with the authority of the Holy Ghost. They utterly denied the continuance of authoritative inspiration even in the *true* Church, how much more in the false! They maintained that such inspiration ceased with the Apostles, when the Canon of Scripture closed. The accrediting as divinely authoritative any thing that might come from a Pope or a Council, or from a German or Coleridgean mystic, or even from the holiest of true Christians, they would have deemed an act of fatuity as well as sin. They would have said, If there be Apostolic authoritative inspiration, where are the *signs* thereof? Where are the attesting *miracles?* Where also is the accordance with Holy Scripture in doctrine and in conversation?

But to acknowledge that inspiration, in its true and proper sense, ceased with the Apostles, suits neither the Neologian, nor the Romanist, nor the fanatic: for the necessities of their respective systems demand that their authorities should be elevated into co-equality with the Apostles and Prophets.

Rome, of course, must assert the continuance of authoritative inspiration, for without it what becomes of the decrees of her Popes and Councils, her infallibility and such like? No one who, on any grounds whatsoever, asserts the continuance of an authoritative inspiration, like to that of the Apostles and Prophets, or in any sense authoritative, could own the Scripture as *alone* authoritative. And no one who owns the Scripture as *alone* authoritative, could own the continuance in the Church of authoritative inspiration. Therefore, seeing that the Court of Appeal admit and assert *on Dr. Williams' behalf*, that he does affirm the continuance in the Church of the same kind of inspiration as was vouchsafed to the writers of Scripture, it follows that Dr. Williams is by the Articles condemned. For the Articles pronounce the Scripture to be *alone* authoritative, and this they could not have done, if they had recognised the continuance of authoritative inspiration. Take from Protestantism the doctrine that Apostolic and authoritative inspiration did with the Apostles cease, and you take from it its foundation. What do we find in the nineteenth Article? "As the Church of Jerusalem, Antioch, and Alexandria have erred, so also the Church of Rome has erred, not only in their living and manner of ceremonies, but also in matters of faith." And again, in Article xxi.: "General Councils . . . . . . may err and sometimes have erred . . . . . . wherefore things ordained by them as necessary to salvation have neither strength nor authority, unless it may be declared that they are taken out of Holy Scripture." How could the framers of the Articles have written thus—how could they have exalted Scripture into this supremacy over Churches and Councils if they had believed that the same authoritative inspiration that was granted to the writers of Scripture was continued through every age, and was to be found in Luther and Milton, and every one else who might be supposed to possess "devout reason"? The Reformers admitted no such thing. They admitted it neither of Churches nor of Councils; neither of Convocations nor of individuals; neither of pretended Christians nor of real Christians. They would have counted the notion profane—destructive alike to God's honour and to His people's peace. It would be destructive to God's honour, for it would drag down His holy Word from its supremacy: it would be destructive of His people's peace, for how could they ever rest, how could they ever be sure of attaining Truth, if daily they were presented afresh by all those who had, or pretended to have, "devout reason," with ten thousand new and doubtless conflicting rules,—all of which must, on this hypothesis, be accepted as authoritative? In that case, I think, we should somewhat dread coming into contact with any one reputed to possess "devout reason," for we should be reasonably unwilling to multiply our masters; nor would it be very apparent why our own "devout reason" might not be as worthy of regard as that of another. Would the Lord Chancellor be willing to admit that every clever, honest citizen in the realm has, in virtue of his integrity and cleverness, authority to make ordinances binding on the nation? This is not one whit more absurd than to affirm that any one who has "devout reason" has a title to speak with authority—authority equal to that of the inspired writers of the Word of God. Alas! How could I ever understand, much less obey the utterances that "devout reason" would every moment multiply around me. It is no wonder that Dr. Williams should take refuge in his "verifying faculty." *That*, no doubt, opens a door of escape and an effectual one. For it nullifies utterly all external authority, and makes every man an authority to himself. It is something higher and better than "devout reason"—higher and better than that from which, according to this theory, Scripture comes. What it pleases each possessor of this "verifying faculty" to believe, he believes; and what it pleases him to reject, he rejects. Sufficient liberty this! It certainly secures to men the advantage (if advantage it be) of becoming "as the fishes of the sea, as the creeping things that have no ruler over them." Yet we afterwards read of those fishes being caught in a drag-net, and a terrible drag-net too. If this be the end sought after —$\tau a \gamma a \theta o \nu\ \dot{o}\ \pi a \nu \tau a\ \epsilon \phi \iota \epsilon \tau a \iota$, we in this country are certainly in a fair way for reaching it. For if the Clergy are to be permitted to teach (and by the recent judgment they *are* permitted) the continuance of the same kind of inspiration as was granted to the writers of Holy Scripture, and to ascribe such inspiration to the possessors of "devout reason," and to magnify the supposed "verifying faculty" into the place of God, we have opening made for any and every form of error to enter which the morally diseased hearts of fallen men may choose, under Satan's guidance to imagine. The Babel of confusion that must follow, one can well conceive. But it will not be of long duration. It will be stilled by the dread and mighty voice of one who shall command that all who will not worship him "shall be killed;" and "all shall worship him whose names have not been, from the foundation of the world, written in the book of life of the Lamb that hath been slain." Rev. xiii. And they shall worship the devil too. This is the end to which the "verifying faculty" will bring. But I turn to another subject.

The doctrine of Propitiation by sacrificial substitution, was justly regarded at the Reformation as the key-stone of Christianity. Without this the Bible could have revealed no salvation; for, apart from sacrificial substitution, Christ could not have been a Saviour. Justification through faith, on account of Christ (per fidem propter Christum, or propter meritum Christi) were words of no ambiguous meaning either to the Reformers or to their adversaries. They were words well understood in all their bearings and connexions. Propitiation ($\iota \lambda a \sigma \mu o s$) in the language of the Reformers, denoted not, as Dr. Williams says, a "recovery of peace of heart," but that one appeasing, satisfying oblation which Christ on the Cross once and for ever offered unto God. Justification was not with the Reformers what it is with Dr. Williams, "a verdict of forgiveness upon our repentance, and of acceptance upon the offering of our hearts:" on the contrary, they affirmed that it was a judicial declaration on the part of God that He accounts believers righteous before Him solely because of the merits of Another. This the Reformers explained in their writings, and this they briefly embodied in the words of the eleventh Article. "We are accounted righteous before God only for [propter] the merit of our Lord and Saviour Jesus Christ, by faith [per fidem] and not for our own works and deservings." In the Latin edition of the Articles the words stand thus: "Tantum propter meritum Domini et Servatoris nostri Jesu Christi, per fidem, non propter opera et merita nostra, justi coram Deo reputamur."

Now let us compare with this Article the words of Dr. Williams; first, respecting "Propitiation;" and secondly, respecting "Justification." Dr. Williams writes as follows:

"If our philosopher [Bunsen] had persuaded us of the moral "nature of Justification, he would not shrink from adding that Re-"generation is a corresponding giving of insight, or an awakening of "the forces of the soul. By the Resurrection he would mean a spi-"ritual quickening. Salvation would be our deliverance, not from "the Life-giving God, but from evil and darkness which are its finite "opposites. (ὁ ἀντικείμενος) Propitiation would be the recovery of "that peace which cannot be, whilst sin divides us from the Searcher "of hearts." *Dr. Williams as quoted by Dr. Lushington in Judgment, p. 24.*

On this passage Dr. Lushington passed Judgment thus:

"It is apparent that Dr. Williams is here speaking of Justification, "Regeneration and Salvation, as doctrines to which he might give a "peculiar construction—in other words, the leading doctrines of the "Church are adverted to, and a meaning ascribed to them very dif-"ferent from that usually received. In a similar way is the word "'Propitiation' used. Propitiation is by the thirty-first Article of "Religion the oblation by Christ finished upon the Cross for sin. "Dr. Williams declares it to be 'the recovery of that peace which "cannot be, whilst Sin divides us from the Searcher of hearts.' Such "may be a consequence from Propitiation or the oblation of Christ, "but it is not Propitiation itself. I think such declaration is incon-"sistent with and contrary to the thirty-first Article." *Dr. Lushington's Judgment, p.p. 24, 25.*

On the charge against Dr. Williams touching the doctrine of Justification, Dr. Lushington observed thus:

"The charge is, that Dr. Williams in the extract pleaded did main-"tain that justification by faith means only the peace of mind or "sense of Divine approval which comes of trust in a righteous God; "and that 'justification is a verdict of forgiveness upon our repent-"'ance, and of acceptance upon the offering of our hearts.' It is "said that the doctrine so alleged to be set forth is contrary to the "eleventh Article of Religion,—on the justification of man: 'We "'are accounted righteous before God only for the merit of our Lord "'and Saviour Jesus Christ by faith, and not for our own works or "'deservings' I entirely concur that such opinion set forth in the "charging part of this Article [of accusation] is contrary to, and "inconsistent with, the eleventh Article, but then the question "remains, is the charge preferred a fair representation of the passage "extracted? The passage is as follows:

"'Why may not justification by faith have meant the peace of mind, or sense "'of Divine approval, which comes of trust in a righteous God, rather than a "'fiction of merit by transfer? St. Paul would then be teaching moral responsi-"'bility, as opposed to Sacerdotalism.'"

"The words are suggested by Dr. Williams as words which Baron "Bunsen might speak in reply to a charge of using evangelical lan-"guage in a philosophical sense. But looking to the whole context, "I cannot doubt that Dr. Williams employs these words as a form "of declaring his own sentiments. He is therefore responsible for "them."

"Then as to the construction of the passage. I think the passage "is repugnant to the eleventh Article; for in it justification is not "represented to be justification for the merit of our Lord by faith, "but is represented to be something distinct from it, namely, peace "of mind, or a sense of Divine approval, which comes of trust in "a righteous God. I think this construction is clear from the "words which follow, viz., 'rather than from a fiction of merit by "'transfer.' These words seem to me to express an idea wholly in-"consistent with the eleventh Article." *Dr. Lushington's Judgment, p.p.* 26, 27.

Such was the Judgment pronounced by Dr. Lushington. Is it not just? Is not the argument by which it is sustained irrefutable? Yet it was summarily set aside by the Court of Appeal. It will be observed that the Court of Appeal says,—"even if Dr. Williams be taken to approve, &c."* Therefore, we are allowed to assume that Dr. Williams does define justification by faith as meaning "the peace of mind, or sense of Divine approval, which comes of trust in a righteous God, rather than a fiction of merit by transfer." Nevertheless, with this doctrine on his lips he is acquitted, and we are told that "it would be unjust to him to take his words as a full statement of his belief or teaching on the subject of justification." Who wishes so to take his words? We are not concerned with statements that he has *not* made, whether full or partial: we have to do only with that which he has published, and to which he adheres. Dr. Williams has given us two propositions respecting Justification, one of which seems to be intended as a definition of Justification—the other, of Justification by faith.

As regards the first, Dr. Williams states that "justification" is "a verdict of forgiveness upon our repentance and of acceptance upon the offering of our hearts." Now although "verdict" is not a word that properly denotes the sentence of a Judge pronouncing judgment, we will pass that over and take "verdict" as meaning "sentence." Is it then true that "justification is a sentence of forgiveness *upon our repentance, and of acceptance upon the offering of our hearts?*" Observe the word "*upon.*" It is clearly used to indicate that our justification results from, and is founded on our repentance and the offering of our hearts? Not a word, observe, is said respecting Christ, nor even respecting faith. How by any possibility can such a statement be made to agree with an Article that declares that we are accounted or reputed righteous before God *only* on account of (propter) the merit of our Lord Jesus Christ through faith (per fidem) and not on account of our works or merits. "TANTUM propter meritum Domini et Servatoris nostri, Jesu Christi, per fidem, non propter opera et merita nostra, justi coram Deo reputamur." Dr. Williams' statement is, as Dr. Lushington rightly judged, in direct contravention to this Article. It is very obvious that they who affirm that we are justified *only on account of the merit of our Lord,* must be at irreconcileable variance with one who asserts that we are justified on the ground of, or as the

---

* The precise words are: "But, even if Dr. Williams be taken to approve of the arguments which he used for his supposed defence [of Bunsen] it would, we think, be unjust to him to take his words as a full statement of his belief or teaching on the subject of justification." *Judgment of Judicial Committee in Weekly Reporter. Vol. xii p.* 449.

result of " the offering of our hearts." And further, inasmuch as such offering of our hearts is unquestionably *a work*, and (on Dr. Williams' hypothesis) a work done before justification, his doctrine must be in direct opposition to the Article which declares that "works done before justification are not pleasing to God, but have in them the nature of sin." See Article xiii. " *On works before Justification.*"

Nor is Dr. Williams' second statement respecting justification *by faith* at all more in accordance with the Articles or with the Truth. He says · " Why may not justification by faith have meant the peace of mind or sense of Divine approval, which comes of trust in a righteous God, rather than a fiction of merit by transfer. St. Paul would then be teaching moral responsibility as opposed to sacerdotalism."

This sentence is so strangely worded, that I admit the difficulty of determining with certainty what the grammatical connexion of the words is. The general sense, however, is plain, and quite sufficient for our present purpose. In the first place, it is quite clear that Dr. Williams considers "merit by transfer"—that precious truth which lies at the foundation of all our hopes, to be *in some sense or other*, " *a* FICTION." Whatever be the grammatical connexion of the words, *that* is evident. Secondly, it is manifest that a definition of "justification " as used in the expression, "justification by faith" is given : and it is defined to be not a judicial sentence of God attributing righteousness to the believer nor a condition of righteousness attributed to the believer by such judicial sentence of God, but it is defined as meaning an inward condition of soul, viz., " peace of mind, or sense of Divine approval "—a definition of justification destructive of its true forensic sense, contradictory to the eleventh Article, and to the Homily on Justification, and repugnant to all that the Reformers ever wrote.

It might be sufficient to say this, but it would be scarcely fair to Dr. Williams himself thus summarily to dismiss the subject. In order to arrive at a just apprehension of his meaning we must compare his two definitions of justification together. In one place he defines justification as being a verdict or sentence, thereby retaining its forensic meaning : elsewhere, he defines it to be a state of mind, thus varying apparently his definition. His answer to this would, no doubt, be, that he varies it not at all; for that in the one case he is defining justification *per se*, in the other, justification by faith—that the first is a judicial sentence, the latter a state of heart. His system of doctrine, therefore, is this. When we repent and offer our hearts to God, God as being *righteous* pronounces a sentence of forgiveness and acceptance. This constitutes our justification *before Him*. But further, when we trust in God as having pronounced this sentence, the peace that flows from such trust is justification by faith—a justification or peace that comes not from a mere phantasy of having merit by transfer through vicarious atonement, but from trusting in a righteous God, righteously owning the offering of our hearts—such offering having justly a value in His sight.

Such is the system. That it utterly sets aside salvation *by grace*, atonement, and every thing else that distinctively marks Christianity as revealed in the Scripture, is obvious. According to this system, justification by *faith* has nothing to do with our forgiveness or acceptance *before God*. We are forgiven and accepted upon our repentance and the offering of our hearts, and are so justified before God. Justification by faith comes when we believe that we have been so justified before God, so that faith has nothing whatever to do with our justification *before God*. Is this the doctrine of the eleventh Article? Are the words "before God through faith" (coram Deo per fidem) found there or not? Why then am I mocked by being asked to believe that the doctrine of Dr. Williams is in accordance with the eleventh Article? Moreover, the eleventh Article affirms that we are justified before God "ONLY on account of the merit of our Lord Jesus Christ." Dr. Williams denies this, and says that we are justified "upon our repentance and the offering of our hearts." And yet I am asked to believe that the statements of Dr. Williams do not contradict the Articles!!

Even then if we had not been told that the conviction that he has "merit by transfer" is, in the mind of every one who has such a conviction, a "phantasy,"—even if such an opinion as this had never been advanced* nothing can be more demonstrable than that the doctrine contained in the passages quoted is in direct contravention of the eleventh Article. Are we to be told that the eleventh Article does not affirm the doctrine of merit by transfer? "We are accounted righteous before God *not* on account of our own merits"— that is the *negative* statement. "We are accounted righteous before

---

* It is in this way that Dr. Williams attempted in his defence to explain what he had said respecting "fiction." See this further referred to in following note. It will be seen that the Court actually allows to Dr. Williams more liberty as to this point than he ventured to claim for himself.

God ONLY on account of the merit of our Lord and Saviour Jesus Christ"—that is, the *positive* part of the Article. And then it is added that we become connected with that Saviour's merit simply through faith—*per fidem.* Now I ask if these words do not teach the transfer of the merit of Christ to a believer, what words could be devised that would teach transfer? The Article tells me that I have no merit, and yet it tells me that I am justified before God on account of merit—merit found in our Lord and Saviour. If transference of merit be not here taught, what is it that is taught? Yet the judgment of the Court of Appeal has now made it lawful (though they admit that it may be somewhat unseemly) for any Clergyman to affirm that "merit by transfer" is a "fiction." He need not even resort to the contrivance by which Dr. Williams sought to soften the force of these words.*

---

* Never perhaps was a more extraordinary judgment pronounced than the following. It is the judgment of the Judicial Committee of the Privy Council delivered through the Lord Chancellor. It is as follows: "The Eleventh Article "of Religion which Dr. Williams is accused of contravening, states, 'We are "'accounted righteous before God only for the merits of our Lord and Saviour "'Jesus Christ, by faith, and not for our own works or deservings.' The Article is "wholly silent as to the merits of Jesus Christ being transferred to us It asserts "only that we are justified for the merits of our Saviour by faith, and by faith "alone." [I have already shown the falseness of this statement. It does not only speak of justification *through faith* (per fidem). It also speaks of that "*on account of which*" (*propter* quod) we are accounted righteous, viz., the merit of our Lord and Saviour Jesus Christ, and opposes to this our own works and merits, and says that *not* on account of them are we accounted righteous. "Tantum propter meritum Domini et Servatoris nostri, Jesu Christi, per fidem et non propter opera et merita nostra, justi coram Deo reputamur." This is the first clause of the Article, and in *it* the instrumental place of faith as linking us to the merit of the Saviour is spoken of only *subordinately.* It is not *the* subject of *this* clause. In *this* clause the believer is told that he has no merits on which to ground a claim of justification before God, but that he is "*reputed righteous*" on account of the merit of Another. If I have no merits of my own and yet am "reputed righteous" on account of (propter) the merits of Another, is not this a transfer of merits? Yet I am told in this so-called "Judgment," that "the Article *is wholly silent* as to the merits of Jesus Christ being transferred to us." It is certainly silent as to those merits being transferred to them that believe not, but I know not what words could be devised to give a testimony more clear and precise as to the transfer of the Saviour's merits to *believers.* If one did not know the ignorance that prevails as to the *true* doctrine of justification one might marvel that this point which is one of the most flagrant, if not the most flagrant, of the perversions of judgment

It is vain to close our eyes to the consequences of the Judgments that have been pronounced. The feeble and imperfect barrier that Dr. Lushington's Judgment allowed to stand, has been utterly thrown down by the Court of Appeal. Technically it may be true that no judicial opinion has been expressed on "the Essays and Reviews" *as a whole*, but *virtually* a judgment has been pronounced, for in the

---

in the "Judgment" has attracted so little attention. Why was it unnoticed in the Oxford protest?]

After having asserted that the Article is silent as to the transference of Christ's merits the Judgment proceeds "We cannot say, therefore, that it is penal in a "clergyman to speak of merit by transfer as a fiction, however unseemly that "word may be when used in connection with such a subject. It is fair, however, "to Dr. Williams to observe that in the argument at the bar he repudiated the "interpretation which had been put on these words that the doctrine of merit by "transfer is a fiction; and he explained fiction as intended by him to describe the "phantasy in the mind of an individual that he has received or enjoyed merit by "transfer" [Observe, even if the "transfer of merit" be spoken of as "a fiction" in the worst sense that can be assigned to "*fiction*," even then *no* sentence of condemnation is to be pronounced. It may be "*unseemly*" in a clergyman to use such words, but he is not to be condemned for it. There was, therefore, really no need for Dr. Williams to endeavour to lessen the force of the expression. But what, after all, does the extenuation amount to? "Phantasy" cannot be predicated of the apprehensions of any one who apprehends what is true. Dr. Williams asserts that every one who enjoys peace of mind from the conviction that he is justified on the ground of the transfer of Another's merit, is deluded by 'a *phantasy* or *fiction*' Why? Certainly because he recognises as the ground of his justification something that God has not made the ground of his justification, viz., the merits of Another. The comfort is a phantasy because that on which it is founded is according to Dr. Williams, something unreal. For if Dr. Williams were to admit that the doctrine of "transfer of merit" was a reality, he must admit that a soul that derived comfort from such a doctrine was not deluded by a phantasy. Therefore he does hold that the doctrine "of transfer of merit" is a fiction]

The Judgment proceeds. "Upon the whole we cannot accept the interpretation "charged by the promoter as the true meaning of the passages included in the "fifteenth Article of charge, nor can we consider those passages as warranting the "specific charge which in effect is, that Dr. Williams asserts that justification "means only the peace of mind or sense of Divine approval which comes of trust "in a righteous God. *This is not the assertion of Dr. Williams*. We are, there-"fore, of opinion that the Judgment against Dr. Williams must be reversed." *Judgment of Privy Council, Vol xxii. p* 449 *of Weekly Reporter.*

The Chancellor says, "*this is not the assertion of Dr. Williams*" It is not difficult speaking ex cathedrâ to give forth an authoritative dictum like this. But we may be permitted to ask for some proof. Dr. Lushington has affirmed (and he

extracts presented to Dr. Lushington and to the Court of Appeal for judgment, the poison of the whole volume is contained. The very pith and sinews of neology are found in those extracts. By the permission accorded to use such words and advance such doctrines as are found in those extracts, a legalized standing in the Established Church of this country is secured for Neology. All its *essential* doctrines may be freely taught. Is this no triumph for Antichristianism?

The *immediate* effect in this country will probably be an increase of Romanism both within and without the pale of the Establishment. It could scarcely be expected that the Sacerdotal party within the Establishment, when they see what a non-natural interpretation of the Articles has effected for the Neologians, should be satisfied unless similar liberty were accorded to themselves. Accordingly, they intend no longer to submit to the restrictions they have hitherto endured. Some have avowed their purpose of teaching openly for the future, things that they have hitherto taught indirectly, or in secret. If the Articles, say they, are not made binding upon others, why should they be made binding upon us? If it be a day in which every bond is to be broken and every band loosed, we certainly will not be slow to avail ourselves of the universal license. Can we marvel at this resolve? The sacerdotal party had previously a firm footing in this country, and now it will receive into its ranks many, who, though not quite prepared to sanction its extreme pretensions, do neverthe-

---

has given his reason) that Dr. Williams *does* assert that wherewith he was charged. Is Dr. Lushington's Judgment to be thus summarily set aside without any reason being assigned for its rejection? Any one who examines the subject will be inclined to say that no reason could be assigned. Consequently, if set aside, it must be set aside *authoritatively—without reason*. And this has been done. Dr. Williams' words are, "Why may not justification by faith have meant the peace of mind, or sense of Divine approval which comes of trust in a righteous God, rather than a fiction of merit by transfer." Dr. Lushington says, and says most truly " I think the passage is repugnant to the Eleventh Article, for in it justification is " not represented to be justification for the merit of our Lord by faith, but is re-" presented to be something distinct from it, namely, ' peace of mind, or a sense of " Divine approval which comes of trust in a righteous God.' I think this con-" struction is clear from the words which follow, ' rather than from a fiction of " merit by transfer?' These words seem to me to express an idea wholly incon-" sistent with the Eleventh Article." *Dr. Lushington's Judgment, p.* 27. And Dr. Lushington is right. Whether you supply "from" before " fiction," or whether you read " peace of mind" rather than a fiction, &c., the conclusion is the same.

less so dread the change that would come over society if brought under the negations of scepticism, as to be willing to accept instead, almost any form of ancient dogmatic theology; and that proposed by Rome is deemed the most respectable, and comes nearest to hand.

Yet the very activity and increase of the sacerdotal party will in the end contribute greatly to the strengthening of the influence of Neology. Who can tell the effect that the high pretensions and sophistical subtleties and exclusiveness of sacerdotalism in Oxford had in driving Arnold and others into the abysses of Bunsenism. Minds less discerning and less sensitive than that of Dr. Arnold, might well be disgusted by all that preceded and followed the production of Tract 90. Men of high natural conscientiousness, and sufficiently intelligent and self-possessed to distinguish between superstitious credulity and real faith—between trust in God and trust in the fictions of a pretended Church, are little likely to be satisfied either with the *past* or *present* path of Sacerdotalism. Such men, unless through God's grace they become real servants of the Truth, will certainly be tempted to rally round that new banner of rebellion which Rationalism has reared against the King of kings. Nor can it be doubted that the principles of Neologianism are far more in unison with the spirit of the age than the restrictiveness of Sacerdotalism. Neology is in profession, at least, wide and comprehensive. It is in every sense broad; desiring to exclude from the circle of its privileges none except convicted criminals or the few insignificant sectarians who trace their origin to Calvin and Geneva. It is quite willing to welcome and honour Sacerdotalism itself, if it will only abate its exclusiveness.

Sacerdotalism, on the contrary, is narrow and restrictive to the very extreme of exclusiveness, and therefore must jar with the governmental arrangements of every country that, like England, treads persistently the path of Latitudinarianism. Think of England's course in India, in the Colonies, and in Ireland. Can England then, governmentally, look with complacency on the narrow exclusiveness of Sacerdotalism? And if its importunities should become excessive, will she not find in the energy and talent of the Neologian a ready and available ally? Moreover, it must be remembered that in this country society is emphatically utilitarian. Commerce has created in England a large and influential class who by means of their riches are fast becoming the great pillars of the State—the very key-stone of the political arch. Devoted to the acquisition of wealth, and to the advancement of the "material" interests of men, they eschew contention of every kind. Religious contention they especially abhor; and are, consequently, ready to surrender, or force into the background, every principle or doctrine that tends to gender strife. Looking on the Establishment as a mighty organ for securing social order; for diffusing education and ameliorating the condition of the people physically, they are willing and anxious to uphold it, provided that no religious party exclusively dominates, and that due subservience be enforced to the will of the State. As to Truth, they deem its attainment to be a matter too problematical, and of too uncertain value, to be for one moment compared with the advantage of quiet; for quiet promotes "material" prosperity, whilst too close adherence to Truth leads to aggressiveness and conflict, whereby progress is impeded. To men with thoughts like these, the breadth and comprehensiveness of Neologianism must be far more welcome than any system of exclusiveness. There can be little doubt, therefore, that Neologian Latitudinarianism has attained in this country a standing that it will retain until it be swallowed up in the black vortex of matured Antichristianism. At present, both Romanism and Neology may be said to have attained a recognised standing in the Established Church of this country—I say *recognised* standing, for when any have assumed a position and no effectual attempt is made to displace them, we may regard their standing as recognised. That which authority refuses to silence, it must be held to sanction.

It is indeed marvellous that they who fear God and reverence His Word, should remain passive and inert whilst these things are being accomplished. The blessed truths of the Reformation are being cast to the winds, and the Bible has by the recent Judgment of "the highest Court which can exercise ecclesiastical jurisdiction in this realm," been deprived of that place of honour which in this country has for ages been assigned to it as the infallible witness of Truth. And yet no great united effort is made to stop the progress of governmental Apostasy. Mere protestation is not action. It seems strange and very sorrowful, that the Churches of Scotland and the Wesleyans, and the various evangelical Churches and organisations throughout the Empire, should witness this *national* degradation of the Word of God, and this installation of Infidelity and of Popery into the high places of the Establishment, and remain passive. Could they not unite and demand the reversal of this "Judgment?" The circumstances that called forth the Confession and Protestation of Augsburgh were not so dark and threatening as those that now surround us. Yet there is no confederated action. " Public opinion" whose influence is so much vaunted, is dormant here; nor is any effectual attempt made to arouse it. The desire for united action in the Truth seems departed even from the Truth's own servants: nor does any hope seem left of arresting, even temporarily, this onward movement of Apostasy. Christians—true, real Christians are so little aware of what is written in the Scripture respecting the close of the present dispensation—so little aware that " an hour of temptation is coming on the whole world to try them that dwell upon the earth "—so little instructed in that which the Scripture teaches respecting Antichristianism and Antichrist, that they ignore the most evident signs of the approach of that Apostasy of which he is to be the embodiment and head. Ignorant of what the Prophets have spoken respecting the closing hour, they speak of the darkness which they cannot deny to be ominously deepening, as if it were a mere momentary gathering of black, it may be, but temporary clouds, soon to give place to lasting brightness.

Among the servants of Christ there are of course none so nearly interested in these questions as the evangelical Christians who continue within the pale of the Establishment. Would to God that they might have grace to look with a clear and steady eye upon the circumstances of the hour. Surely if they have heretofore clung to the hope that the work commenced at the Reformation would be perfected by remaining corruptions being removed and errors rectified, they must now see that the hope was fallacious. They have over them an iron ruling power that is resolved not only to protect old errors, but to introduce new.

For the intervention of God's mercy and power at the time of the Reformation, there are millions who in eternity will bless His holy name for ever and ever. But the Reformation was checked in its outset. Even if the revision of doctrine had been more complete than it was, yet revision of doctrine (vitally important as it is) is not the only thing needful when an attempt is made to recall from darkness to paths of separateness and light. The manner in which the doctrines of Truth are used and *applied* is a question no less important than the maintenance of the doctrines themselves. No one who knows the Gospel of the grace of God can read the first eighteen Articles of the Church of England, without being struck by their simplicity and excellence. But Christian truths belong to Christians. To apply to the unbelieving world truths which belong only to them who, being justified by faith, have peace with God, is deception. It is an attempt to effect that which our Lord has forbidden. A new patch is not to be sewed on an old garment: new wine is not to be put into old bottles. If, at the Reformation, the true servants of Christ had had sufficient light, and sufficient power, to search out and extirpate all Popish leaven; if they had been permitted to send into the dark parishes only those who were really, by God's Spirit, qualified to teach and to preach; if the attempt to allure, or to force the unconverted into the assumption of a Church-position had been abandoned; if the unconverted had been assembled in order to hear the Gospel of the grace of God, and distinct meetings held for the further instruction of those who credibly professed the name of Christ; if none but those who made such credible confession had been baptized and gathered around the Table of the Lord; if godly discipline, such as the Apostle enjoins to the Corinthians, had been there exercised; if the great principle that the law of the Church is contained in the Bible alone had been practically carried out, and the work of the Church, through her ministers, had been acknowledged to be, not legislation, but administration; if the Spirit of God had been owned by seeking to recognise as ministers those only whom He had qualified to minister; if it had been remembered that His gifts are diverse, and that every evangelist is not necessarily a pastor, and teacher; nor every pastor, or teacher, an evangelist, if the Apostle's charge to Timothy to commit the truth that he had himself received, " to faithful men suited or qualified to teach others," had been taken as the only means for the perpetuation of true ministry; if such perpetuation had been recognised as dependent on God alone, and beyond the scope of any power that had been committed, even to the Apostles; and if secular rulers, *as such*, had been admitted to no place of headship or rule, or authority in the Church of God; if all these things had been remembered and acted on, the Reformation in England would have been a Reformation indeed. But, alas, how different its history! The secular power demanded a place of sovereignty, and it was accorded by those who, as to all things connected with Truth and order *in the Church*, owned allegiance to another Head. And what was the result? No sooner did any seek after increased purity of practice or of doctrine, than they were repressed and persecuted. Think of the treatment of Bishop Hooper. Think of the Non-conformists and their sufferings. Chains, hunger, misery, death, became their portion. But the persecution of the Protestant Non-conformists was not unpunished. It was followed by a season of deep spiritual gloom. Indeed, until near the time of the French Revolution (when as if to stem the tide of blasphemy thence originated, Whitfield and others were raised up to proclaim afresh the Gospel of the grace of God) the condition of England generally was one of intense spiritual darkness. Since the days of Whitfield much increase of most precious light has been mercifully vouchsafed to the Christians of our land: but our *collective* condition has not improved. The Bible, even when truly owned as the Word of God, has not that place of actual supremacy over our thoughts and ways which God claims for it. Consequently, throughout a large mass of active Christianity, disorder and confusion reign. In the meanwhile, in the mere professing Church, Sacerdotalism and Infidelity give by their contests an opportunity to the secular power to interfere as arbiter: an opportunity of which it is not slow to avail itself, and the present Judgment is one of the results. A world-wide platform is being established; and Evangelicalism may, if it please, take its stand thereon, by the side of Sacerdotalism, and Neology, and form *with them* a so-called Church; and receive *with them* like honour. Will the servants of Christ be content with this position? Will they own such a confederation? Questions far, far, less extensive than these have, in former times, caused martyrs to seal their testimony by their blood.

APPENDIX A.

Note on Mr. Wilson's Rejection of the Doctrine of Eternal Punishment.

In the foregoing observations, I have confined myself to the Judgment pronounced by Dr. Lushington and the Committee of the Privy Council *on the Essay of Dr. Williams;* and therefore have not referred to another most important question that was made very prominent in the Judgment of the Council, viz., the denial of the doctrine of eternity of punishment—that denial being found, *not* in the Essay of Dr. Williams, but in another written by Mr. Wilson, who is also a clergyman, and whose case formed the subject of a separate trial. The tests having been, as in the case of Dr. Williams, relaxed, Mr. Wilson also obtained a ready acquittal.

Holiness and justice are as much attributes of God as love. He may be pleased, in the riches of His wisdom and grace, to find a way of manifesting His love toward sinners without compromising His righteousness, and this He has done: but as it pertains to Him alone to devise the method, so He only is competent to declare what that method is, and what are the consequences of rejecting it. He has revealed that the only means of deliverance from the wrath to come is faith in a substitutional *wrath*-bearer, and he has declared that they who reject this one way of reconciliation, must themselves meet His wrath and bear it for ever and ever.

Few, I believe, reject the doctrine of everlasting punishment without also manifesting a tendency, and more than a tendency, to reject the doctrine of Christ being in any real sense, a wrath-bearer. The same habit of mind that refuses to bow to the plain declarations of Scripture respecting everlasting punishment, finds equal difficulty in recognising that such passages as Ps. xxii. 14, 15, reveal the action of God's hand in bruising the Son of His love—"I am poured out like water, and all my bones are out of joint: my heart is like wax; it is melted in the midst of my bowels. My strength is dried up like a potsherd; and my tongue cleaveth to my jaws; and THOU hast brought me into the dust of death." Can we wonder that they who scorn the salvation thus provided for them through the sufferings of the Holy One, should themselves be left to experience that eternity of wrath, of which God has warned them, and from which He has sought to deliver.

When we read in Matthew xxv. 46, "These shall go away into everlasting (αιωνιαν) punishment, but the righteous into life everlasting" (αιωνιαν) are we to believe that in these two conjoined clauses, the same word "everlasting" varies in its sense? Are we to say that in the last clause it means never-ending duration, but in the former not? Surely if language be subject to such arbitrary variations as this, it must cease to be useful as a medium of instruction, for if the contextual association of words affords no indication of their meaning, to what else are we to appeal? Are the varying fancies of each individual reader to be our guide? In the passages in which we read of "the everlasting God" (Rom. xvi. 26.)—"who liveth for ever and ever" (Rev. xv. 7), and of "everlasting life," and of "everlasting punishment," our thoughts are in each case called away from this sublunary sphere, and consequently, we have to attach to these expressions, that sense which they *must* bear in that world which stands in emphatic contrast with the present, as being one in which transitoriness of existence is unknown.

Some, indeed, admit that the punishment spoken of in Matthew xxv. is "everlasting," but say that the punishment indicated is to be *annihilation*—a punishment not involving infliction of torment, but simply deprivation of blessing. The annihilated, they say, will lose the life, glory and blessing prepared for the righteous, and *so* be punished; but that by ceasing to exist, and therefore to feel, they will be incapable of torment. Now, in the first place, this system requires us to admit that the soul of man is perishable—a doctrine which even the Pagans hesitated, and in many instances refused, to maintain. Further, this doctrine is at utter variance with the words of our Lord when He says: "where their worm dieth not, and the fire is not quenched," as likewise with Rev. xx. 10, where we find the words, "tormented day and night for ever and ever." "Torment" is not annihilation: it is a word that necessarily implies existence and feeling: nor does a "never-dying worm," and "fire unquenched," imply either the extinction of the instrumental means of the torment, nor the cessation of feeling in those who are tormented. Why should the fires of torment be declared to be *unquenched* fires if there were none to be subjected to the power of their burning? In these and in like questions, are we to become judges of God, or are we to bow with implicit subjection to the declarations of His Word, and to say, Shall not the Judge of all the earth do right? He shall be justified in His sayings, and overcome when He is judged. (Rom. iii.) It is no less a sin to alter or to conceal that which He has revealed respecting His judgments, than to alter or conceal that which He has written concerning His love.

In the case of Mr Wilson, as in that of Dr. Williams, the Court refused to try the question submitted to them, *by Scripture.* Their province, they said, was merely to determine whether such of the standards of the Church of England as were affirmed in the pleadings to have been violated by Mr. Wilson, had been violated. The passages quoted were, first, from the Catechism, where the child is taught that in repeating the Lord's Prayer he prays unto God "that He will keep us from all sin and wickedness, and from our ghostly enemy, and from *everlasting* death." Also the Commination Service: "O terrible voice of most just judgment, which shall be pronounced upon them, when it shall be said unto them, Go, ye cursed, into the fire everlasting, which is prepared for the devil and his angels:" and also the Athanasian Creed, "they that have done good shall go into life *everlasting:* and they that have done evil into *everlasting* fire." No one who knows the sentiments of the Reformers can for a moment question that they understood the word "everlasting" in its proper sense, and sanctioned its use in the passages just quoted in order that the doctrine of everlasting punishment might be unequivocally taught in the Formularies of the Church of England. Yet the Chancellor, speaking as the organ of the Committee of the Privy Council, says: "We are not required, or at liberty to express any opinion upon the mysterious question of the eternity of final punishment further than to say, that we do not find in the Formularies to which the Article [of charge] refers, any such distinct declaration of our Church upon the subject as to require us to condemn as penal, the expression of hope by a clergyman, that even the ultimate pardon of the wicked who are condemned in the day of judgment, may be consistent with the will of Almighty God."

"The Lord Chancellor," says Dr. Pusey, "has as far as in him "lies, poisoned the springs of English justice for ages in all matters "of faith. Not only has he done this in his own person, but he has "virtually ascribed the same trickery with words to our Redeemer "Himself; for he avers that the word 'everlasting,' as used in the "Athanasian Creed, is to be taken with the same ambiguity of mean-"ing, as 'learned men' have taken it in the Gospels. In other words, "because heretics have affixed a non-natural meaning to our Lord's "words, therefore it is to be ruled, that our Blessed Lord, when re-"vealing the final issue of our state of trial here, used the selfsame "word in the selfsame sentence, once in its natural, once in a 'non-"natural' meaning. 'These shall go away into everlasting punish-"ment; but the righteous into life eternal.'"

"On such a system of interpretation, no one could be found guilty "of any charge, except Almighty God of the one sweeping charge, "that He either did not reveal Himself to His creatures at all, or "like the Pythian Oracle, used ambiguous terms, which may be taken "any how,—until the Day of Judgment."

"Yet further, the Lord Chancellor laid down the principle, that a "word, whose meaning was not laid down in the formularies them-"selves, might be taken in any sense of which it was capable. But "since Theological terms, not only in our formularies, including "the Creeds, but in Holy Scripture also, are used in their known "Theological sense, and, being known, are not defined (for men "define what is really ambiguous, not what is known), then it follows, "that every word may be taken in a non-natural sense. And this has "a direct practical bearing on the misbelief of the present day, because "it is an avowed plan, 'to win' (as it is said) 'new senses for received "Theological terms,' i.e. to take them in 'non-natural' meanings; so "that, in this new Babel-din of Theology, every one is to be able to "veil his meaning at least from the understanding of human justice."

"These are the principles to which the present Lord Chancellor "stands committed; this is the injustice, which by those principles "he is held bound to measure out to the English Church: this the "profanation of justice, which he stands pledged to counsel to the "Supreme temporal authority of this realm." *Preface p.* 12.

"This choice" (I continue to quote from Dr. Pusey) "alone stands "before us. Either, as heretofore, men's consciences must restrain "them from taking obligations upon them, which it is a burden to "discharge, from pledging themselves to read, as God's Word, what

"they believe to be the word of man, and from uttering to God, as the
"truth of God, what they take upon themselves to pronounce to be
"alien to His Nature;—either the consciences of the Clergy must
"conform themselves to our Prayer Book, or we must be prepared for
"the claim that prayers should be disused, whose natural sense men
"shall be allowed to disbelieve, and therewith that the faith, which
"those prayers express, should be obliterated."

"The present stage is but a stepping-stone. Will the Church of
"England require that the Court which has shown itself so partial, so
"dishonest, which, had it been a matter of human property, would
"not have dared so openly to profane justice, should be reformed? or
"will it acquiesce in such unprincipled principles, as the Lord Chan-
"cellor enunciated in its name? If it does, every attempt to require
"that the Clergy should not deny what they profess to God and man
"that they believe, must throw open a fresh article of the Creed. It
"must have been in irony, that one, advocating recently the abolition
"of subscription, proposed that errors as to doctrine should be left to
"Courts of Law.* It would be curious to see, what denials of truth
"he would think to be errors, or likely to be condemned. Mr. Wilson,
"who does not think it essential to any National Church, that it should
"be Christian, speaks of the 'meshes of the law' which requires sub-
"scription, as 'too open for modern refinements,' and teaches how to
"evade the statements as to the faith, without directly impugning
"or contradicting them. The Lord Chancellor follows his lead, and
"teaches how every statement of faith may be evaded, if only the old
"words be kept, and new meanings affixed to them.

"Is then the Church of England to be really a mere arena for jug-
"glers' tricks, sporting with the meanings of words, as if there were
"no truth, no faith, no Word of God, no God, to whom men are re-
"sponsible? If it is not to be such, the course must be arrested at
"once. The principles enunciated by the Lord Chancellor would
"make Articles, Creeds, Prayers, Scripture, a mere superficial mirror,
"in which any one, instead of seeing the truth of God, is to see only
"the reflexion of his own mind. As he looks in to them, so are they
"to look out to him. . . . . . Let men bind themselves not to give
"over, but to continue besieging the House of Parliament by their
"petitions, and beseeching Almighty God in their prayers, until they

---

* The present Dean of Christ Church. [Liddell.] In Macmillan's Magazine.

"shall obtain some security against this State-protection of unbelief. Better be members of the poorest Church in Christendom, which can repel the wolves which spare not the flock! than of the richest, in which the State forces us to accept as her ministers, those whom our Lord calls 'ravening wolves.' Withal see we to it, that we pray God earnestly day by day to stem this flood of ungodliness, and to convert those who are now, alas! enemies of the faith and of God." (*Preface** p p. 18, 19, 22.)

---

* See "Case as to the Legal force of the Judgment of the Privy Council *in re* Fendall v. Wilson;" by Rev. E. B. Pusey, D.D.

APPENDIX B.

Doctrine of the English Reformers on Baptism.

An attempt has been made to justify the *non-natural* interpretation of the Formularies in the case before us, by reference to the decision of the Privy Council in the case of Mr. Gorham, when, it is argued, a *non-natural* interpretation was put upon certain passages in the Prayer Book, in order to retain in the Church those who refused to admit that regenerating grace is necessarily bestowed in Baptism: why, then, it is said, should not a *non-natural* interpretation be put on the other parts of the formularies in order to retain the Neologian party in the Church?

There is a certain plausibility, perhaps, in this argument: but it will not bear a moment's examination.

In the first place, the questions are not parallel. As regards the sacraments, the question in dispute is, whether the language used respecting them, both in Scripture and in the Formularies, is, or is not, *symbolic*. Is Baptism a *symbolic* washing away of sin, or an *actual* washing away of sin? In the Lord's Supper, in eating the bread, do we eat the *symbol* of the Lord's body, or do we *actually* eat His body? Is the language used of such eating or washing to be understood symbolically, or literally?

Now, inasmuch as no one can pretend that any question about symbol or figure can be raised respecting such parts of the Articles and Formularies as have been cited in the case before us, the questions are not parallel. No figurative meaning is supposed by any one to attach to the words, "Dost thou unfeignedly believe all the Canonical Scriptures of the Old and New Testament?" All agree that the words are to be understood literally.

But further: I suppose that no one, even in these days of reckless assertion will pretend that the statements of Dr. Williams and Mr. Wilson are not diametrically and essentially opposed to the sentiments of those Reformers from whom the Articles and Formularies proceeded. Does any one doubt that, if the Reformers could rise from their graves and themselves interpret the Formularies by them sanctioned, Dr. Williams and Mr. Wilson would be condemned? Unquestionably the Reformers did by their Formularies intend to exclude such as hold the opinions of Dr. Williams and Mr. Wilson. If, therefore, there had been any point on which the language seemed uncertain, the *animus imponentis* (and of this there could be no doubt) should have been scrupulously regarded.

That it was the design of the Reformers to condemn and to exclude those who impute falsehood to the Word of God, is beyond a question. But is it equally certain that they intended to condemn and exclude those who taught that Baptism does not *actually* regenerate? Unquestionably not; for in that case they would have condemned and excluded themselves.

No one of impartial judgment can read the following quotations from Bullinger and affirm that the doctrine of Baptismal Regeneration could be accredited by those who sanctioned and enforced the doctrines taught by Bullinger. The fifth book of Bullinger's "Decades," from which the following extracts are taken, was received in England in 1551; and in the next year Cranmer after having previously sanctioned the publication of Bullinger's "Tract on the Sacraments," invited Bullinger to England to " devise the means by which . . . . . . in England, or elsewhere, there may be convoked a Synod of the most learned and excellent persons, in which provision may be made for the purity of ecclesiastical doctrine, *and especially for an agreement upon the Sacramentarian controversy.*" (Cranmer's Works ii. 431. Parker Society.) And thirty-five years later, in 1586, an order was issued entitled, "Orders for the better increase of Learninge in the Inferior Ministers, and for more diligent Preachinge and Cathechisinge." This order was introduced by Archbishop Whitgift, and is as follows:—
"Everie Minister, havinge cure and beinge under the degrees of Master of Arte and Bach. of Lawe, and not licensed to be a publique preacher, shall, before the second daye of Februarie next, provide a BIBLE and BULLINGER'S DECADES in Latin or Englishe, and a paper booke; and shall everie daye reade over one chap're of the Holie Scriptures, and note ye principall contents thereof brieflie in his paper booke; and shall everie weeke reade over one sermon in the said

Decades, and note likewise the cheife matters therein conteyned, in the saide paper And shall once in everie quarter, viz within a fortnight before or at the ende of the quarter, shewe his said note to some preacher neere adioyning, to be assigned for that purpose." *Gorham's Gleanings p.* 497.

Nothing therefore can be more evident, as Mr. Gorham observes, than "that the selection of the DECADES of Bullinger, as the only Examination Text Book, besides the Bible for the inferior Clergy—and that by the whole bench of Bishops assembled in Convocation, is a clear proof that the Church of England deemed Bullinger's doctrines to be generally in accordance with her own, in the judgment of the Prelates of that day.*

The doctrine of Bullinger on Baptism will not be doubted by any who read the following extracts. They are taken from the fifth book of his Decades :—

EXTRACTS FROM BULLINGER.

"The Lord, doing after the manner of men, hath added signs of His faithfulness and truth, in His everlasting covenant and promises of life; the Sacraments, I mean, wherewith He sealed His promises, and the very doctrine of His Gospel." *Bullinger's Decades as quoted in Gorham's Gleanings,* p. 249.

"If any should go obstinately to affirm, that the sign in very deed is the thing signified, because it beareth the name thereof, would not all men cry out that such a one were without wit or reason, and that he were to be abhorred by all means as an obstinate brawler? Those, therefore, that are skilful in the things, understand that that is and hath been Catholic, received of all men, and also sound . . . . . . to wit, that the signs do borrow the names of the things, and not turn into the things which they signify . . . . . the Apostle, speaking of Baptism, saith, 'We are buried with Christ by Baptism into His death' He doth not say, 'We signify the burial;' but he doth flatly say, 'We are buried.' Therefore he calleth the

---

[* "These Orders were introduced by Whitgift into the Upper House of Convocation, in its 13th Session, December 2nd, 1586 ; they were transmitted to the Secretary of State for the Queen's information (and possibly approval, though it is not recorded) in January, 1587 ; on the 10th of March, in that year, in the seventh session of the same Convocation by prorogation, the Prolocutor of the Lower House ' prayed that they might be read, which was done, and then the Archbishop exhorted the Clergy to do their duty.' On, or about the 27th of March, they were registered at Lambeth ; in the course of the summer they were transmitted to the several Dioceses ; and in 1588, the Archbishop sent a Circular to the Bishops to enquire strictly how they had been observed."]

Sacrament of so great a thing, no otherwise than by the name of the selfsame thing." *Ibid.*

"The common sort of priests and monks have taught, that the Sacraments of the new law are not only Signs of grace, but together also causes of grace, that is, which have power to give grace. For they say, that they are as instruments, pipes, and certain conduits of Christ's passion, by which the grace of Christ is conveyed and poured into us." *Ibid*

"This is undoubtedly true, that the Apostles with no other forcible engine [battering-ram] more strongly battered (as it were) and beat down flat to the ground their adversaries' bulwark in defence of Sacraments that purify, than with this, 'That we which believe shall be saved by the grace of our Lord Jesus Christ;' and whereas in every place almost they add, 'Not by the law, not by ceremonies, or other ritual observations,'—do we think that they will admit Sacraments to the partaking of such power and virtue, seeing they be comprehended under rites and ceremonies, and so accounted? Christian faith doth attribute the grace of God, remission of sins, sanctification, and justification, fully and wholly to the free mercy of God, and to the merits of Christ's passion; yea, in such sort doth Christian faith attribute these spiritual benefits unto it, that beside it nothing at all is admitted to take part with it. Therefore, whereas Lombard (Sent. iv., Dist. ii.) saith, 'that Sacraments have received power to confer or give grace by the merit of the passion of Christ,' it is of his own forging. For as Christ giveth not His glory to any, either saint or mortal man, much less to a creature without life, even so, he that believeth to be fully justified by the death and resurrection of the Lord, seeketh no further grace and righteousness in any other thing than in Christ only, upon whom he stayeth; whom also by faith he feeleth in his heart or mind already, to exercise His force by the Holy Ghost." *Ibid.*

"Whereas it is objected,—that by a certain heavenly covenant, it is so appointed by God that Sacraments should have grace in themselves, and should from themselves, as by pipes, convey abroad the water of grace unto those that are thirsty,— that is alleged without warrant of the Scripture, and is repugnant unto true religion. . . . . The holy and elect people of God are not then first of all partakers of the grace of God, and heavenly gifts, when they receive the Sacraments. For they enjoy the things before they be partakers of the Signs. For, it is plainly declared unto us that Abraham our father was justified before he was circumcised. And who gathereth [not] thereby, that justification was not exhibited and given unto him by the Sacrament of Circumcision, but rather that that righteousness which he by faith before possessed, was by the Sacrament sealed and confirmed unto him? And, moreover, who will not thereof gather that we, which are the sons of Abraham, are after no other manner justified, than it appeareth that our father was justified; and that our Sacraments work no further in us than they did in him? especially since the nature of the Sacraments of the people of the Old Testament and ours is all one. . . . . . The Eunuch [Acts viii. 36] believed before he received Baptism therefore, before he received Baptism he was born of God, in whom he dwelled and God in him; he was just and acceptable in the sight of God; and, moreover, he had also life in himself; and therefore the Baptism which followed did not give that to the Eunuch which he had before, but it became unto him a testimony of the truth, and a seal of the righteousness which came by faith, and therewithal to assure unto him the continuance and increase of God's gifts." *Ibid.*

"Sacraments do neither confer, nor contain grace." *Ibid.*

"They [the Sacraments] be testimonies of God's truth, and of His goodwill towards us, and are seals of all the promises of the Gospel, sealing and assuring us that faith is righteousness, and that all the good gifts of Christ pertain to them that believe." *Ibid.*

"They which before by grace are invisibly received of God into the society of God, those selfsame are visibly now by Baptism admitted into the selfsame household of God." *Ibid.*

"We do say, that it [Baptism] is an holy action, instituted of God, and consisting of the word of God and the holy rite or ceremony, whereby the people of God are dipped in the water in the name of the Lord; to be short, whereby the Lord doth represent and seal unto us our purifying or cleansing." *Ibid*

"By Baptism we are gathered together into the fellowship of the people of God. Whereupon, of some it is called the first sign or entry into Christianity; by the which an entrance into the Church lieth open unto us. Not that before we did not belong to the Church for whosoever is of Christ, partaker of the promises of God and of His eternal covenant, belongeth unto the Church. Baptism, therefore, is a visible sign and testimony of our ingraffing into the body of Christ." *Ibid.*

Such are the doctrines which in 1552 obtained the sanction of Cranmer, and thirty-six years later the formal sanction of the Archbishop of Canterbury and the Upper House of Convocation, resulting in an order that Bullinger's Decades should be obtained and read weekly by all the inferior Clergy. It is very evident that they who did this could not have accepted the doctrine of Baptismal Regeneration as the doctrine of the Church of England. The statement of Peter Lombard "that Sacraments have received power to confer or give grace by the merit of the passion of Jesus Christ," is, says Bullinger, "OF HIS OWN FORGING." And again; "the holy and elect people of God are not "then first of all partakers of the grace of God and heavenly gifts, "when they receive the Sacraments . . . . The Eunuch (Acts viii. "36) believed before he received Baptism: therefore, before he re- "ceived Baptism, he was born of God in whom he dwelled, and God in "him; and moreover, he had also life in himself: and therefore, the

"Baptism that followed did not give to the Eunuch that which he "had before; but it became to him a testimony of the truth, and a "seal of the righteousness which came by faith, and therewithal to "assume unto him the continuance and increase of God's gifts." *Bullinger*.

It is very evident, therefore, that the Reformers must have regarded the words used in the Prayer Book and Catechism as "sacramental and figurative" language. They must have regarded Baptism as regeneration *in figure;* believing that the mercy which Baptism shadowed forth had been previously received.

It may be said that if this was the doctrine of the Reformers, common prudence would have dictated the rectification of the language of the Prayer Book and Catechism. Unambiguous words should have been used, and the plainest explanation given of the *figurative* sense in which they intended the expressions to be understood. The expressions as they now stand both in the Prayer Book and Catechism have, no doubt, blinded myriads unto eternal death. They have been and are being the inlet of incalculable evil. To have expected that such language as that contained in the Baptismal Service and in the Catechism would be understood as *figurative*, and that too without any appended comment or explanation, seems indeed most extraordinary: yet no one who candidly peruses the extracts from Bullinger can doubt, that such was the thought of the Reformers. The result has indeed been most fearful. Here again we learn a lesson which the history of Christianity has often taught, that in the Church of God ambiguities are to be avoided, and "great plainness of speech" used, especially on subjects on which it is known, that Satan has successfully blinded and beguiled. If the Catechism and Prayer Book had been made unmistakeably to declare the sentiments of Bullinger's Decades, what woes, what ruin might have been avoided! An attempt to bring the language of the Prayer Book into accordance with the Scripture on this subject, and with the Article on Justification would, if thoroughly persevered in, have shown, that although it is the privilege and duty of Christian parents to consign their children to the care and love of Jesus from the moment of their birth, yet that children are not to receive the sign and seal of baptism until they are of sufficient age to return personally, "the answer of a good conscience unto God." It would have been found that the promise "made unto our children" is not different from the promise made unto ourselves, viz., the promise of eternal life to all who turn in repentance and faith to the one salvation provided in the blood of the Lamb. It would have been found that no promise is made to Christian parents that all their offspring, simply because they are their offspring, should be regenerate; for in that case, no child of any real Christian could ever perish. It would have been acknowledged that even if, in the case of any given infant, a revelation from heaven were made that it was regenerate, yet that we should not on that account be justified in baptizing it, because one of the things appointed to be required in baptism is, "the answer of a good conscience unto God." Consequently, although infants may be, and often are regenerated whilst infants (else those who die in unconscious infancy could not be saved, as they surely are) yet personal confession being requisite for admission both to Baptism and to the Table of the Lord, they who are incapable of making such confession, are not in a condition to be admitted to either.

But it is not my present object to discuss this question.* I wish only to show that the doctrine of Baptismal Regeneration as now taught, was not held in the time of Cranmer and of Whitgift, when the foundations of the Church of England were being laid. Consequently, the Judgment pronounced in the case of Mr. Gorham, interpreted and applied the Formularies in the manner in which the Reformers intended that they should be interpreted and applied: whereas, the present Judgment not only alters the Formularies, but destroys the very key-stone on which the Reformers rest the whole of their structure—the authority of the Word of God. No parallelism, therefore, can be drawn between the Gorham Judgment and this.

---

* See it further discussed in "Doctrine of Scripture respecting Baptism" as advertised at end.

APPENDIX C.

Dr. Pusey and his "Eirenicon."

The hearts of all who reverence and love "the Word of God," will respond to the words of solemn protest just quoted from Dr. Pusey.* Although spoken, it is to be feared, to deaf ears, they are true words —words that will finally rise up in judgment against those who may now read and despise them.

But Dr. Pusey has done more than protest. His work on Daniel is a triumphant refutation of Neologian folly. His opponents ought to be shamed by it, not only into silence, but into confession. It would scarcely be too much to say, that with the failure of their attack on the Book of Daniel falls their whole system. Few will have the effrontery to affirm that there is no "secular prognostication" in Scripture if the Book of Daniel be proved to be genuine and true. And if such prognostication be admitted, what becomes of their doctrine about Scripture being the result of "devout reason" and the like?

Dr. Pusey's Preface, too, to his work on Daniel, contains remarks of exceeding value. Take for example, the following passage. "A writer, who seems to think exclusive adherence to definite truth the great antagonist to the mind of Christ, would have us agree to differ in every particle of faith, yet to hold ourselves to be in one 'common Christianity.' Like the Pantheon of Old Rome, everything is to be enshrined in one common Temple of Concord, not of faith or minds or wills, but of despair of truth. Nothing, in this new school, is to be exclusively true, nothing is to be false. No words are to have any

---

* See p. 114 preceding.

exclusive meaning. Every one is to decypher the old inscriptions as he likes, so that he do not obtrude that meaning upon others as the *sole* meaning. 'Everlasting' is to one to mean 'lasting for ever,' to another, for what seems to be 'an age,' as men say, 'atonement' is to one to mean only 'being at one' with God somehow, by imitation, or admiration of the 'greatest moral act ever done in this world;' to another, if he likes, it is to be that Act of God's awful Holiness, which human thought cannot reach; to one the Bible is to be, if he wills, 'the word of God,' so that he allow his neighbour to have an equal chance of being right, who holds that it 'contains' somewhere 'the word of God,' *i.e.*, a revelation, of no one knows what, made, no one knows how, (it may be through man's natural faculties, or his own thoughts or mind,) and lying no one knows where, except that it is to be somewhere between Genesis and Revelation, but probably, according to the neo-Christianity, to the exclusion of both. We are to recognise together, that God the Holy Ghost, 'spake by the prophets,' yet not so as to exclude their being fallible in matters of every-day morality. The authority of Jesus is to be respected; yet not so far but that modern critics may be held to know more than He, our God. These things (as far as they have been yet applied,) are, of course, the beginning, not the end. On the same ground that 'everlasting,' in the mouth of Jesus, is to be an ambiguous word, so, and much more may we be called upon to hold that 'grace,' 'faith,' nay 'God' are ambiguous words, and to harmonize with those who hold like the Pelagians of old, that 'grace' is God's gracious help through man's natural powers, and only so far the help of God, in that man received those powers from God; or that, 'faith' is faithfulness; or that 'god' may (as the Arians taught) designate a secondary god, and that the Mahommedans may perchance hold the right faith, since the Socinians declared themselves their nearest fellow champions for the faith of one supreme God without personalities or pluralities."*

What can be more true than this? Would that these words were engraven not only on the hearts of Neologians, but on the hearts of many true Christians also who seem to think that there can be right unity in the Spirit without unity in the Truth.

"Non-natural" interpretation also is thus denounced by Dr. Pusey. "Most of us remember the burst of indignation, the shock to the reli-

---

* Preface to Dr. Pusey's "Daniel the Prophet," p. xxvi.

gious mind of England, when the Rev. W. G. Ward avowed that he held the sense, in which he subscribed the Articles, to be 'non-natural.' It was not the claim to hold all Roman doctrine, which swelled or occasioned that decided majority in the Oxford Theatre. It was the implied want of honesty in the claim to hold an endowment by virtue of subscription, and yet to take the Articles subscribed in a non-natural sense. 'Non-natural' has, since that time, been a by-word for dishonest interpretation of words. Mr. Ward used no defence, except that, in his opinion, all parties in the Church of England were, of necessity, in one way or the other, equally dishonest. He left no plea to his defenders, except that one-sided justice was injustice. The Lord Chancellor has now reversed the decision in the Oxford Theatre, as well as that of the Court of Arches, and has established the principle (unless the influence of his decision is shaken, and this 'judge-made law' die with himself), that in English courts of law words may be taken in 'non-natural' senses. He has, as far as in him lies, poisoned the springs of English justice for ages in all matters of faith."

Not a few, when they first read these, and like words, were disposed to indulge the hope that Dr. Pusey after having in his more early days tasted of the waters of German Neology and found them bitter, had discovered that the waters of Ritualistic Sacerdotalism of which he next drank, are bitter too, and that now he was renouncing them and that he had begun to turn to Holy Scripture as the one well-spring of Truth. But there were others who had sadder thoughts. They remembered the course that Dr. Pusey has for the last thirty years persistently trodden. They called to mind how earnestly he has longed and laboured to unprotestantize Protestantism, or else to crush it by reproach. They remembered Tract XC. and his connexion therewith. It was observed too, that in the recent Oxford Protest (in determining which his influence was believed to be great) that it passed over that all-important point, so shamefully treated in the Judgment respecting the justification of believers by the transference to them of the merits of Christ. They remarked, too, with pain, though not with surprise, his acquiescence in the remarks of the Lord Chancellor respecting the continuousness of authoritative inspiration. These, and other like things, seemed to indicate that there was no disposition to confess the error of the past, or to acknowledge those two foundation truths (without the acknowledgment of which all other acknowledgments are vain) first, that we are reputed righteous before God only *on account of* the merits of our Lord Jesus Christ *through* faith; and secondly, that the written Word of God is *alone* authoritative, and that there is in no sense a continuation in the Church of such inspiration as would enable it to issue authoritative decrees, or to stamp Divine authority on Tradition.

Yet, however sorrowful were the thoughts of many respecting Dr. Pusey, few if any, I suppose, were prepared for the appearance of such a book as his "Eirenicon." How could it be supposed that one who had a few weeks ago denounced so earnestly and forcibly the sin of non-natural interpretation, should himself adopt a system of non-naturalism, or worse—which, if it were followed, would leave the world truthless, because we should be able neither to form conceptions, nor to use words in which the distinctness between any one truth and its opposite error could by any possibility be maintained.

Well was it said by one whose name was once well known in Oxford, and that as a preacher of the Gospel of the grace of God, which he preached to the salvation of many souls.

> "Hear this, deluded Newman,
> Hear this, ye priestly host,
> A Jesuit's acumen
> Is not the Holy Ghost."

For the Holy Ghost seeing that He is holy, hateth sophistry; He abhorreth all subtilty. It would scarcely perhaps be true to say that Dr. Newman and Dr. Pusey in their mode of explaining, or rather explaining away the Protestant and Popish Articles of faith, have shown any very especial "*acumen;*" but certainly as regards sophistical perversion of fact we must search the records of Jesuitism, as given in Pascal's Provincial Letters and elsewhere, if we would find anything like a parallel to their interpretations. Dr. Newman, whilst yet remaining in the Church of England, wished to show how Protestant Articles might be signed by persons who secretly held Catholic doctrine, as he was pleased to term it. The XXII. Article stood somewhat in his way. It is this: "The Romish Doctrine concerning "Purgatory, Pardons, Worshipping and Adoration, as well of Images "as of Reliques, and also invocation of Saints, is a fond thing vainly "invented, and grounded upon no warranty of Scripture, but rather "repugnant to the Word of God."

Dr. Newman admits that this Article condemns the Romish doctrine of Purgatory, but he asserts that it need not be understood as condemning *every* doctrine of Purgatory. We may maintain the doctrine of Purgatory if we do not maintain it precisely in the *Romish* way. Thus if a man were to hold the doctrine of Purgatory in a form more horrible (were it possible) than that in which Rome holds it, he might yet, according to Dr. Newman sign the Protestant Article above cited, because his doctrine being in excess of that of Rome could not be said to be absolutely identical with it.

So as regards Pardons or Indulgences: Dr. Newman admits that the Article condemns the *Romish* doctrine of Indulgences. But if any one hold the doctrine of Indulgences ever so strongly, he may still swear to the truth of this Protestant Article, provided his doctrine do not in every jot and tittle accord with that of Rome.

Respecting the adoration of Images and Relics he argues in the same way. He may adore and invoke them *ad libitum*, if it be not in the identical manner in which Rome adores and invokes them.

Such are Dr. Newman's principles. And what are Dr. Pusey's?

"The pathway of Dr. Pusey," says a recent writer,* "is widely different. He has, indeed, re-published Tract XC. with approval, and adopted its principles, but his own independent line of argument is different. It all tends in the same direction,—Romewards. If Mr. Newman explained away the Articles so as to enable men to evade them, Dr. Pusey explains away the Decrees and Canons of the Church of Rome so as to enable men to accept them."

"The key-note is one of the strangest passages that ever fell from a member of a Reformed Church. It refers to Art. XIX., which says, 'As the Church of Jerusalem, Alexandria, and Antioch have erred, so also the Church of Rome hath erred, not only in their living and manner of ceremonies, but also in matters of faith.' This Article simply states that all these four Churches have erred, implying that there is no infallibility in any of them Dr. Pusey seems to feel this was a lion in his path, and deals with it in these strange words:—'The Article says nothing about formal errors or decrees. This Article was a puzzle to me when young . . . . . I found there were no canons of Jerusalem, Alexandria, and Antioch, which were intended; then it followed, on the same principle of the correspondence of the two clauses, that neither were canons of the Church of Rome spoken of. The Article, moreover, does not say that *the Church of Rome is in error at present*, but ' hath erred,' *in time past*, just

---

* Rev. Hobart Seymour

"as it says of the other Patriarchates, that they 'have erred, i.e., in
"time past.' This passage is without parallel. It certainly has never
"been surpassed in the way of evasiveness. It distorts the Article so
"as to put on it a meaning the very reverse or opposite of what was
"designed, for while the Convocation plainly designed it as a reason
"for the Church of England withdrawing from the Church of Rome,
"on the very account of her then present errors, this evasion is de-
"signed to show they had at that very present time no reason to
"separate from her, as all her errors were in the past and none in
"the present."

This example may for the present suffice. *Ex uno disce omnia.* Dr. Pusey has discovered a way in which we may openly declare our adhesion to the Articles of our Protestant Confession, and to the Decrees of the Council of Trent *also;* although those decrees have in numberless instances pronounced the doctrines of our Articles "*accursed.*" That however matters little, for non-natural interpretation can effect any thing in the way of transubstantiating doctrines or statements of doctrine. It is a power before which any mountain may be made a plain. Truth and falsehood can be so melted in its crucible and fused, or metamorphosed, that no *fixed* form either of falsehood or truth can be affirmed to exist. The negations of Neology do not leave the earth more Truth-less than does this system of Dr. Pusey. If there be no opposedness in contraries, how can we form a distinct notion about any thing? We should find ourselves in a moral and intellectual vacuum, in a world of nonentities with nothing on which to base a settled judgment, or else (seeing that "non-natural" interpretation is as arbitrary, and as little really subject to an external rule as the supposed "verifying faculty") I must become a rule to myself by interpreting words and facts in whatsoever "non-natural" manner it may best suit me to interpret them. Thus non-naturalism opens as wide a door as Neology to the licentiousness of human thought. If, for example, in reading the Tridentine Decrees in which Purgatory is expressly defined to be a "locality," we are at liberty (as Dr. Pusey contends) to understand "locality" as if it meant "a state of mind:" if Indulgences (than which there is nothing of which Rome has more distinctly defined the character) are to be understood as merely a very solemn kind of prayer: if the due honour and veneration which Rome requires to be given to Images may be regarded as having no "religious" character in it—if, I say, in expounding Romish doctrine such license be allowed in dealing with facts and words, how can we

R

refuse the same license to those who wish to subject Scripture to the same process? If the Church of Rome in defining Purgatory to be "a locality" is to be understood as meaning thereby "a state of mind," how can I find fault with those who affirm that "hell fire" is a "state of mind?"

Dr. Pusey inveighs bitterly against the Judgment pronounced by the Lord Chancellor. "The Lord Chancellor . . . . . . has established the principle (unless the influence of his decision is shaken, and this 'judge-made law' die with himself) that in English Courts of Law, words may be taken in non-natural senses. He has as far as in him lies, poisoned the springs of English justice for ages in all matters of faith. . . . . . It is an avowed plan 'to win' (as it is said) 'new senses for received Theological terms,' i.e. to take them in 'non-natural' meanings; so that, in this new Babel-din of Theology, every one is to be able to veil his meaning at least from the understanding of human justice."

Such is the protest of Dr. Pusey against the Judgment of the Chancellor. But if the Chancellor has done all this (and I do not deny it) I ask who have been his instructors? In what school has he learned this lesson? Who are the grand masters in the school of non-natural interpretation? I reply, Dr. Newman and Dr. Pusey. It is they who have poisoned, and are poisoning, the springs of truthful thought in this country. The Lord Chancellor has but imitated *them*, and that, but feebly. That dread outbreak of atheistic phrenzy which was seen in France in 1792 was but the consequence of the public mind having been demoralized and debased, years previously, by the Jesuitry and Priestcraft whose workings Pascal describes. Nor has the effect even now worn off. It exists still, and has prepared France for Antichrist. An analogous result by analogous means is taking place in this country. Non-natural interpretation is demoralizing minds, and causing them to lose themselves in that "Babel-din" of sophisms in which "every one is able to veil his meaning at least from the understanding of human justice;" and it may be added, from the judgment of his own conscience. What can be expected of such, but that they should go from misbelief to unbelief, and so be prepared for the atheism of Antichrist The "Eirenicon" will work no less potently than Neology towards this end, though by a different path.

After being made aware of Dr. Pusey's principle of interpretation we are in some degree prepared to expect extraordinary results.

Nevertheless, it is difficult to read without amazement such a passage as the following: "I believe that we the Churches of England and "Rome have the same doctrine of grace and of justification. There "is not one statement in the elaborate chapters on Justification in "the Council of Trent which any of us could fail of receiving; "nor is there one of their anathemas on the subject, which in the "least rejects any statement of the Church of England." *Eirenicon*, p. 19.

One can scarcely read these words without feeling some degree of astonishment; for we naturally ask, How has it come to pass that the whole Protestant world and the whole Romanist world have always imagined that there was a difference, and a vital difference too? How strange that they should have been for so many centuries mistaken? Well: they were not exactly mistaken, only they were not acquainted with Dr. Pusey's new transubstantiative process. They did not know his system of verbal alchymy. If we will only enter his school he will soon show us how to change contraries into identities. But no. Through God's grace we will never enter that school, for it leads to eternal death. It teaches "another Gospel, which is not another." We call to remembrance the words of the Apostle; "though we, or an angel from heaven, preach any other gospel unto you than that which we have preached unto you, let him be accursed" Gal. i. 8.

The doctrine of the Church of England is sufficiently, though briefly expressed in the eleventh Article. "We are accounted righteous before God ONLY for the merit of our Lord and Saviour Jesus Christ by Faith, and not for our own works or deservings. Tantum propter meritum Domini et Servatoris nostri Jesu Christi, per fidem, non propter opera et merita nostra, justi coram Deo reputamur." Clear, simple and blessed words! But in Homily iii. ratified by the xxxv. Article, we find the following more amplified statement. "In "these foresaid places, the Apostle toucheth specially three things, "which must go together in our justification. Upon God's part, his "great mercy and grace; upon Christ's part, righteousness,[*] that "is, the satisfaction of God's righteousness, or the price of our re- "demption, by the offering of his body, and shedding of his blood, "with fulfilling of the law perfectly and throughly; and upon our "part, true and lively faith in the merits of Jesus Christ, which yet

---

[*] I have, throughout this quotation, substituted the word "*righteousness*" for the more antique word "*justice*," which the Homily uses.

"is not ours, but by God's working in us: so that in our justification,
"is not only God's mercy and grace, but also his righteousness, which
"the Apostle calleth the righteousness of God, and it consisteth in
"paying our ransom, and fulfilling of the law: and so the grace of
"God doth not shut out the righteousness of God in our justification,
"but only shutteth out the righteousness of man, that is to say, the
"righteousness of our works, as to be merits of deserving our justifica-
"tion. And therefore St. Paul declareth here nothing upon the
"behalf of man concerning his justification, but only a true and
"lively faith, which nevertheless is the gift of God, and not man's
"only work, without God. And yet that faith doth not shut out re-
"pentance, hope, love, dread, and the fear of God, to be joined with
"faith in every man that is justified; but it shutteth them out from
"the office of justifying. So that, although they be all present together
"in him that is justified, yet they justify not altogether. Nor the
"faith also doth not shut out the righteousness of our good works,
"necessarily to be done afterwards of duty towards God; (for we are
"most bounden to serve God, in doing good deeds, commanded by
"him in his holy Scripture, all the days of our life;) but it excludeth
"them, so that we may not do them to this intent, to be made good
"by doing of them. For all the good works that we can do be im-
"perfect, and therefore not able to deserve our justification: but our
"justification doth come freely by the mere mercy of God, and of so
"great and free mercy, that, whereas all the world was not able of
"theirselves to pay any part towards their ransom, it pleased our
"heavenly Father of his infinite mercy, without any our desert or
"deserving, to prepare for us most precious jewels of Christ's body
"and blood, whereby our ransom might be fully paid, the law fulfilled,
"and his righteousness fully satisfied. So that Christ is now the
"righteousness of all them that truly do believe in him. He for them
"paid their ransom by his death. He for them fulfilled the law in
"his life. So that now in him, and by him, every true Christian
"man may be called a fulfiller of the law; forasmuch as that which
"their infirmity lacked, Christ's righteousness hath supplied."

No statements can be more plain than these. Will any one say that they do not teach that we are justified *only* by the ascription to us of the righteousness of Another? Will any one say that they do not altogether exclude every thing, that grace may work in us "*from the office of justifying*"? But does the Council of Trent teach this doctrine, or anathematize it? Their words are: "If any one shall say "that men are justified, either by the imputation of the righteousness of Christ alone, or by the remission of sins only, to the exclusion of grace and charity, to be shed abroad in their hearts by the Holy Ghost and to inhere in them; or moreover, that the grace whereby we are justified is merely the favour of God, *let him be accursed.*"

These words are certainly not deficient in plainness. But they are extraordinary words; for they assume that it is possible for a man to have the merits of Immanuel, God manifest in the flesh, imputed to him, and yet that he would not stand in a perfectly justified condition before God. If the Council had said, that the doctrine of the imputed righteousness of Christ was altogether a fiction, *that* we could have understood, but for any to affirm that the meritorious righteousness of our God and Saviour can be imputed to us, and yet that we are not thereby brought into a state of justification before God, seems like blasphemy—for is the righteousness of our God and Saviour imperfect? Is it needful that any thing else should be added thereunto? Can that which *is* perfect be made more perfect? And what could be added? God will not accept for justification any thing that is not absolutely perfect. However, I pursue not this subject now. My present object is merely to show that Rome *anathematizes* the statements of the Homilies and Articles above quoted. Yet Dr. Pusey asserts that there is no difference on this point between the two Churches.

He would have been far nearer the truth if he had said that there was no point of agreement. The Church of Rome dares to assert that concupiscence (evil desire) is not sin,* even though God has said, "Thou shalt not be concupiscent." The Articles of the Church of England, following the Scripture, maintain that concupiscence, even though restrained, is sin; though to believers it is not imputed for Christ's sake. Here then there is a vital difference respecting the nature of sin. Furthermore, the Church of Rome asserts that the human will since the fall, is not so in bondage to sin but that it can "co-operate" with the grace of God, (See Council of Trent, Sess. vi. Canons iv. and v) whereas the Articles of the Church of England say, that "man is gone *as far as possible* (quam longissime) from original righteousness"—which would not be true if he had naturally

---

* "That concupiscence, however, or the fuel of sin, still remains, as the Council declares in the same place, must be acknowledged *but concupiscence does not constitute sin.*" *Catechism of Council of Trent, p.* 178. Donovan's Translation.

a will able to co-operate with God. See Art. ix. And again, in Art. x. "We have no power to do good works pleasant and accept-"able to God, without the grace of God by Christ preventing us, *that* "*we may have* a good will," &c.—words which distinctly teach, not merely that the results of having a good will are assignable to grace, but that *the will itself* is the gift of grace.

Furthermore, the Church of England says: "Works done before "the grace of Christ, and the Inspiration of His Spirit, are not "pleasant to God, forasmuch as they spring not of faith in Jesus "Christ, neither do they make men meet to receive grace, or (as the "School-authors say) deserve grace of congruity: yea rather, for that "they are not done as God hath willed and commanded them to be "done, we doubt not but they have the nature of sin." Art. xiii. In direct contradiction to this the Church of Rome says, "If any "one shall affirm that all works which are done before justification, "on whatsoever principle done, are truly sins, or that they deserve "the hatred of God . . . . . *let him be accursed.*" (Council of Trent. Canon vii.) Wide differences these as concerns the state of man *by nature*

Then as to the meaning of the word "justify," as used in Rom. v. and viii. The Romanists assert that it means "*to make righteous:*" whereas the Church of England maintains "*to repute righteous*" because of the merits of Another. "We are reputed righteous before God only on account of the merits of our Lord Jesus Christ, through faith." (Art. x. Latin.) "Yea, 'there is none other thing that can "be named under heaven to save our souls, but this only work of "Christ's precious offering of his body upon the altar of the cross.' "(Acts iv. 12.) Certainly there can be no work of any mortal man, "be he never so holy, that shall be coupled in merits with Christ's "most holy act. *Hom*. xxv. 1.

"Q. Dost not thou then say, that faith is the principle cause of "this justification, so as by the merit of faith we are counted righte-"ous before God? A. No: for that were to set faith in the place of "Christ. But the spring-head of this justification is the mercy of God, "which is conveyed to us by Christ, and is offered to us by the Gospel, "and received of us by faith as with a hand." *Nowell's Catechism*, p 73

Such is Protestant doctrine. Mercy from God, operating through Christ, proposed to us in the Gospel, received by faith as by a hand; such, according to Nowell, is the method of a sinner's justification. According to this, justifying faith is simply *reliance*—fiducia—"reliance on the Divine mercy remitting sin for Christ's sake: and such was the definition the Reformers gave. But what does Rome say to this definition? Does she accept it? No: she rejects and anathematizes it. "If any one shall affirm that Justifying Faith is nothing "else than reliance on the Divine mercy remitting sin for Christ's "sake . . . . . . *let him be accursed.*"

Yet the Council of Trent, whilst pronouncing thus their curse on the true definition of Justifying Faith, have nowhere condescended to give us a definition of their own. Bellarmine, however, (whose authority no Romanist will question) says that the Romish divines teach that "Justifying Faith" is nothing more or less than historic faith—"fidem historicam et miraculorum et promissionum unam et eandem esse docent . . . . . et hanc unam esse fidem justificantem." *Bellarmine de Justif. lib. I. cap.* 4. They who define faith thus do thereby sufficiently show that they are utter strangers to the Gospel of God: for one of the earliest distinctions apprehended by a truly converted heart is that which distinguishes reliance of soul on God through the blood of the Lamb, from that historic faith wherewith devils believe and tremble.

Again, as to the completeness of justification when received, the Church of England teaches that it is a *fixed* condition, because resting on the finished meritorious righteousness of Another already presented and accepted on behalf of all believers—a righteousness which, seeing that it is perfect, admits of no augmentation. After He (Christ) had constituted us righteous by means of His sacrificial work on earth, "He rose from death (I quote from Dean Nowell), and we also are "risen again with Him, being so made partakers of His resurrection "and life, that from henceforth death hath no more dominion over "us. For in us is the same Spirit which raised Jesus Christ from the "dead. Beside that, since the ascension, we have most abundantly "received the gifts of the Holy Ghost. He hath also lifted and carried "us up into heaven with Him, that we might, as it were with our "head, take possession thereof. These things indeed are not yet seen; "but then shall they be brought abroad into light, when Christ which "is the light of the world, in whom all our hope and wealth is set "and settled, shining with immortal glory, shall shew Himself openly "to all men." *Nowell,* p. 58. See also Art. xvii.

The fixedness of the condition of the justified and their sure preservation unto eternal life is distinctly taught in these passages. Rome, on the contrary, says, "If any one shall affirm that righteousness re-

"ceived [in justification] is not *preserved*, nay more, *increased* before "God by good works, but shall say that good works are merely the "fruits and signs of justification that has been acquired, but not the "cause of augmenting it, let him be accursed." *Canon xxiv.* False and heretical doctrine this: strange to the Articles of the Church of England—subversive of all that Christ and His Apostles ever taught.

Again, after asserting that the grace of justification is received by baptism (Catech. Coun: Trid. p 181; Donavan); and that by the sacrament of baptism sin is utterly "*eradicated*" (ibid, p. 179), and that the grace of which the baptized are the subjects, "not only remits "sin, but is also a divine quality inherent in the soul, and, as it were "a brilliant light that effaces all those stains which obscure the lustre "of the soul, and invests it with increased brightness and beauty," (ibid, p. 183); they go on to say that "for those who fall into sin "after baptism, the sacrament of penance is as necessary to salvation, "as is baptism for those who have not been already baptized. On this "subject the words of St. Jerome, which say, that penance is 'a second "plank,' are universally known, and highly commended by all who "have written on this Sacrament. As he who suffers shipwreck has "no hope of safety, unless, perchance, he seize on some plank from "the wreck; so he that suffers the shipwreck of baptismal innocence, "unless he cling to the saving plank of penance, may abandon all "hope of salvation." (Ibid, p. 251.) Thus, the so-called justified, by the first sin committed after baptism, lose all their blessings and need to be re-justified. Hence the need for penance and the pretended sacrifice of the mass, and purgatory, and all that other machinery of falsehood whereby souls are deceived into perdition, and Christ's work made of no effect. Accordingly, Bellarmine affirms that Christ's work on the Cross was impetratory merely of grace, and that it did not by itself secure salvation to any. Salvability, according to him, not salvation, was its result. The doctrine of a finished salvation accomplished for all believers by the one offering on Calvary, is the key-stone of Christianity. But it is utterly denied by Rome. It is a truth they abhor; for before it, as they well know, their whole system falls—vanishes, leaving not a wreck behind.

Dr. Pusey's assertion, therefore, about the agreement of the Churches of Rome and England on the doctrine of justification is utterly untrue. There is not a point in the whole question on which they are agreed. Where the one says *yea*, the other says *nay*. When affirmation on one side is met by negation on the other, it used to be thought that difference, not agreement, was implied: and I believe it is still thought so except in Dr. Pusey's transubstantiative school.

The real truth is that it would be difficult to find one single point on which the doctrines of the Church of England, as expressed in her Articles, agrees with those of Rome. Even as regards the Divine Persons in the Godhead, difference is beginning to appear. The Church of England holds that there is one God who is from everlasting, and that in the unity of the Godhead there are three Persons, co-equal and co-eternal, and that those three Divine Persons are alone God, and alone to be worshipped. A little while ago it might have been truly said that Rome accepted this truth. But recently, teachers have appeared within her borders who say that in the sacramental bread, which they affirm to be God and which they worship as God, there is not only Christ, "the divinity and humanity entire, the soul, the body and blood of Christ with all their component parts, such as bones and nerves, (see Cat. Con. Trent, p. 226) but that there is also a co-presence of Mary. In this case either a creature is worshipped as God, or Mary is God—and the doctrine of the Trinity ceases to be true; for there must be a fourth Person. Dr. Pusey at present declines to believe all this about Mary. And it is not to be supposed that any reflective mind does believe it: but the effect of promulgating these blasphemies is clearly this, that less advanced statements of falsehood become, in contrast with these outrageous forms of error, looked upon as comparatively harmless. Dr. Pusey gains a certain credit for candour and discernment in not going all the lengths of all the Roman teachers: and his partizans are able to lull the suspicions of his victims, and to say, "Surely you need not fear that he will lead you to Rome, for, see, he disagrees with Rome! He is fair, candid, reflective. He does not accept every dogma. He makes distinctions."

As respects the doctrine of the Trinity, and the true humanity and Deity of Christ, Dr. Pusey, no doubt, accepts at present the statements of the English Articles. But on what other point does he agree with them? Does he hold the doctrine of the Church of England as to the *sole* authority of Scripture? Does he reject Tradition and every form of doctrine that teaches the continuance in the Church of infallible authority either to decree or to interpret? Does he hold the sinfulness of concupiscence,—the bondage of the human will, the doctrine of the Articles and Homilies respecting Justification and its results? Does he not utterly repudiate the 17th Article, and does he not equally reject the doctrines of the Church of England respecting Baptism and the Supper of the Lord?

Dr. Pusey, no doubt, abhors the name of *Bullinger*: yet that very fact proves that he abhors the doctrines of the English Reformers; for they sanctioned and adopted Bullinger's doctrines both as regards Baptism and the Eucharist. His doctrine respecting Baptism may be seen on a previous page.* Of the Lord's Supper *Bullinger* writes as follows: "Wherefore those solemn words, 'This is my body which "is broken for you;' and likewise, 'This is my blood which is shed "for you,' can have none other sense than this,—This is a commemora-"tive, memorial, or remembrance, sign or sacrament of my body "which is given for you. This cup, or rather the wine in the cup, "signifieth or representeth unto you my blood, which was once shed "for you . . . . . But let us leave off to cite men's testimonies con-"cerning the proper and most ancient exposition of Christ's words, "'This is my body.' Let us rather proceed to allege sound argu-"ments out of the Scriptures, as we promised to do, thereby to prove "that we must sometime of necessity depart from the letter, *and that* "*Christ's words are accordingly, as I have said, to be expounded by a* "*figure.*" Bullinger as quoted by Goode on the Eucharist, vol. ii. p. 736.

That the English Reformers utterly rejected the doctrine of Transubstantiation; that they maintained that the Table in the Lord's Supper was a Table merely, and not an altar; that they rejected the offering of the Mass and denounced as blasphemous the doctrine, that therein was "offered a propitiatory sacrifice for the living and the dead;" that they regarded the worship of the consecrated elements as Idolatry, are facts which will be controverted by few. And can any read the extracts from Bullinger which I have just given and also those in page 119 without being convinced that the Reformers *wished* the language of Scripture in Acts xxii. 16 to be regarded as figurative, and also the words which they adopted in the formularies by them sanctioned?

No one can regret more unfeignedly than myself the language retained in the Catechism and in the Prayer Book respecting Baptism and the Lord's Supper. To expect that such language would either by Sacerdotalists, or by the unthinking multitude be received as figu-

---

* See page 119, as also "Gorham's Gleanings," published by Bell & Daldy.

rative, is to expect an impossibility. Yet there can be little doubt that if the Reformation had not been hindered in its progress, and the Reformers had been allowed to perfect their work, we should have found all Lutheran as well as Romanistic mystifications removed. How can we think otherwise when we read the words of Bullinger, and find the Regius Professor of Divinity at Oxford writing thus: "Atque etiam loquutionem illam, quâ isti (the Schoolmen) frequenter utuntur, Sacramenta remittere peccata, aut conferre gratiam, non facilè admittimus: nisi fortè in eam sententiam, quâ Paulus prædicat, Evangelium esse vim Dei ad salutem: utque lectio sacrarum literarum ad Timotheum dicitur, servare. Quod sanè nihil aliud est, quàm vim, et potentiam Dei, (quâ peccata remittit, gratiam largitur, et denique servat) his instrumentis et mediis uti ad salutem nostram. Ad quod efficiendum, quemadmodum utitur verbo Evangelii, et prædicatione sacrarum literarum, ita etiam adhibet sacramenta. Per utraque enim prædicatur nobis liberalis Dei promissio. Quam si fide complectimur, et salutem, et remissionem peccatorum obtinemus. . . . . . . Tunc aiunt, (the Schoolmen) sacramenta Evangelica conferre gratiam. Atqui hoc nihil aliud est, quàm creaturis tribuere causam nostræ salutis nosque nimium obligare symbolis, et elementis hujus mundi." *Peter Martyr in Epist. ad Romanos, cap. IV.*

Would to God that every expression and every practice that was not in harmony with these and like statements had been extirpated from the services and formularies of the Church of England. The language that was retained in the Catechism and Prayer Book has been, no doubt, the means of deceiving multitudes unto eternal death. They have deemed themselves regenerate and made partakers of Christ, whilst utter strangers to His true salvation. For my own part (God giving me grace) I would rather be burned at the stake, than consent to the use of words that have worked so destructively, and are still made the great fulcrum of the attack that Sacerdotalism is making against Scripture Truth.

If Dr. Pusey had truly prized the principles of the Reformation; if he had discerned in it the grace and mercy of God in restoring the light that ecclesiastical apostasy had quenched, he would have spent his days in freeing that light from obstructions, and in giving it its full, proper development. But he has not done this. Whilst professing Protestantism, he has done every thing in his power to destroy it. He has sought to discover every point in which its foundations may be weak, not in order that he might remedy the weakness, but that he might assail and destroy strength. As regards the destruction of our national Protestantism, no doubt he will succeed. He will have the pleasure of seeing Protestantism in England deprived of its dominancy. But what will finally be reared upon its ruins? Idolatrous Ecclesiasticism? No. *Infidel Antichristianism.* Dr. Pusey is in truth labouring for Antichrist. That great impulse to Infidelity given by the late Judgment about the Essays and Reviews would probably not have been given, if it had not been discerned that Puseyite Romanism required for its shelter the shield of non-natural interpretation, and that therefore consistency demanded that Neology should not be deprived of a like protection. Moreover, where Protestantism lingers, the ground is not well prepared for the fulness of Antichristianism. It is in hearts well debased by priestcraft, idolatry and superstition, that Antichristianism finds the sphere suited to its matured developments. France has supplied fearful examples of this. There can be little doubt that a large and influential section of society in England, before the fulness of Antichristianism sets in, will pass through the school of Sacerdotalism, become thereby thoroughly alienated from the Scripture, be delivered over to priestly traditions, become debased by superstition, and so prepared to be the victims of the last great lie of Satan. Thus Apostasy from the Truth under the profession of the name of Christ, will culminate in a naked, undisguised Apostasy in which the name of Christ and the name of God and all revealed Truth will be renounced and blasphemed.

What then does it profit, that Dr. Pusey has girded on his armour against Neology? We have to enquire not only what he assails, but what he defends. Sadducceanism of old found a potent enemy in the Pharisee. The Pharisees could argue, and did argue well in defence of the resurrection and many like truths; but what was *their* relation to Truth? Did not Pharisee and Sadducee alike band together against Christ? Did they not both say, "Crucify Him, crucify Him"? Men's relation to Truth, not their relation to any one special form of falsehood, is the true measure of their relation to God.

"The Eirenicon" has been applauded not merely by the organs of Dr. Pusey's own party: it has been equally greeted by his Neologian opponents, who welcome its aid in the war they are waging against the definiteness and certainty of Truth. Dr. Stanley, for example, writes as follows:

"The most striking result of the 'Eirenicon' and its acceptance is
" the effect on the future position of the Thirty-nine Articles, and with

"them, of ecclesiastical Confessions generally. It is not necessary to
"go through in detail the explanations by which at least twelve of
"the thirty-nine are reduced in this learned work to mere truisms,
"which, under such explanations, certainly no one would think it
"worth while to retain, as no one would originally have thought it
"worth while to issue them. It is enough to say that Tract XC. has
"been re-affirmed, and the general result is that stated by a well-
"known quarterly journal,* the recognised exponent of the views ex-
"pressed by the 'Eirenicon,' in an article which is one sustained
"eulogy upon it, and which I believe has never been disavowed by
"any of the school which it represents." The reviewer says:—

"' One is tempted to ask with wonder, How is it that men ever have
"placed such implicit belief in the Articles? . . . . . No other answer
"can be given than that they have been neglected and ignored. . . . .
"It is impossible to deny that they contain statements or assertions
"that are verbally false, and others that are very difficult to reconcile
"with truth. . . . . . What service have they ever done, and of what
"use are they at the present time? . . . . . Their condemnation has
"been virtually pronounced by the 'Eirenicon.' Virtually, for it is
"after all only an implicit, not an explicit condemnation of them that
"the volume contains. . . . . . We venture to go a step further, and
"boldly proclaim our own opinion, that before union with Rome can be
"effected [that is, before that can be effected which the reviewer thinks
"most desirable], the Thirty-nine Articles must be wholly withdrawn.
"They are virtually withdrawn at the present moment, for the en-
"dorsement of the view of the 'Eirenicon' by the writer in the *Times*
"proves that, as far as the most important of the Articles are con-
"cerned, there are persons who sign them in senses absolutely con-
"tradictory.'—*Christian Remembrancer, as quoted below.*

"The peculiar position thus assigned to the Articles," continues
Dr. Stanley, "is rendered doubly important by the contrast between
"the furious outcry with which this dissolving and disparaging pro-
"cess was received twenty years ago, and the almost complete acqui-
"escence with which it has been received now. There are many of
"us old enough to remember the agitation in 1841, and still more in
"1845, when the matter was brought to its final issue in the famous
"Oxford Convocation of the 13th of February. We have seen many

---

* *Christian Remembrancer*, January, 1866, p. 188.

"theological disturbances in our time, but nothing equal to that.
"The religious and secular press were up in arms. The Bishops in
"their charges charged long and loud. I do not mean with ab-
"solute unanimity; there was at least one Bishop who abstained
"then, as he would have abstained now, had he still lived, from join-
"ing in any of the indiscriminating Episcopal denunciations which
"have been so common in the last few years. If ever there was a
"theological treatise under a ban it was Tract XC. And now it is re-
"published, virtually, in the 'Eirenicon,'—actually, in the pamphlet*
"which may be called a postscript to the 'Eirenicon.' Not a word
"of remonstrance. The Heads of Houses are silent. The Bishops are
"silent. The leading journals even approve it, and consider the
"former outcry 'as ludicrously exaggerated and onesided.' The
"learned author of the 'Eirenicon' has, I believe, received no serious
"annoyance from this bold step. 'The explanations' (I quote again
"from the same journal) 'which in Tract XC. were regarded as
"pieces of the most subtle sophistry, are repeated in the 'Eirenicon'
"not only without rebuke from anybody, but with the approving
"sympathy of thousands† . . . . . What the Bishops and others in
"a panic of ignorance condemned in 1841 is accepted and allowed
"to be entirely tenable in 1865.'

"Such a phenomenon in itself, irrespectively of the subject, is of a
"most reassuring and pacificatory kind. It is interesting and con-
"soling to trace such a palpable instance of the total collapse of a
"great theological bugbear, such a proof of the ephemeral character
"of protests and denunciations and panics, such an example of the
"return of public and ecclesiastical feeling to the calm consideration
"of a topic which once seemed so hopelessly inflammable. The Hamp-
"den controversy, the Gorham controversy, the 'Essays and Reviews'
"controversy, the Colenso controversy—all have had their turn; but
"none excited such violent passions, and of none would the ultimate
"extinction have appeared so strange whilst the storm was raging, as
"the extinction of the controversy of Tract XC.

"But still more interesting in the cause of peace is it when we
"regard the subject-matter. It was the question of the binding,
"stringent force of our chief historical Confession of Faith. It had

---

* Tract XC. Republished, with a Preface by the Rev. E. B. Pusey, D.D. 1866.
† *Christian Remembrancer*, January, 1866.

"appeared in 1841, that this Confession had suddenly given way on
"the points on which it was thought the strongest; that eminent
"divines had burst through the bonds with which the old Philistines—
"the Earl of Leicester and King James I.—had bound them, 'as a
"thread of tow is broken when it toucheth the fire.' On no theological
"question was it believed that the Articles had spoken more certainly,
"and with a more deliberate intention, than against the doctrines of
"the Church of Rome; and Tract XC. announced that they had been
"so carelessly or so ambiguously framed as to admit those who held
"these very doctrines. This it was which produced the alarm. What
"has produced the calm? Many causes have contributed;—the re-
"crudescence of the High Church party; the charm thrown over the
"history of that time by the 'Apologia;' the exhaustion of the odium
"theologicum in another direction. But mainly, and beyond all ques-
"tion, and long before these events, it was the growth of the convic-
"tion, that such formularies must not be overstrained; that their
"chief use is that of historical landmarks of the faith of the Church
"at a given time, but that they cannot, by the very nature of the
"case, bind the thoughts and consciences of future times. This con-
"viction had already begun to prevail even when Tract XC. appeared.
"By the time of the fierce and final attack in 1845, what has since
"been called the Liberal party in the Church was sufficiently power-
"ful to make a strong rally in favour of toleration. The first force
"of the intended blow against Tract XC. was broken by two vigorous
"pamphlets from this quarter—one by the present Bishop of London,
"the other by Mr. Maurice. It was resisted in the Oxford Convoca-
"tion by almost all those who have since been most vehemently as-
"sailed by those whom they then defended—by four out of the five
"Oxford Essayists, and by others of like tendencies, but who have
"been fortunately less conspicuous. The good cause has triumphed
"at last. It is true that the particular form which Tract XC. and the
"'Eirenicon' take of dissolving the Articles may not be—I think it
"is not—historically tenable. It is true that the vehement attack
"upon them in the *Christian Remembrancer* is exaggerated in tone and
"substance. But the general principle of the inefficacy and inade-
"quacy of such Confessions is the same as that which has been stated
"in the most lucid and energetic language by the Dean of St. Paul's,
"in his speech on the Thirty-nine Articles in the Royal Commission,
"and by Principal Tulloch in his Address on the Westminster Con-
"fession to the students of Divinity in the University of St. Andrews;

"and this change of feeling has coincided with, and resulted in, the
"fundamental change in the terms of subscription effected by the
"Legislature last year."

Such are Dr. Stanley's notes of triumph over the rejection of God and of His Truth.

Few will imagine that Dr. Pusey was not aware of the effects that would follow on the establishment of his "non-natural" principle. He could not but forsee that a system of interpretation such as the "Eirenicon" advocates, is, and must be, destructive of all dogmatic statements of Truth, whether primitive, mediæval, or modern. The definiteness of Scripture, and the definiteness of Creeds must alike fall before it. What then could have tempted him to employ an instrument so formidable, even to his own position; for is not fixed dogmatic Truth the very thing that he is so anxious to uphold? Is there any thing that causes him to expect that a weapon mighty and irresistible against the Creeds of Protestantism should be found useless and impotent when directed against formularies which, in his judgment, embody Catholic Truth?

We shall be assisted in answering this question if we remember that there is, by and by, to be established in the earth, a body of which the Scripture uses such words as these. "No weapon that is formed against thee shall prosper; and every tongue that shall rise against thee in judgment thou shalt condemn." Dr. Pusey refuses to apply these words to those to whom they alone belong; that is, to God's ancient people Israel in the yet future day of their forgiveness and restoration. The prospects of Israel Dr. Pusey persistently ignores. He believes that Israel have forfeited those blessings which the faithfulness of God has pledged to them for ever; and thinks that they have been transferred to that body called out from among the Gentiles which he denominates Catholic, and imagines to be the indefectible witness of Divine Truth in the earth. We cannot wonder that with this conviction in his heart, he should be impatient of all arrangements, whether secular or religious, that interfere with the recognition of such a body, and the acknowledgment of its rightful supremacy. We cannot wonder that he and all who sympathize with him should welcome rather than dread the approach of revolutionary storms and convulsions, because they believe that however society may be deranged, however its order may be overthrown, they have in their hands the sure power of rectification. They, and they alone, are able to point out the body which shall withstand, rock-like, every storm—shall preserve through every trial its consistency and strength, and become at last, the point around which the chaotic elements of human society shall be gathered—there to find a stable and everlasting centre.

But notions such as these are not the fruits of wisdom, but of fanaticism: for when persons or systems are by our imaginations, invested with attributes that fact, reason, and Scripture prove not to pertain to them, we are justly chargeable with fanaticism. And what more dangerous than a fanatic? He may destroy, but he cannot restore. He may kill, but he cannot revive. He may level, but he cannot raise.

APPENDIX D.

The future of Israel ignored by the Modern Maintainers of Catholicity.

ONE of the most solemn, as well as blessed truths revealed in Scripture, is the purpose of God respecting Israel, His chosen earthly people. He has said that a day is coming when He will forgive them; bring them under that new covenant of grace sealed in the blood of Jesus under which believers now stand; regather them to their own Land and plant them there with His whole heart and with His whole soul, so that they shall not be rooted up nor cast down any more for ever. This re-establishment of Israel is the one bright spot in the earth's future for which faith waits. It will be the great turning point in the world's history, when at last a governmental centre worthy of God and of His truth shall be established in the earth, around which all nations shall be gathered "The law shall go forth from Zion, and the word of the Lord from Jerusalem."

The purposes of God respecting the earth and all things, are so much bound up with Israel, that a peculiar solemnity attaches to all their future history. He that toucheth them, God hath said, "toucheth the apple of His eye." Yet, notwithstanding this and like warnings in the Word of God, one of the earliest efforts of Dr. Newman and his party in Oxford, was to set aside the promises made to Israel. At the same time the Irvingite Prophets in London, and elsewhere, were doing the same thing—and for a like reason. Supremacy is the object at which Puseyism and Irvingism, and all like systems aim. They covet the supremacy which God has appointed to Israel, and therefore arrogate to themselves the place reserved for Zion and Jerusalem. Accordingly, the defenders of these systems argue, that Israel having sinned, have for ever forfeited their standing, and that a transfer of Israel's blessings has been made to others, who, consequently, are to be recognised as the Zion of God. In saying this, indeed, they do but imitate Rome. She long ago saw the importance of claiming for herself the latter-day promises of Israel; and the Catechism of Pope Pius IV., so far as it has in it the semblance of Scripture truth, derives it from a perverted use of passages which speak of the future glories of Israel. If Rome's title to appropriate these passages be admitted, she can soon prove that she is to be the centre of the earth's government, and that to her all nations are to be gathered—before her all things are to bow. Dr. Pusey's dream of the supremacy of Catholicity, would so be realized.

Ecclesiasticism, in every form in which it has developed itself among the Gentiles, has ever blinded itself as regards the prospects of Israel, and also as respects its own future. Can Christendom, or any of those in Christendom who talk so loftily about Catholicity and the like, dare to read and expound faithfully the eleventh chapter of the Romans? They dare not; for therein they would find the record of their own doom. Gentile Christianity is there represented by a branch graffed into the Abrahamic olive tree, which, if it did not continue in God's goodness—if it became like the Israelitish branch before, cankered and corrupt, should be cut off under judgment Has there been a continuing in God's goodness? Is there any likeness between secularized, corrupt, idolatrous Christendom now, and the Churches originally gathered under the Apostles? While the Apostles lived, the Church could be spoken of collectively as the pillar and ground of the Truth: but with the Apostles the Catholic testimony of the Church to Truth died. The Gentile Churches lapsed; their candlesticks were removed: and ever since the Catholic testimony so much vaunted, has been a testimony to worldliness and to falsehood.

Ecclesiasticism has always pretended that an absolute promise of indefectibility was made by God to the visible Church of this dispensation. But the very reverse is the truth. Not only did God threaten the visible Church with excision if it did not continue in His goodness, but He has also distinctly spoken of the corruptions that would abound and stamp its history with apostasy and failure. The place of the faithful servants of Christ throughout the greater part of the Gentile Church period, has been as isolated as was that of faithful Israelites of old through the greater part of Israel's history. "Lo, I am with you alway, even to the end of the age," was a promise made to those who should truly abide in the Apostles' doctrine, not to those who should apostatize from the faith, and give heed to seducing spirits, having, it may be, a form of godliness, but denying the power thereof.

Would to God that Dr. Newman and Dr. Pusey would even now (though it be late) apart from Tradition and as before God, read and meditate on, the eleventh chapter of the Romans. If they would only receive and bow to the truth there revealed, every thought that they have ever formed respecting Catholicity and its future, would vanish as the dream of a night vision. They would see that (however grievously the principle of Protestantism may have been departed from in practice) its principle is nevertheless true, viz. that separation in the midst of Christendom from the corruptions of Christendom, is the absolute duty of all who fear God; and that the extent and character of such separation must be determined by Holy Scripture, and by that alone. Protestantism is not to be valued merely because it is Protestantism. Its value depends on the measure of its conformity to the Word of God.

I would not for a moment deny that the adversaries of Evangelical Protestantism have too much reason to speak of its "*declension and secularization*" in many things. It has longed for *influence*, and has, not unfrequently, sought to gain that influence by unlawful means. It seems to be forgotten that God hath said, "If there come any unto you, and bring not this doctrine, receive him not into your house, neither bid him God speed: for he that biddeth him God speed is partaker of his evil deeds." This commandment is fearfully transgressed. On the occasion of religious celebrations, held professedly in honour of the God of Truth, we see publicly associated with the servants of Christ, men who either profess not to know, or else openly reject and oppose, His truth. We see the Jew and the Neologian standing by the side not only of the professing, but of the real Christian. We see them received, fêted, honoured together, and that in the name of God, as if there was no difference between Truth and Falsehood—Christ and Belial. We cannot marvel that enemies of the Gospel should point the finger of scorn at such exhibitions and say "Aha, aha, so would we have it," whilst others who fear God and love His truth retire; and weep in secret places, seeing what the end of these things must be.

Salvation by Substitution.*

THE first anxiety of an awakened soul, when it has begun to discover the iniquity that is *within*, as well as around it, is to ascertain what way God hath provided (if indeed He has provided any) for access unto His mercies. Is there any method by which He that is holy and righteous can receive *the guilty*, and deliver from the deserved wrath to come? Can He be a just God, and yet a Saviour? These enquiries are instantly met by the declarations of the Gospel. God Himself hath undertaken " the ministry of reconciliation:" He Himself "preaches peace through Jesus Christ." I know no text that more plainly sets forth the relation of God in love and mercy towards man as man, than this. He Himself proposes to the sinner peace and reconciliation through Jesus Christ. Standing, as it were, by the side of the Cross of Jesus, He by His Word, and by His servants, points thereunto; declaring that it is intended not for the righteous (for there are none) but for the guilty; so that the perishing find in the fact that they are perishing, their title to look to that saving object of faith. Nothing is more important than for the soul ever to remember that its *title* to look is found in the fact of its ruin. No title can be found in any *good* thing connected with ourselves, for there is no good: therefore it must be found, if found at all, in the fact of our unworthiness and guilt. No message respecting the Brazen Serpent was sent to any except the bitten—those into whose life-blood the poison had entered, working sure and certain death. But for all such the Brazen Serpent was prepared, and all such were commanded to look. The river that cleansed Naaman from his leprosy was needed by him, and appointed for him, *because he was a leper*. As a leper he went; as a leper he washed; and as soon as he had washed, the leprosy departed. He was no longer the

---

* Compiled from notes of a Lecture delivered on Christmas Day, 1865.

plague-stricken leper. There can be no question, therefore, either respecting the efficacy of that saving power which God hath provided in Christ crucified; nor respecting the readiness of God to shelter sinners under its efficacy. Accordingly, we ever find God spoken of in the Scripture, as the final object of the soul's rest through Christ. See for example 1 Peter i. 21. "Who by Him do believe in God that raised Him up from the dead and gave Him glory; that your faith and hope might be in God." And in "the Acts" (which is *the* part of Scripture to which we turn for instruction as to the manner of preaching the Gospel) we find the Apostle saying to a mingled multitude: "Men and brethren, through this man is preached unto you the forgiveness of sins, and through Him all who believe are justified from all things." Acts xiii. 38. On the other hand we read, that on him that believeth not, "the wrath of God *abideth*." See John iii. 36. No one, therefore, except he believe, is brought out of that unpardoned and guilty state which naturally attaches to us all: for we are born "*children of wrath.*" I mention this, because some, who do not avowedly adopt the heresy of universal pardon (as taught by Mr Erskine and others) do yet maintain a doctrine kindred thereunto, by teaching that men are justified, not *when* they believe, but *before* they believe. Faith is by them compared to a telescope. The telescope may enable you to discern an unseen star, but it creates it not. The star exists whether you discover it or no. So in respect of justification: it is a condition, according to these teachers, which faith, like a telescope, enables us to discover and recognise, but it exists previous to and apart from, such recognition. If this be so, we must either say that *all* men are justified whether they believe or not, or we must say that all God's elect are justified apart from, and previous to, repentance, belief, or confession. In that case, we could no longer speak of them as being when in their natural condition, "children of wrath even as others;" nor could we speak of them as having guilt needing to be removed. They would need no saving object like the Brazen Serpent to be presented to them; for if justified they are pardoned—and the pardoned can have no guilt attaching to them, and therefore need not salvation. The reasons that lead to conclusions such as these are, no doubt, different in different minds. But not a few are led into this train of thought by refusing to receive the declarations of Scripture respecting sin. They look on it simply as a moral disease, not as a condition of criminality involving guilt, penalty, and wrath. The sinner is spoken of as a child whose relation to his father has become morally disturbed, but not as a rebel standing as a criminal before the bar of a righteous judge. Hence, it is not admitted that there is any wrath needing to be removed by the intervention of a substitutional *wrath*-bearer. The heart disorganised by sin, say they, will soon be restored to healthfulness when it is taught to recognise that God has loved, pardoned, and blessed it. Faith is nothing more than the recognition of the fact that it is the subject of such love and mercy: it is a recognition that will act like a medicine upon the soul, healing and recovering it to God. Such is the doctrine which not unfrequently lurks in minds that are fascinated by the "telescope" illustration. But in whatever form presented, it is a doctrine altogether false. Not one truth that God has taught respecting the condition of sinners, or the method of their justification remains intact, if this evil doctrine be received.

God commands us to preach Christ to sinners, and to *all* sinners. We say, "Look unto Him and be ye saved, all ye ends of the earth." We are sent forth to command impossibilities—to bid the blind to look, and the deaf to listen; to prophesy unto dry bones and to say, "O ye dry bones, hear the word of the Lord." We expect to meet with multitudes who put from them the things that we preach, and judge themselves unworthy of everlasting life. Often we may have to say, "Who hath believed our report?" But we also expect to find *some* who shall be as Lydia, whose heart the Lord opened to receive the things spoken by Paul. Lydia believed, that is to say, she credited the message brought to her by Paul, and *relied* on that which God by the lips of His servant proposed to her to be relied on—even the free salvation provided by Him in Christ crucified; and *so* having believed, she became justified by faith: faith being the link which connected her with that which God had provided in Christ for justification—a link formed by God in the power of the Holy Ghost, and therefore a link that abideth for ever.

But the justified need instruction. How little did Lydia, how little did Paul when suddenly forgiven through faith in Jesus, know of the methods of God's mercies in Christ, or of the depth and extent of their own sin. Yet, unless these things are well understood, there can be no stability of soul, no proper testimony to God and to His Truth. Accordingly, the Epistles, and more especially, the Epistle to the Romans, unfold the methods of God in justifying His people. We are taught in what manner we, who are both naturally and by practice *criminals*, unable to meet the claims of God's holy Courts, are yet, according to principles which those Courts recognise, "constituted (and that for ever) righteous."

God is our Creator. As such, He is good and beneficent to all His creatures. He feeds even the young ravens when they cry unto Him. But He is not only our Creator; He is also our Lawgiver and our King. We have therefore not merely to think of His love or His goodness, but to consider how we who, through the sin of our first parent, are born sinful and corrupt, respond to that love and goodness. We stand related to Him not merely as a Father, but as a Judge. Accordingly, He has established towards us Courts of Judgment and made known to us their demands. Are we, or are we not in relation to those Courts, *criminals*?

The principles of the Courts of His Judgment are not mutable. They are founded on that which He essentially is as the Holy One, and are therefore as unchangeable as Himself. The claim therefore of His Courts can never be lowered or withdrawn. They must be met in all their fulness. God must be righteous and prove His righteousness before He will exercise grace. Nor is any one excepting Himself competent to determine what is needful to the maintenance of His own governmental holiness—a holiness which He hath declared it to be His purpose to uphold and to glorify.

The principles of the Courts of God's judgment in their relation to us as men, were revealed at Sinai; and they were as immutable as the stone tablets on which they were written. There were mandatory, and there were prohibitive enactments. The great mandatory commandment was, Thou shalt love the Lord thy God perfectly. Perfect love, perfectly proved in perfect action was demanded. Nor was the demand other than right and fitting; for God, from the very fact of being what He is, merits all love and all perfect development of love in action. Perfect love, perfectly developed, implies inward perfectness of motive; perfectness in the selection of the end; perfectness in the choice of the means; perfectness maintained throughout the whole course of action, without intermission and without flaw; in a word, perfectness that falls in nothing short of the perfectness of Heaven. Nor does the Law's great *prohibitive* commandment involve less. "Thou shalt not be concupiscent," that is, thou shalt not desire nor have any tendency or bias towards any thing that is evil. Such is *righteousness*—the righteousness that the Courts of God demand; and if we have it, our claim, seeing that those Courts are holy, just, and true, will surely be recognised. God hath said,

"The man that doeth these things shall live by them." Blessing was pronounced from Mount Gerizim upon all who should keep this holy Law to do it. But if it were not kept, then there was curse. "Cursed be he that continueth not in all things that are written in the book of the law to do them." "He that offendeth in one point is guilty of all." Here then is blessing and curse: blessing on perfectness, but curse upon the most trivial, the most temporary failure. Which do we claim to inherit? Trying ourselves by this standard (and God will permit no lower one) must we not say that hopelessness is stamped upon every attempt to establish a claim of righteousness before God? All but hypocrites will say so. And if we are not righteous, then are we guilty. Absence of perfectness is criminality; and criminality involves penalty. Apart therefore from the imputation of Adam's first sin, and apart from the depravation of nature from him received, we are by our actual shortcomings and trespasses also marked as guilty, and as deserving all the penalties which the Law has appointed to transgression.

If we could say respecting God's judicial Courts nothing more than this, we might give ourselves up to anguish and to despair for ever. "Weeping and gnashing of teeth" would surely be our portion. But God in the infinitude of His mercy has made known to us this great and blessed fact—that His Courts admit of vicarious or substitutional action being pleaded, when personal action has failed. How blessed this principle! What a sure ground of hope it affords if only a suited substitute can be found. Yet how great the difficulty! For not only must the claim of God as to perfect unfailing obedience be met by our Substitute, but (seeing that we have sinned and thereby incurred penalties) our debt of incurred penalty must also be discharged. Is there any one competent for this?

No one whom *we* could find: no one whom *we* could provide. Jehovah-jireh—"Jehovah will provide," is the name which the Lord our God hath assumed in reference to this very thing. He hath provided the Son of His own bosom—the man that is His fellow. Immanuel was appointed to undertake the Suretyship. Of His own free will He undertook it. He undertook as a Substitute to meet every claim and to bear every appointed penalty in the stead of those who should not despise this method of mercy, even those who should believe on Him unto life everlasting.

In order that God's Law might not be abrogated or "made void," in order that God's avowed resolve "to magnify the Law and make it honourable" might be accomplished, the Son of God was both "born of a woman," and also "made under the Law." He was made under the Law in order that He might honour and magnify it by keeping it. And He did keep it. In announcing His entrance on His appointed path of obedience and suffering He says; "Lo, I come, in the volume of the book it is written of me, I delight to do thy will O my God: yea *thy Law is within my heart*." He does not say that it was *written* there, but that it *was* there. It was essential to Him; it was part of His nature to have it there; for He was by birth the Holy One of God. And afterwards when He Himself took the place of legislation and sat on the mountain and taught, what did He say of the Law? "Think not that I am come to destroy the Law, or the Prophets: I am not come to destroy, but to fulfil. For verily I say unto you, Till heaven and earth pass, one jot or one tittle shall in no wise pass from the Law, till all be fulfilled." These are emphatic and solemn words. Have they, or have they not been verified? Has the Law been perfectly kept, or no? And if it has been, by whom, save Immanuel? And did He keep it on His own behalf, or on behalf of His people?

"As by the disobedience of one man many were constituted sinners, so by the obedience of One shall many be constituted righteous" Such are the words of the Apostle in the 19th verse of the fifth of Romans. In the immediately preceding verse he had spoken of this justifying obedience as being "one righteousness," saying that as "by one offence" judgment had come, so "by one righteousness ($\delta\iota'$ $\dot{\epsilon}\nu o \varsigma$ $\delta\iota\kappa\alpha\iota\omega\mu\alpha\tau o \varsigma$) the free gift had come unto justification of life." From the first moment, therefore, that Jesus came into the world, He was a Representative Person. His very object in coming was that He might act as the Representative of others. He came to do what they could not do; to bear what they could not bear. He came to render unto God an unbroken "obedience," by means of which all His believing people were to be "constituted righteous." That obedience, therefore, seeing that it had for its object the provision of a *completed* righteousness for His people, had a period of commencement and of end. It commenced when He said, "Lo, I come to do thy will, O God:" it terminated when He said, "It is finished: and bowed His head, and gave up the ghost." The obedience required of our Surety was at that time fully rendered. The "one righteousness" was *then* complete. The obedience required was an obedience unto death, even the death of the Cross—death under wrath. He had not only to magnify God's holy Law by keeping it so as to secure that not one jot or tittle thereof should pass away, but He had also to bear all that it was appointed to Him to bear of suffering and of penalty—penalty incurred by our disobedience. Thus he was at once the Obedient One and the Sufferer. Through Life and through death He obeyed: through life and through death He suffered. The difficulties of His obedience and the character of His sufferings were not always the same. They greatly varied. It was the Cross that peculiarly made manifest the intensity of His love in obeying, as well as the intensity of the anguish which such obedience entailed. Yet He was ever the Sufferer as well as ever the Obedient One; and thus was wrought out that which the Apostle terms "one righteousness"—His life being throughout one prolonged unbroken act of righteousness, whereby has come unto us the free gift "unto justification of life."*

It had been condescension and humiliation unspeakable for Him whom the Heaven of heavens cannot contain, to take into union with Himself the nature even of angels; but He descended lower in the scale than angels, and took upon Him *man's* nature; and that, not whilst it retained the beauty and honour proper to it in Paradise before Adam sinned, but *after* it had lost its primœval strength and beauty. He came "in the likeness of *sinful* flesh;" being "in all things made like unto His brethren, sin excepted;" of which He was clearly void both in flesh and spirit. *Morally*, He was not in the likeness of sinful flesh. Though "made of a woman," yet by virtue of His miraculous generation, there was in Him no sin, no taint of sin; no proclivity to sin. It was said to Mary, "The Holy Ghost shall come upon thee, and the power of the Highest shall overshadow thee: therefore also that Holy Thing that shall be born of thee shall be called the Son of God." Yet His humanity, though holy, was weak humanity—weak in order that He might suffer. It was not humanity in strength, such as we now see in Him glorified, nor even that form of humanity that was seen in Adam in Paradise.† He was

---

* See this further considered in tract entitled, "Christ our Suffering Surety," as advertized at the end of this volume.

† "Moreover, Jesus Christ did not only assume the human nature; but He also assumed its nature, after sin had blotted its original glory, and withered its beauty and excellency. For He came not in our nature before the fall, whilst as yet its glory was fresh in it; but He came, as the apostle speaks, "in the likeness of *sinful* flesh," Rom. viii. 3, that is, in flesh that had the marks, and miserable effects,

"crucified in weakness." His humanity was pure, holy, and perfect, but it was true humanity. It was not "heavenly humanity" as some have said; for how then could He have taken part of *the same* flesh and blood that pertained to them whom He came to save. *We*, certainly, have not "heavenly humanity," nor humanity different in any respect from that of other men, and it is written, that "inasmuch as the brethren were partakers of flesh and blood, He also Himself likewise took part of THE SAME." If it had been otherwise, He neither could have suffered nor have died. All His sufferings would have been semblance merely—not reality, and redemption would be a dream. Nor was there as some (so far following the Socinians) teach, a commingling of Divine and human elements in His human NATURE. If we were to say, that in virtue of His being begotten by the Holy Ghost, elements of Divine *nature* were commingled with His human *nature*, as oil in the meat-offering was mingled with fine flour, we should in that case deny that He was truly *man*, just as much as we should deny that He was truly God, if we were to say that human elements were commingled with His Divine *nature*. Christ is one Per-

---

and consequents of sin upon it I say not that Christ assumed sinful flesh, or flesh really defiled by sin. That which was born of the virgin was a holy thing. For by the power of the Highest, that whereof the body of Christ was to be formed, was so sanctified, that no taint or spot of original pollution remained in it. But yet, though it had not intrinsical native uncleanness in it, it had the effects of sin upon it; yea, it was attended with the whole troop of human infirmities, that sin at first brought into our common nature, such as hunger, thirst, weariness, pain, mortality, and all these natural weaknesses and evils that clog our miserable natures, and make them groan from day to day under them.

"By reason whereof, though He was not a sinner, yet He looked like one; and they that saw and conversed with Him, took Him for a sinner, seeing all these effects of sin upon Him In these things He came as near to sin as His holiness could admit. Oh what a stoop was this! To be made in the likeness of flesh, though the *innocent* flesh of Adam, had been much; but to be made in the likeness of *sinful* flesh, the flesh of sinners, rebels, oh what is this! and who can declare it! And indeed, if He will be a Mediator of reconciliation, it was necessary it should be so. It behoved Him to assume the same nature that sinned, to make satisfaction in it. Yea, these sinless infirmities were necessary to be assumed with the nature, forasmuch as His bearing them was a part of His humiliation, and went to make up satisfaction for us Moreover, by them our High Priest was qualified from His own experience, and filled with tender compassion to us. Oh the admirable condescensions of a Saviour, to take such a nature! to put on such a garment when so very mean and ragged!"—*The Fountain of Life, by Flavel, p.* 164. *Edited by Religious Tract Society.*

son; but He has two *natures,* which two natures, though intimately and inseparably united, are not confounded. "The right Faith is, that we believe and confess; that our Lord Jesus Christ, the Son of God, is God and Man: God of the substance of the Father, begotten before the worlds: and Man, of the substance of his Mother, born in the world. Perfect God, and perfect Man; of a reasonable soul and human flesh subsisting. Equal to the Father, as touching his Godhead: and inferior to the Father, as touching his Manhood. Who although he be God and Man; yet he is not two, but one Christ: one, not by conversion of the Godhead into flesh: but by taking of the Manhood into God: one altogether; not by confusion of Substance: but by unity of Person." Such are the statements of the Athanasian Creed. They ought, as the English Article says, "thoroughly to be received and believed, for they may be proved by most certain warrants of Holy Scripture."

There are also some who affirm that because the humanity of the Lord Jesus was united to His Deity, therefore His humanity was not the same as ours. But this is to confound between, that which things are in themselves, and that which they are in their relation to other things. Doubtless, the humanity of Jesus, seeing that it was taken into personal union with Godhead, stood and stands in a relation to Godhead in which the humanity of no other has ever stood, or ever will stand. The relation of Christ's humanity to Deity is utterly different from the relation of our humanity to Deity; but that does not make His humanity in itself different *as to its substance* from our humanity. "If He was God of the substance of His Father begotten before the worlds, He was also Man of the substance of His Mother, born in the world." Yet peculiar as is the *relation* of humanity to Deity as seen in Christ, and great as is its exaltation as found in union with the Eternal Word, yet it was, and is, essentially the same humanity as ours. And although "many glorious effects proceeding from so near a copulation with Deity" [Hooker] were found in the humanity of Christ, which "by its union with Deity became replenished and filled with an unparalleled measure of Divine grace and excellencies;" [Flavel] and although "the Spirit was given to Him without measure" (John iii. 34) so that there thus became inseparably connected with Christ's humanity, heavenly and Divine developments that pertain to none excepting Himself, yet His humanity though unspeakably different from ours *in its characteristic developments and relations,* was nevertheless *essentially* the same as ours. All the heavenly excellency that He caused to dwell in it, and to be exhibited in it, did not invalidate the everlasting truth, that because "the children were partakers of flesh and blood, He also Himself likewise took part of THE SAME." " If therefore," says Hooker, " it be demanded, what the Person of the Son of God hath attained by assuming manhood, surely the whole sum of all is this, to be as we are *truly, really, and naturally man*, by means whereof He was made capable of meaner offices that otherwise His Person would have admitted, the only gain He thereby purchased for Himself was to be capable of loss and detriment for the good of others." (p. 264.)

One of the most marked types of the humanity of Jesus was the beauteous veil of the Tabernacle. It represented, not His Person (as some, strangely contradicting Scripture, have recently affirmed)—it represented Him not in the integrity of His Person as God and Man, but it represented (as we are taught by the Apostle himself) His humanity. "The veil, that is to say, His flesh." (Heb. x.) It was frail in its texture, for it was formed to be rent. No wires, therefore, of gold or of any metal were interwoven with the fine white linen which formed the basis of its structure. That could not be; for it would have implied that His humanity was commingled with Deity. But though no gold was found in the texture of the veil, yet it was suspended on gold. As typically displayed in the Tabernacle it was inseparably connected with gold. Gold was, so to speak, its sustaining strength: gold in the Tabernacle being continually used as a type of Divine nature. And how beauteous was its aspect! Its basis was fine white linen, representative of a purity fit for God in heaven. Its colours were blue, purple, scarlet; all indicating qualities of dignity, or of moral beauty developed in unqualified perfectness through and in the humanity of Immanuel. Cherubic forms, also, were depicted thereon. Indeed, forms of Cherubim covered it. It was made up, so to speak, of Cherubim. "He made it Cherubim," is the expression used. Exodus xxxvi. 35. Thus it presented to the eye of the beholder the type of an excellency that could be displayed only in One whose humanity was such as necessarily to exhibit in all *its developments*, characteristics that were not only superhuman, but Divine. The character of Jesus not only displayed a moral perfectness that was equal to the perfectness of God, but there was in Him likewise (although for the most part hidden) all *glorious* power. "In Him dwelleth all the fulness of the Godhead bodily." Col. ii. That wondrous and almighty power denoted by the Cherubim which were shown in vision to Ezekiel, and which he saw depart, grieved away from the guardianship of Israel by Israel's sins, returned in the Person of Jesus to the earth again. The power denoted by the Cherubim was all concentrated in Him. He was able to exercise it, and He did from time to time exercise it; as when He rebuked the winds and the waves, or fed the multitudes, or raised the dead, or caused the barren fig tree to wither. Divine power, therefore, as well as Divine perfectness was found in the man Christ Jesus. His ways, His looks, His actings, in a word, every thing that constitutes developed "*character*" in the sight of God and of man, exhibited traits that proved to all whose eyes were opened to see the truth, that He who stood before them, whilst truly and strictly human, was also as truly and really *Divine*. The consciences of men recognised it. "Never," said they, "did man speak as this man." John could not only say, "The Word was made flesh and dwelt amongst us full of grace and truth," but he could add likewise, "and we beheld His glory, the glory as of the only begotten of the Father."

Dangerous, however, as is the doctrine that the humanity of Jesus, because of its relation to the Divine, was not the same humanity as ours, there is yet another doctrine more deadly still. Some have imagined that the Eternal Son in taking what has been called, "the first Adam-life," in other words, the life which He had as man, did thereby assume a life with which sin was in such sort connected, that it became needful to lay down the life so assumed, and not to take it again. This, it is said, Christ did. At His death He laid down "the first Adam-life," and by resurrection assumed another life, and *so* effected the justification of His people.

Few doctrines ever promulgated are more dangerous. Shall we indeed say that coming to be the Substitute of His people, the Lord assumed a life which He laid down, and *took not again;* and that because sin in some sort was connected with or attached to it? Does He not Himself say, speaking of the life which as man He possessed, and which as man He laid down, "no one taketh it from me: I lay it down of myself. I have power to lay IT down, and I have power to take IT again?" Do not these words show beyond all question, that He took again the very same life which He laid down? Irving's doctrine, though stated perhaps in a more naked and repulsive form, was scarcely more dangerous than this. Irving strenuously asserted that Christ did not sin, though he averred that the humanity of

Christ was full of sin, which He repressed: and repressed sin, repressed concupiscence, said Irving, (following Rome in this) is not to be regarded as sin. The system to which I am referring, is not the same as this; yet it is scarcely less distant from the truth. Its teachers, it is true, are not wont to use "great plainness of speech;" but their doctrine appears to be this. Instead of saying (what would be true) that Christ as the Substitute of His people had imputed to Him, as something that did not attach to Him personally, the guilt of their "old man," that is, their corrupt carnal nature, they seem to think that the life which Christ took as man, was so associated with the condition of "the old man," that it was needful that He should divest Himself of this life, and assume another life in order that He might bring Himself into a condition meet for God. I scarcely need say to any one who knows the truth, that if our Substitute in taking on Himself the imputation of our guilt did, in any sense whatever, take into union with His Person our old man, or our morally tainted life, He would then Himself have stood in "the actual condition of a sinner," and would have Himself needed reconciliation. But the whole system is false. Christ never took upon Him our old man In taking our flesh He did *not* take its corruption. He never took a life that needed, because of sin in it to be laid down in order that another life might be taken up. The life that He had as man was as pure and morally perfect as that which He had with the Father before the world was. His flesh in all its connexions was as the veil of the sanctuary. If He had separated Himself from His people, and received that which was due to His own individual position, He would never have tasted death, but have been taken without death into glory. "Thinkest thou that I cannot now pray to my Father, and He shall presently give me more than twelve legions of angels: but how then shall the Scriptures be fulfilled, that thus it must be?" It was by the laying down of a life essentially perfect and holy, and not by the assuming a holy life after He had laid down a tainted one, that the great Substitute accomplished the work whereby the ground on which the justification of His people rests was perfected. Nothing subsequent to His death added any thing thereunto. God reconciled to Himself all His believing people, "in the body of Christ's flesh through death, so as *thereby* to present us holy and without blemish, and uncharged ($ανεγκλητους$) in His sight." No words can be more plain than these. Take from the work of Christ on the Cross its prerogative; say that it did not by itself alone, "perfect," as to acceptance, God's believing people for ever; assign that "perfecting" to any thing else whatsoever, and you destroy the very foundation on which the whole fabric of Truth has been made by God to rest.

Some from misapprehension,—others with the intent of deriding the doctrine of the vicarious obedience and suffering of our Substitute, have affirmed that all who teach it must say that Jesus filled and discharged perfectly all the identical offices and duties in which His people have failed; and that He must have suffered also the very identical sufferings that His people would have known if He had not delivered them. But His people, if He had not delivered them, would have known *eternal* wrath. They would also have known the bitterness of personal *remorse*. Neither of these things could Jesus know: for none can know remorse except those who have personally sinned. The sufferings, therefore, of Jesus, were not and could not be in all respects identical with the sufferings that we should have known, if He had not redeemed us. Nor was it needful that He should obey in the very same relations and circumstances in which we have failed: for many of the relations filled by His people He never held. That which it was needful for Him as the Substitute to do and to suffer in order that He might secure the justification of His people,—and at the same time uphold the governmental holiness of God, was determined in the counsels of eternity by the Father, the Son, and the Holy Ghost, before the world was. Jesus came to fulfil all that was *written* of Him. His path of suffering-obedience was an appointed path; the circumstances thereof, and the length thereof, being predetermined. It had a beginning, and it had an end. It began when He came, saying, "Lo, I come to do thy will O God." It ended when He said, "It is finished, and bowed His head, and yielded up the ghost." The work that He had undertaken to accomplish for the justification of His people was then *finished:* and therefore He neither obeyed nor suffered for it any longer. It was a work terminated because the end was reached. It was not needful that the sufferings of the Substitute should be eternal in order that God's Law should be magnified. It was in the dignity of the Person of the Sufferer, not in the length of the sufferings, that the Law found its honour. Angels recognised it to be so when they saw Him, whom they adored and worshipped as their Creator, take upon Himself the form of a servant and become obedient unto death, even the death of the Cross. They well understood, and so did Satan, that the governmental holiness of

God was more magnified by the obedience and sufferings of the man who was Jehovah's "fellow," than it could be dishonoured by any thing that had been done or could be done by creatures.

And when we speak of the sufferings of Christ we must remember that it is not sufficient to speak of them in a vague and general sense merely. None who believe that He ever came in the flesh at all, will deny that He in some sort suffered; but multitudes have denied (and their numbers increase daily) that He suffered *penally* under the hand of God in order to make satisfaction for sin. They admit that He suffered under the hand of man and from pressure of surrounding circumstances, but the truth taught in Isaiah, that "it pleased Jehovah to bruise Him, and to put Him to grief, and to make His soul an offering for sin," they reject. This is the habit of the whole Neologian School, from the somewhat moderated statements of Coleridge and Archdeacon Hare, down to the more advanced infidelity of Stanley, Maurice, Kingsley, and Jowett Such writers may well refuse to see in the Psalms and in the Prophets any testimony to Jesus and to His sufferings: for if it be once admitted that the great Sufferer in the Psalms is Jesus, their system is scattered to the winds. And what says the Scripture? "Those things that God before had spoken by the mouth of *all His prophets*, that Christ should suffer, he hath so fulfilled." And again, Jesus said, "These are the words which I spake unto you, while I was yet with you, that all things must be fulfilled, which were written in the law of Moses, and in the Prophets, and in the Psalms, concerning me Then opened He their understanding that they might understand the Scriptures." It is from the testimony of the Psalms and the Prophets, added to the historic narrative of the Gospels, that we derive our knowledge of the real character and depth of the sufferings of Jesus both in life and in death. How little could they who stood by the side of the Cross and discerned merely the outward circumstances as described in the Gospel narrative, have inferred that His sufferings were such as the following verses from the Psalms describe. "I am poured out like water, and all my bones are out of joint: my heart is like wax; it is melted in the midst of my bowels. My strength is dried up like a potsherd; and my tongue cleaveth to my jaws, and THOU hast brought me into the dust of death." Ps. xxii. 14. If we had been there present and witnessed His calm collectedness—how He remembered to fulfil every relation in which He stood, whether to man or to God, caring even for His mother, we should little have inferred that all His bones were out of joint, or that

His heart was as melted wax. The full character of His sufferings is not to be learned from those parts of Scripture whose object is to record those outward circumstances which were presented to the eye of man: we must turn to those other parts which reveal His inward experiences and secret cries. The Psalms, more especially, declare that hidden sorrow and anguish—the true intensity of which was known only to Himself and to God. "Save me, O God; for the waters are come in unto my soul. I sink in deep mire, where there is no standing: I am come into deep waters, where the floods overflow me. I am weary of my crying: my throat is dried mine eyes fail while I wait for my God. . . . . . O God, thou knowest my foolishness; and my sins (literally guiltiness) is not hid from thee:" (Ps lxix.)—not His own foolishness or guiltiness, for He had none, but that which pertained to His people, and which He thus appropriated to Himself as the Substitute who had undertaken to bear the penalties. So also in Ps. xl. "Innumerable evils have compassed me about: mine iniquities have taken hold upon me, so that I am not able to look up; they are more than the hairs of mine head: therefore my heart faileth me." Such were His sufferings: such His cry. It was because of the ascription to Him of sins which indeed were more in number than the hairs of His head, but which were not His own sins, but the sins of others—the punishment of which He had undertaken to bear. Hence the penal action of the hand of God against Him. All this, of course, will be denied by those who meet the descriptions of the sufferings of Christ in Scripture with the same kind of unbelief that once met the great Sufferer Himself. There is an increasing disposition to deny that sin is in any case met by God either with wrath or penal infliction. Hence the denial of eternal punishment by so many. They speak of sin as a disease needing remedy, but they refuse to recognise it as *criminality* meriting and receiving curse. They admit of punishment if it be merely remedial, and intended to reclaim and to restore: but punishment that is strictly penal and the result of wrath, they refuse to acknowledge. Hence they who reject the doctrine of eternal punishment cannot, if consistent, receive the doctrine of Scripture respecting the Cross, nor believe in Jesus as the *wrath*-bearer: for they admit not the existence of wrath in God, and therefore must reject every thing that is founded on that truth.

But we have to believe Scripture and not the thoughts of men. The words which I have above quoted from Ps. xxii., "Thou hast brought me into the dust of death," are words too plain to be evaded. We see in them Jesus, the holy and beloved Son, ascribing to the hand of His God and Father (who loved and delighted in Him as the Son of His bosom) those bitter sufferings which the connected verses describe. It was the Father not sparing His own Son. In all His sufferings, Jesus recognised the hand of His Father. The means employed might be various; the intermediate links many; but it was God that appointed, and God that controlled. Apart from Him, not a sparrow falls unto the ground. Satan and his angels might be among the instruments employed, but they were no less under the supreme control of God than when, for a season, Job was delivered into their hands. It was appointed that the Seed of the woman should be "bruised," and He *was* bruised.

And if this be true respecting His sufferings on the Cross, it is no less true respecting His lesser, yet most bitter sufferings in life. From the moment of His first appearance on the earth, He was the Representative of His believing people, discharging for them their obligations: a sufficient proof of which is that if he had not been their Representative He never would have suffered at all. Joy, honour, and glory, would have been His portion. As the Head and Representative of elect Israel, He was called out of Egypt. "When Israel was a child, then I loved Him and called my Son out of Egypt." As representing others, He received from the hands of John the baptism of repentance for the remission of sins—a baptism which One who had no sin, and needed no repentance, could only receive as the Representative of others. As the Second Man, the Representative of God's believing people, He overcame in the wilderness that same Tempter before whom the first man in Paradise fell. His path was always a path of obedience, but it was equally a path of suffering. *Before* He was led away to be crucified, He was known as "the poor or afflicted One," Ps. xli. 1: as One that had "eaten ashes like bread and mingled His drink with weeping." Ps. cii. It was true of Him long before the Cross, that "His visage was more marred than any man, and His form more than the sons of men." Nor could the words, "O my God, I cry in the day-time and thou hearest not, and in the night season and am not silent," be interpreted of the Cross *only*. He who personally deserved all honour, glory, and manifested blessing, is in the Psalms known as "the afflicted One" throughout the whole period of His earthly sojourn. How could this be? Only because He was the Substitute: only because He was suffering in the stead of others. It mattered not what the instrumental agency might be that caused the suffering. It might proceed from man, or from Satan, or from circumstances, but He who appointed it was God. And although it be true that the depth of His suffering in life was not manifested to the outward eye any more than the depth of His suffering in death, yet it was not on that account the less real. They who stood by His side whilst He testified in the midst of Jerusalem against the sins of her people and her priests, might not have inferred from any thing that met the outward eye, that He was saying in His heart, " Oh that I had wings like a dove! for then would I fly away, and be at rest " Yet the 55th Psalm gives as true a picture of His sufferings in life as the 22nd Psalm does of His agony in death. Shall we then reject the instructions of the Psalms as to the obedience and suffering of the great Substitute?—extending as they do not only over the years of His public ministry, but even those previous years of sorrow, during which He dwelt as the witness of righteousness in the midst of unrighteousness—as a lamb in the midst of lions, being ever " the faithful and true witness," testifying and acting for God against evil.

And as Jesus was from the beginning of His course on earth, the Surety and Representative of His people, so His appearance was the evidence that the long promised operation of Divine power in creating " a new thing " in the earth, had at last been put forth. "How long wilt thou go about, O thou backsliding daughter? for the Lord hath created a new thing in the earth, A woman shall compass a man." Jer. xxxi. 22. The character of the Divine acting was new, and the result thereof was also new; for the result was the manifestation of One, who though truly having " flesh and blood" even as we, was nevertheless a Person altogether " new,"—for He was Immanuel— God manifest in the flesh. He was the Eternal Son—the being One (ὁ ὤν) in the bosom of the Father; and as such could say, " I came down from heaven." " I am from above." " No one hath ascended up to heaven, but He that came down from heaven, even the Son of Man that is in heaven." Resurrection into glory might be the occasion of bringing His humanity into a condition of majesty, strength, and power, suited to the excellency of the life that was in Him, but it did not give to Him that life, for He was from everlasting the Living One. He was " the Light " and " the Life " from everlasting, before the world was. The circumstances might be different, but the " Light" and " Life " were the same. Though now no longer known " after the flesh " (2 Cor. v. 16.), but separated from the earth by the defining limit of resurrection-glory* (Rom. i. 4.), His personal condition is not one of more essential distinctness and isolation now, than it was when He tabernacled below. He stood on earth as the new covenant Head of His believing people, in whom they had life, although He was not preached as the Second Man and last Adam, until He had taken that place in glory which befitted Him as the Head of the new creation of God.

Some with the design of overthrowing the true doctrine of the Cross, maintain that the Son of God by the fact of assuming humanity, did thereby reconcile humanity and all who have it unto God: in which case redemption by shedding of blood would not have been needed, nor could any one who had human nature be lost. But to those who know the Scripture I need not say, that it never speaks of the reconciliation of an abstract nature. It speaks only of the reconciliation of *persons*. "You," saith the Apostle, "hath he reconciled, &c." The Apostle does not say, God hath reconciled humanity, and so reconciled you: nor is there any common nature, as the Realists dreamed, giving unity to all the individuals who possess it. It is a mere fiction. The reconciliation effected by Christ is effected for believers only. He hath not reconciled them that believe not: on the contrary, the "despisers wonder and perish." And for believers reconciliation is effected, not by the Incarnation of the Son of God, but by His *death*. "You who were sometime alienated, &c. . . . . yet now hath He [the Father] reconciled in the body of His [Christ's] flesh through death, to present you holy and without blemish, and uncharged in His sight" (Col ii 22.) If the Son of God in becoming incarnate had taken the position which personally pertained to Him as the Holy One, and had not acted in the power of His pre-appointed redemption, no sinner could have drawn nigh to Him in peace: for the holiness of Immanuel was as the holiness of God. The sudden exclamation of Peter, "Depart from me, for I am a sinful man, O Lord," expressed his sense of the moral distance which separated him from his Lord. and the apprehension was a true one, if Immanuel were to be viewed only in the heavenly perfectness of His own personal position, and not as the One who came to take on Himself the guilt of Peter's sin. If Jesus had separated Himself from His people and claimed that which was due to His own individual

---

* Ὁρισθείς—see the force of this word considered in Notes on the Greek of the first Chapter of Romans, page 23, as advertised at end.

condition, He might without death, have gone into heaven, and into glory, but He would have gone alone. "Except a corn of wheat fall into the ground and die, it abideth alone, but if it die it bringeth forth much fruit." It was not His purpose to return alone. He came to fulfil His Father's will, and that will was the eternal reconciliation and sanctification of His people "by the offering of His body once."

Therefore, although the Incarnation was necessary in order to effect the appointed reconciliation, yet the Incarnation by itself would have reconciled none. "Without shedding of blood is no remission." It was needful that an appointed course of obedience and suffering, consummated by the Cross, should be fulfilled, in order that the just wrath of God, to which the slightest falling short of His glory exposes us, should be appeased,* and it cannot be appeased except by all the claims of His holy Courts being fully *satisfied*. We owe unto God a double debt; a debt of obedience, and having failed in that, a debt of suffering: and unless these two debts are duly paid, the claims of God not being satisfied, wrath must be our portion. The penal suffering, therefore, of our great Substitute was as needful as His obedience; and His obedience as His suffering, to provide that reconciliation which is founded on the appeasement of wrath by a satisfaction rendered to both the claims of God's Courts—the claim of penalty, and the claim of perfected obedience, seeing that the Courts of God never separate these claims, but enforce both. Consequently, the blood of the Cross is not only the evidence of punishment borne, it is also the evidence of perfect obedience fulfilled. To believers the value of their Substitute's sufferings and of His obedience are alike imputed; *both being needful to their justification*, and being so intimately associated together that they cannot be separated except in thought; for as He obeyed He suffered, and as He suffered He obeyed. Thus in the sacrificial types we see not only the victim stricken, but we see also part thereof burned on the altar for a sweet savour; and both these things were needful in order to secure the reconciliation. That which covered over the guilt of the offerer did also cover him with acceptable fragrance. In the methods of God's grace non-imputation of guilt

---

* Ιλαος and its cognates, ιλασκω, ιλασμος &c are the words by which appeasement is signified in the New Testament Wherever these words are used, placation of wrath is indicated. See further observations on the meaning of ιλαος in *Notes on the Greek of Romans I.* as advertised at the end of this volume.

exists not apart from the imputation of righteousness. The same authority that tells us that Christ was "made a curse for us," tells us also that He offered Himself for us, "an offering and sacrifice to God for a sweet-smelling savour." His sacrifice abolishes the ill-savour of our sin, but it leaves instead thereof (and that for ever) the sweet-smelling savour of its own excellency. Our justification, therefore, is founded as much on the perfect obedience of our Substitute, as on His sufferings; and on His sufferings as much as on His obedience. The value of the obedience, and the value of the sufferings are alike found in the blood. The "one righteousness" whereby we are constituted righteous, is made up of all that the Obedient One did and all that He suffered from the moment He became flesh, until He said, "It is finished."

There are some who object to its being said that Christ's righteousness is imputed to us, on the ground that the expression "imputed righteousness" is unscriptural. It is nowhere, they say, found in Scripture. Are we then contending about *words*, or about the verities conveyed by words? We do not find in Scripture the words, "Trinity," nor "Incarnation," nor "Satisfaction," yet shall we on that account refuse to use these words? or say that they are unsuited to convey the truths expressed by them? We are told by the Apostle that we (i.e. believers) are "constituted righteous" before God "by means of the obedience" of Another. If this statement be true, the obedience of Christ must be transferred to us, reckoned to us, or set down to our account. Is not this imputation? And this is the more evident, because in the fifth of Romans, the imputation of Christ's righteousness is spoken of as correlative to the imputation of Adam's first sin. Shall we deny the fact of the imputation of Adam's sin whereby we are "constituted sinners?" We must, if we deny the imputation of that righteousness whereby we are constituted righteous. How is it possible to hold the one and reject the other? Shall we then reject it? If we do, if we reject *imputation*, we incur the guilt of rejecting that which God has distinctly revealed as the ground of our condemnation on the one hand, and the ground of our justification on the other. By imputation we were ruined, and by imputation we are saved.

I have argued on the supposition that the expression "imputed righteousness" is not found in Scripture. Even *then*, the truth would be the same; for we are concerned not with words, but with things. In the fourth of Romans, however, we do find the very words, "impute righteousness":—"David also describeth the blessedness of the man to whom the Lord IMPUTETH RIGHTEOUSNESS without works." The expression that occurs in the preceding and following verses where faith is spoken of as being "imputed FOR righteousness," is not identical with this, and is to be distinguished from it.* We are taught in this chapter that to the believer his faith is "imputed or reckoned for (λογίζεται ΕΙΣ) righteousness." Now it would be impossible for faith to be thus imputed FOR righteousness, unless there were an actually subsisting righteousness of which, faith so imputed FOR righteousness is regarded as the representative. God whose governmental holiness demands that His mercy should not be so exercised as to derogate from His righteousness and who sanctions no fiction, could not recognise faith as having a value which *intrinsically* it has not, except something that had a real value existed, of which faith is regarded as the token ; just as a bank note is looked upon as having the value of the gold which it is legally authorized to represent.

Faith is the instrumental means that connects us with the justifying merits of Christ. Under the expression, "justifying merits," I include His active and His passive righteousness, that is to say, His obedience and His suffering. When therefore the soul enters its plea in the Courts of God, and saith, "Lord I have believed, and therefore I have that righteousness which Thy Courts acknowledge," the plea is recognised. It is a valid plea. But how ? Is it because faith is *in itself* righteousness ? No ; but because it is imputed *for* righteousness, inasmuch as it doth connect us with, and is looked on as representing that real righteousness—that true gold which is found in the obedience unto death of Immanuel ; *that* being the "righteousness" by means of which grace reigneth unto eternal life. See Rom. v. 21. Seeing, therefore, that faith is imputed to us for righteousness, and that Christ's righteousness is imputed to us *as* righteousness, God is able on this ground, without sanctioning any fiction, to impute to us righteousness without works.

We are sinners · that is no fiction. And we have believed : that is no fiction. Through faith we have become connected with no fictitious righteousness, but with a righteousness actually wrought out for us by our God and Saviour in the days of His flesh. And having that righteousness imputed to us, we stand before God, even now, in true actual possession of righteousness bestowed on us freely by God—as

---

* See remarks on this in "Occasional Papers," No. I. p. 89.

the result of which bestowment, we are to reign in life: "for if by one man's offence death reigned by one, much more they which receive the superabounding ($την περισσειαν$) of grace and of THE GIFT OF RIGHTEOUSNESS, shall reign in life through one, Jesus Christ."

Whilst, therefore, the ascription to us of the righteousness thus wrought out for us by Immanuel, is the sole ground of our justification, we must remember that the riches of God's grace towards us through Christ, extend beyond our justification. He who, in fulfilment of the will of God, voluntarily wrought out for us that righteousness which enables us, even now, to appear before God as those who have all its value attributed to us, has thereby brought us into the possession of that, the value of which is infinite, because it is the righteousness of One whose merits are infinite. Who can search into the depths of the merits of Immanuel? Can any of us say, what is the estimate formed thereof by Him who dwelleth in the Heavens? His merits are as His Person—past finding out; and therefore, the value of the righteousness imputed to us for our justification is *infinite*. Its value is not exhausted in our justification. It is eternal: it abides for ever: and because of it the redeemed receive every favour and every blessing that reaches them, whether in time or in eternity. In the ages of eternity our great Redeemer shall see the fruits of the travail of His soul in seeing His people blessed according to the value of that righteousness which He has provided for them, and whose value can only be estimated by the infinitude of His merits. His people, therefore, shall for ever stand under, and be blessed according to, the value of a righteousness which is not their own righteousness, but the righteousness of Another imputed to them. The love, the life, the glory, which they receive in union with and in fellowship with Christ, are all bestowments that come to them because of God's eternal purpose to bless them according to the value of the merits of Him who is "the Lord their righteousness." The final change which shall bring us into the heavenly likeness of our risen Lord, and give us practical meetness for heaven, is not the cause, but *the result and consequence* of the possession of that righteousness, which in all the infinitude of its value is reckoned to us now, and will equally be reckoned to us then, and for ever. In glory the redeemed will recognise the imputation of the righteousness of Immanuel as the sole ground of all their blessings. All the blessings they will receive, they will recognise as blessings prepared for them by God as the result of His eternal purpose to bless them according to the value of the righteousness by which they were justified; and that value is, as I have already said, to be determined by the value of the merits of the Person who wrought out that righteousness: and those merits are infinite. How then have we to cleave to that great and all-blessed truth which is taught in the word IMPUTATION! It is the great distinctive doctrine of the gospel of the grace of God—the very key-stone of the arch of blessing. Destroy it, and you destroy every hope On it, as on a foundation, God has made to rest the whole economy of grace throughout the whole detail of its ministration and development. There is not a blessing which God ever has dispensed, or ever will dispense to the redeemed, as the redeemed, in time or in eternity, that is not the result of IMPUTATION. However excellent and precious may be that which He *imparteth* to His people in the way of inherent grace, or gift, yet all such bestowments are simply the consequences of imputation. Whatever God thus *imparteth*, is because of that which He *hath imputed.* It is the knowledge of this that enables us to say truly, "*Of* Him, and *through* Him, and *unto* Him are all things; to whom be glory for ever and ever. Amen."

APPENDIX I.

Dr. Steane on Imputed Righteousness.

The following excellent and well-considered observations are extracted from a Tract, to which I have on a former occasion referred, entitled "Imputed Righteousness," by EDWARD STEANE, *D.D., Jackson and Walford, St. Paul's Churchyard, price 1s. 6d. per dozen, or 10s. per 100.*

"SIN is not only depravity, but guilt; not only moral deformity, but legal desert of punishment. A representation is sometimes given of the moral condition and relations of man which is essentially defective; the representation which, while it admits the doctrine of depravity, shuts out the doctrine of guilt. But sin, considered in this light, ceases to be a crime and becomes only a calamity, or at most a fault; an evil, which distorts the character of man and disturbs his happiness, but which is not of a penal nature, and necessitates no judicial condemnation. It puts him out of harmony with the moral law, for he is no longer holy, but it does not bring him under its curse. So that what a man needs, according to this view, is not to be set right with God, but to be made right in himself; and this once accomplished, the other follows as a necessary consequence. His great want is not justification, but personal rectitude. Under these circumstances, of course, no necessity exists for imputed righteousness.

"And this view is commonly connected with another equally defective, of the relations in which man stands to God. These are all resolved into the relation which arises out of the Divine paternity; to the exclusion of that which is involved in the rectoral and judicial character of God, and which regards man as a subject of His moral government, and amenable therefore to law. But if man is to be looked upon only in the light of a child who has broken through some family arrangement, or acted undutifully towards a parent, then certainly it is hard to understand what scope there is in such circumstances for imputed righteousness. The child's father does not demand it. A return to a proper sense of his position in the family, and to a better state of feeling towards his father, may at once rectify the temporary aberration, and the penitent transgressor is restored to favour. No thought occurs to the father's mind that something is due in the case to law and public justice; still less does he dream of insisting on propitiation, the shedding of blood, satisfaction, and atonement. The very conception of such things is abhorrent to the paternal nature, and they are never required by paternal government. Yet these are the things, as we shall presently see, that constitute the righteousness which a man must have imputed to him before he can be blessed.

"God is, no doubt, a loving Father. If His love were not infinitely greater and more ready to spring into exercise towards sinners than we can understand, there would have been no hope of salvation, and no righteousness provided that might be imputed to them in order to their being saved. But that righteousness has been provided, and must be imputed, or salvation is impossible. And since this must be taken to be the statement of the Word of God, it brings us by a direct consequence to the recognition of other relations between Him and man besides that involved in paternity; and of those views of sin in which it is contemplated rather in its aspect towards God, than in its effects upon the character of man. The latter, however, are the views and relations which are almost exclusively exhibited in books and sermons, in which we are taught that we do not need an atonement, nor a righteousness springing out of it. Of course we do not, if there is no guilt to be cancelled, and consequently no punishment to be endured. But if, on the other hand, transgression necessarily draws after it the infliction of the penalty of transgression—if the majesty of God's law demands an equivalent for its violation—if the sinner cannot be legally purged until satisfaction has been made—if the inflexible rectitude of God be imperilled should there be any connivance at sin, and His moral government is overthrown the moment it is removed from the foundations of eternal and immutable law—then the deep necessities of man's condition as a sinner rise to view in their just and vast proportions, and it becomes apparent that nothing can meet them but such a propitiation as the cross of Christ and that alone presents, and nothing save the sinner but that act of God by which He imputes to him the righteousness which results from it, and is intentionally provided by it.

"The necessity, then, for an imputed righteousness arises out of the legal relations which God has established between Himself and man. Those relations the sinner has violated, and their violation not only produces misery, it constitutes guilt. Guilt must be cancelled, and the position of one who has never disobeyed must be regained, before the sinner can be restored to a state of blessedness. By no possibility can he himself re-achieve this position, nor can it be regained by any improvement effected in his personal character.

. . . .

"Pardon and justification are not to be confounded as though they were simply the equivalents of each other. The law which exacts blood shedding, in order to our escaping punishment, equally requires obedience, in order to our being justified; and, therefore, the righteousness which it demands must comprehend a perfect conformity to the precept of the law, as well as the discharge of its penalty. An imperfect obedience, however sincere, will not meet the exigency, for the law must essentially change its nature, and cease to be law, before it can forego or relax any portion of its claims. Eternal rectitude can make no concessions to human weakness; and human weakness, on the other hand, labours under an absolute impossibility of fulfilling the demands of eternal rectitude. Where, then, is the escape from this dilemma? Where is the sinner's hope? Clearly where the Apostle places it, and there only. If he is ever again to know what it is to be blessed, his blessedness must come from some source altogether apart from himself; in a word, it must be 'the blessedness of the man to whom God imputeth righteousness without works.'

. . . .

"Gratuitous as salvation is to us, it has been procured at an infinite cost. The righteousness which God imputes to the sinner, is a righteousness wrought out by the obedience and sacrificial death of His Incarnate Son. It results from both. from His active obedience to the precepts of the law, and from His passive submission to the penalty of the law. By the one He fulfilled its requirements, by the other He exhausted its curse.

. . . .

"Thus the righteousness which God imputes to those whom He justifies, is the righteousness that springs from the spotless obedience and the sacrificial death of the Lord Jesus Christ. And this righteousness is a perfect righteousness, and an everlasting righteousness, and a righteousness intrinsically of infinite value. Perfect,—for it needs no supplement, as indeed it can receive none. It is admitted in the Court of Heaven's jurisprudence as a full acquittal against all charges which, from any and every quarter, may be brought against the man to whom it is imputed. It cancels the guilt of all sin, fulfils all the requirements of law, satisfies all the claims of justice, upholds the integrity of moral government, and makes it not less honourable to the majesty of God's holiness, than to the riches of His mercy, to restore the trangressor to His friendship Everlasting,—for it shall never be superseded, and never exhausted. It will never become obsolete, but be always new, and constitute the title-deed to the saint's inheritance, as long as the inheritance itself shall last. And it is intrinsically of infinite value,—for it is the righteousness not of a man, nor of any creature, however exalted, but of the Eternal Son of God.

. . . .

"The act of imputation is God's:—'The blessedness of the man *unto whom God imputeth* righteousness without works.' But the question arises, is it an act of sovereignty, or a judicial act? Is it an act in which the blessed God proceeds upon the ground of absolute and unexplained prerogative, or upon the ground of rectitude? Not upon the former, but the latter. Antecedently to that arrangement in the eternal councils of heaven, by which the Son of God became the appointed as well as the voluntary substitute who, in the sinner's place, should fulfil the law by His obedience, and endure its penalty in His death, there was scope for the exercise of sovereignty. Divine sovereignty is accordingly to be recognized in the original determination out of which the whole economy of redemption arises. It was Divine sovereignty which, when the question presented itself whether apostate man should be left to perish in his apostasy, resolved that question in favour of the apostate. It was Divine sovereignty which made the distinction between the treatment of sinning angels and sinning men. It was Divine sovereignty which selected the Redeemer, and then in Him, as their Head, chose or predestinated all the redeemed. In these, and other similar instances, sovereignty and the absolute prerogative of God are exercised; exercised, however, let it be said, always in harmony with the personal character of God, as a Being of infinite wisdom, holiness, and love. But when once the system of moral government came into operation, it came into operation necessarily upon the ground not of sovereignty, but of rectitude; not of prerogative, but of equity.

"When, therefore, the Son of God, acting in His substitutionary and representative character, provides the righteousness by which believers in Him are justified, the imputation of it to them becomes a judicial act, or an act of Divine justice. If the sins of believers have been imputed to Christ, it is only just that His righteousness should be imputed to them. This was the very stipulation of the covenant made with Him; the consideration, in view of which He undertook the sinner's responsibilities. If the death of Christ was a judicial transaction, then the justification of believers is a judicial transaction also; for they are but the two parts of the same process of redemption. As in the former, the blessed God acts as a Judge, or in a judicial capacity, so in the capacity of a Judge He acts in the latter; and in both, as the Administrator of that system of moral government, the very glory of which consists in its absolute and unswerving equity. Hence the language of the Apostle John:—'If we confess our sins, He is faithful and just'—not simply merciful, but faithful and just—'to forgive us our sins, and to cleanse us from all unrighteousness.' (1 John i 9.) Our forgiveness, it must ever be remembered, is a propitiated forgiveness; our justification, a justification by righteousness. Every thing in the entire development of salvation is in harmony with rectitude. It is a legalized process, a proceeding according to law, and magnifying law from first to last. And hence the declaration of another Apostle, 'Him hath God set forth to be a propitiation through faith in His blood, to declare His righteousness for the remission of sins that are past, through the forbearance of God; to declare, I say, His righteousness; that He might be just, and the justifier of him who believeth in Jesus.' (Rom. iii. 25, 26.) It is observable with what emphasis the statement is made that the remission of sins, as the consequence of faith in Christ's propitiation, is an exhibition of God's righteousness, and not of His sovereignty; and that it is so in order to this end—that God Himself might be just in the act of justifying believers. This is, in truth, the grand paradox; but it is, at the same time, the sublime triumph of the dispensation of grace, that while under the law God is just in condemning sinners, He is just under the Gospel in justifying them.

"It is proper still further to advert, in a few words, to another point. It may be asked, what is the act itself of imputation, and what is it that we understand to be imputed? Such representations have sometimes been given, in answer to these questions, as seem to me to involve serious error. I cannot, for example, suppose, as some do, that our sins are transferred to Christ in any sense that would make Him to be a sinner, or that His righteousness is so transferred to the believer, as to make him an innocent or righteous man. Imputation, in both cases, must consist with the facts, that Christ, after our sins have been imputed to Him, is personally as sinless as He was before; and that we, after the imputation of His righteousness, are still personally sinners. On neither side does the transaction make any change in character. Christ's actions do not become our actions, nor Christ's sufferings our sufferings. Nor, on the other hand, do the sinner's actions become the actions of Christ, nor is the penalty due to the sinner, and exacted of Christ, to be taken as a manifestation of God's displeasure against Him. But by the imputation of our sins to Him is meant, that He was dealt with by Divine Justice as though He were a guilty person; and by the imputation of His righteousness to us, is, in like manner, meant that we are dealt with as though we were righteous persons. God laid our sins to Christ's account, and to our account He lays Christ's righteousness; and the consequence is, that He is treated as if He had been the sinner, and we are treated as if we had never sinned.

"And now, finally, when does this imputation take place? The unhesitating reply to this inquiry is, that it takes place immediately upon the exercise of faith. Not before. To say that the believer is justified from eternity, is to confound the purposes of God with their practical development. Just as reasonable would it be to speak of him as regenerated from eternity, or even of the world as created from eternity. 'Known unto God,' no doubt, 'are all His works from the beginning;' but it is simply an abuse of language to say, that what God knows, or determines to do, is therefore actually done. He has determined, and eternally determined, for all His purposes are eternal, that those who believe in Christ shall be justified by the imputation of 'righteousness without works;' but it is a contradiction to describe that righteousness as being already imputed, while they are yet in unbelief. 'Abraham believed God,' says the Apostle, 'and it was counted to him for righteousness,' the obvious meaning of which is, that it was so counted to him at the time he believed. And it is thus in every other case. Righteousness is imputed upon believing. When a sinner believes, that is, as soon as he believes, he is justified. From that moment he stands a pardoned and accepted man through the imputed righteousness of Christ; for since nothing but faith is necessary to make that righteousness his own, this result follows, and follows in its completeness, the moment he believes.

. . . .

"And when God imputes that righteousness, He imputes it once for all, and its effect is equally instantaneous and complete. Not at several times, therefore, and in successive acts and instances, does the transition take place, by which we pass out of a state of condemnation into a state of judicial safety, but at one time only. If the translation is effectuated at all, it is effectuated perfectly. Either we are under condemnation, or we are justified; there is no third alternative. Either the unrepealed curse of the law is still suspended over us, or we have received a full discharge from its penal claims; for the supposition is impossible that we should at one and the same time be amenable to punishment, and yet be acquitted; that we should be partly condemned, and in part justified Nothing so anomalous can be conceived in the condition of man, or the jurisprudence of God. Justification, therefore, is from the first an act complete in itself, needing no supplement, and suspended on no future contingency. When hereafter the believer stands at the great tribunal, he will stand there as being already absolved from guilt, and at peace with God. His justification, instead of taking place then, will then be recognized, admitted, and proclaimed as a transaction antecedently accomplished, at once begun and finished, when God imputed to him 'righteousness without works.'"

APPENDIX II.

Clarkson on Imputation.*

"Ask dissenting Protestants, such who have forsaken the doctrine of the Church of England and of all Reformed Churches in this point, whether the righteousness of Christ be imputed to us? No, by no means, will they say; and some of them have the discretion to smut it with black invectives, as a dangerous doctrine of I know not what pernicious consequence; well, but ask them again, Did Christ suffer in our stead? Was what He suffered accepted as suffered in our stead? This they will readily grant, as being maintained by the whole Christian world against the Socinians. The Papists themselves will not have the face to deny it, how much, how satirically soever they write against the imputation of Christ's righteousness; now where is the reason of those men, Papists and others, when they presume so much on the strength and the clearness of their reason? They grant the sufferings of Christ in our stead accepted for us, yet deny they are imputed to us, when the accepting of them for, and the imputing of them to us are the very same thing; they both grant and deny one and the same thing, only expressing it in differing terms; and these terms differing only in the sound when in truth they are of one and the same import.

---

* David Clarkson B.D. was born in Bradford, in Yorkshire, in February 1621-2. He was educated at Clare Hall, Cambridge, and became Fellow and Tutor in that Society in 1645. He was afterwards Rector of Mortlake, Surrey, from which he was ejected by the Act of Uniformity in 1662. After this, in 1682, he was chosen as colleague to Dr. John Owen, in the pastorship of his congregation in London. On the death of Owen in the following year, he became sole pastor of the congregation until his death in 1686. The above extract is taken from his sermon entitled, "Justification by the Righteousness of Christ," as given in Vol. I. of his works recently published in "Nichols' Series of Standard Divines."

This is not to deal like men of reason; it is no more reasonable than to grant that this is a living creature, but to deny it to be an animal. . . . . . . The Socinians are more impious, and bid more defiance to the Gospel, in denying the imputation of Christ's satisfaction, because they deny He made any satisfaction; but those are more repugnant to reason, who grant that He made satisfaction, but deny that it is imputed.

If they will use their reason, they must either fall into the detestable error of Socinus, and deny both, or submit to the doctrine of the Gospel and acknowledge both; both must stand or fall together; and both must be denied, or both must be acknowledged." (p. 287.)

* * * * * * * * *

"It is objected, that if Christ's sufferings be imputed to us, then we must be reputed to have suffered what He suffered, and then we must be accounted to have satisfied justice ourselves, and consequently to be our own saviours and redeemers.

Ans. From imputation in the sense fore-explained, it cannot with any reason be inferred that we suffered personally but only that Christ suffered in our stead. And from thence it cannot be inferred that we ourselves made satisfaction, but only that Christ in our stead satisfied divine justice. And so in short the foundation of this fallacy being removed, the rest of the consequences fall.

Thus much for the imputation of Christ's death and suffering, commonly called His passive righteousness; the truth whereof I hope is rendered so clear and firm, that it cannot (as I said) be denied by any but such as will deny Christ to be a Saviour and Redeemer in the style and sense of Scripture." (p. 290.)

* * * * * * * * *

"I should be sorry to find any Protestant divines denying the merit of Christ's active obedience, for thereby His whole undertaking will be divested of its meritorious excellency. If there be no merit in His obedience, there will be none in His sufferings; for penal sufferings, as such, do not merit, as is confessed on all hands, they are not meritorious but as there is obedience in them. And therefore if His obedience be not meritorious, there will be no merit in His sufferings, and consequently none in His whole undertaking.

And His satisfaction will fall with His merit, for that only is satisfactory which is meritorious; so that, when there is no merit, there is no satisfaction.

This then we may take for granted, as being generally acknowledged, that Christ fulfilled the law, performed perfect obedience on our behalf, so that it was meritorious for us.

Secondly, Christ performed perfect obedience in our stead, not only for us, for our good, but *vice nostrûm,* in our place or stead. This, as to what I intend, is of more consequence than the former, and will clear the whole business before us, if we can but clear it. If we can gain this one point, we shall go near to carry all that we desire; and, if I mistake not, it may be easily done. Indeed, there are divers who stick at this, those who acknowledge that Christ's obedience was for us, and that it was meritorious for us, will scarce grant that it was performed in our stead; but if they take notice what we mean thereby, they will not, they cannot stick at it.

A duty is said to be done in another's stead, when that is performed for him which he was obliged to do himself. As when one pays a debt for another which he himself was bound to pay, it is truly said to be paid in his stead.

Or when one is obliged to do some work, but is some way or other disabled for it, another undertaking to do it for him, doth it in his stead. So Christ fulfilling the law for us, which we were obliged to have done ourselves, He truly and properly did it in our stead.

This seems clear, past all denial; no more is required that it be done in our stead, but that what we were bound to do ourselves be done for us. That it was done for us, all grant; and that we ourselves were obliged to do it, none can deny. Nor can it be denied that He performed it for us but for that end for which we should have performed it, that is, that we might have life, so that He did for us what we should have done, not accidentally, but out of design; for it is acknowledged that His end and design in performing perfect obedience was to merit life for us, that is, purchase for us a title to heaven.

All that I find objected against Christ's obeying in our stead is only this: if He performed obedience in our stead, we shall be thereby exempted from obedience ourselves, as His sufferings in our stead did free us from sufferings.

But this which is alleged to enforce the objection serves to dissolve it. By Christ's suffering in our stead we are freed from suffering anything for that end for which He suffered, that is, for satisfying of divine justice; so by Christ's obeying in our stead we are freed from obedience, for that end for which He performed obedience in our place, that is, that we might have title to life. For these ends for which He suffered and obeyed, it is not required of us either to obey or to suffer, for He alone satisfied justice by the one, and He alone purchased title to life by the other.

For other ends we suffer afflictions and death, not to satisfy divine justice; and so for other ends we are as much obliged to obedience as if He had not obeyed for us, but not to purchase a title to life, not for that end.

In short, I cannot see how those who will have Christ's active obedience to be satisfactory or meritorious for us, can reasonably deny that it was performed in our stead, since they must grant all that is requisite thereto; for no more is necessary that it be done in our stead, but that what we are obliged to do be done for us. That it was done for us they assert; that we ourselves were obliged to do it, they cannot deny.

Thirdly, what Christ performed in observance of the law, is accepted in all points as He did it. What He performed was accepted; what He performed on our behalf is accepted in our behalf; what He performed in our stead is accepted as done in our stead." (p. 291).

* * * * * * * * *

"The Papists grant that Christ's righteousness may be said to be imputed to us, because He thereby purchased, as other benefits, so inherent holiness, which with them is our justifying righteousness."

The Jesuits, Vasquez, Bellarmine, and others, expressly own the imputation of Christ's merits or righteousness in this sense.

So others among us grant that Christ's righteousness may be said to be imputed to us in this sense, and no other; but because He thereby purchased pardon of sin, and title to life, in which they say, consists that righteousness which justifies us, they will have us justified not by a righteousness which Christ performed for us, but by a righteousness which by His performance He purchased for us. Not by His own righteousness, but by that which is the effect of His own.

All these admit not of any imputation of Christ's in itself, but only in its effects and benefits.

But it is plain, by what is premised, that the obedience of Christ itself is imputed; for to be imputed to us is nothing else but to be accepted for us, as performed in our stead. But the obedience of Christ was performed in our stead, and is accepted for us, therefore His obedience itself is imputed to us.

Indeed, either the righteousness of Christ is imputed to us or nothing; for the effects of it, viz., pardon of sin, and title to life,

&c., are not imputed to us, because it cannot be said with any tolerable sense, that right to life, or pardon of sin, were performed in our stead or accepted for us as so performed.

"Besides, that which is imputed to us is not personally or subjectively ours; but the effects of Christ's righteousness, our faith, our inherent holiness, pardon of sin, title to life, are ours subjectively and personally; we are the subjects of them as we are not of that which is only imputed to us; and to say these effects of it are only imputed to us, is to deny all imputation of it." (p. 295.)

APPENDIX III.

Extracts from Bishop of Ossory on Justification.

ARCHBISHOP LAURENCE in his Bampton Lectures, Sermon VI., observes: "Here, to avoid a misconception of the argument, it seems necessary previously to state in what sense the word Justification, which comprehends the sole ground of contention, was used by the opposing parties [i.e. the Reformers and their adversaries]. Upon both sides it was supposed *entirely to consist in* the remission of sins."

These words are thus commented on by the Bishop of Ossory. "This is, certainly, a most extraordinary statement from one who is professedly aiming at exactness; and who shows, elsewhere, considerable acquaintance with works which prove its very great inaccuracy. The fact is, that the early Romish and Protestant divines could not be truly represented as concurring in any view of the *entire* meaning of Justification; but it seems a curious infelicity, that the sense of the term which the Archbishop describes as agreed upon by both, was, in fact, admitted by neither. How far it is from a fair statement of the meaning assigned to this important word by *one* of 'the opposing parties' the foregoing extracts afford ample materials for judging. And how strangely it misrepresents the views of the *other*, will appear by referring to the Canons and Decrees of the Council of Trent. It will be found, not only that the Council expressly decrees (Sess. vi. cap. 7) thus—Justification 'is not the remission of sins only, but is also the sanctification and renovation of the inner man through the voluntary susception of grace and gifts;' but also, that in what Chemnitz happily calls its '*profuse liberality of anathemas*,' it pronounces a distinct *anathema* upon every one who ventures to assert that men are justified by the remission of sins only (solà peccatorum remissione)—Sess. vi. can. i.

If ever, then, Romanists speak of Justification as *consisting entirely in the remission of sins*, it is certainly, only in opposition to the reformed doctrine, that it includes also *the imputation of righteousness;* and, on the other hand, whenever the Reformed writers speak of it in the same terms, they are to be understood as meaning to reject the Romish addition of *the infusion of righteousness.*

From Calvin, for example, very strong declarations that justification *consists entirely in the remission of sins,* might, doubtless, be produced. But, as Bellarmine (De Just. lib. ii. cap. i.) very truly remarks, other and neighbouring parts of his writings do not allow us to fall into any mistake concerning the sense in which such declarations are to be received. "Therefore, when the same Calvin in the same chapter (cap. ii. lib. iii. sect. 21 and 22) and in the Antidote to the Council [of Trent] in the Sixth Session, contends that Justification consists only in the remission of sins, *he does not exclude the Imputation of the Righteousness of Christ,* but he excludes internal renovation and sanctification." *Bellarmine on Justification, lib. ii. cap. i.* . . . . . . And Bull referring to Calvin on Rom. iv. 6, 7, observes: "That which Calvin says in this place, namely, that Righteousness is nothing else than the remission of sins, is to be explained from other passages of the same Calvin, in which he openly confesses, that, besides remission of sins, *the imputation of Righteousness also is contained in the notion of Justification.*" *Bishop Bull, Answer to Animadver.* vii. And the same is true of all the rest [of the Reformers], as a review of the foregoing extracts (see pp. 399-404 in Appendix of work of Bishop of Ossory) from their writings will abundantly prove."*

* * * * * * * *

"It is thought a very strong objection to the doctrine in question, if not a complete refutation of it, that while the law only requires us to obey *or* to suffer, this doctrine seems to require us to obey *and* to suffer, because, according to it, Christ, as our representative, obeyed and suffered for us.

But there is an ambiguity in the word *requires,* which renders it necessary to fix its meaning, before we can judge what this argument is worth. To make it of any value, *requires* ought to mean *requires for our justification.* This is its sense in the second proposition; but

---

* See Appendix to Sermons of Bishop of Ossory on the Nature and Effects of Faith. p. 404.

the same sense cannot be given to the word in the first proposition without making it false. The law does not propose *suffering* as a substitute for *obedience* in procuring *justification;* but sets it forth as the penal consequence of disobedience. If the law says, obey or suffer, it is not as proposing two means to the same end, either of which you may take with the same result. It is an alternative of a different kind—one in which, if you do not choose the first, you must take the second. And the law does not represent those who take the second, and who do suffer accordingly, as objects of God's favour and justified by Him, but as condemned by Him and objects of His wrath. It cannot be said, therefore, that we have suffered in Christ, and are therefore justified before God. No other way of justification but obedience is proposed to us. Reasoning, therefore, on these principles, the conclusion would seem to be that we cannot regard ourselves as justified before God, until we can say that we have obeyed in Christ.

But then it may be said, 'Suppose that in this way you show that Christ's suffering for us does not render His obedience for us superfluous, would not His obedience for us render His suffering for us not only superfluous but something more? If we had ourselves obeyed, could we have been justly punished? And if He has obeyed for us, can it be justly required that He should suffer for us also? This seems to be as good reasoning as the other. And is it not a decisive *reductio ad absurdum?* Is it not enough to overthrow any view of the Gospel plan of redemption, that, according to it, Christ's death was unnecessary, not to say unjust?'

This reasoning appears plausible, but it is really founded upon an inadequate statement of the case. For Christ's obedience has been rendered for man, not simply as subject to the law, but as a sinner against the law. No obedience rendered *by* such a one, and therefore no obedience rendered *for* him could expiate his past guilt, or could secure his justification while his guilt was unexpiated. And for this the other part of the Lord's work was necessary." *pp.* 437-8.*

* * * * * * * * *

---

* If we had been like Adam in his innocency, or like angels who had never sinned, and it had become a question how we could be raised into a condition of higher privilege by rendering an obedience in circumstances that were beyond our capacities, in such a case obedience rendered by a Substitute might have attained the benefit without the addition of penal infliction. But this is NOT our case. We are rebels, transgressors, sinners. Therefore, if we are to be blessed through a Substitute, our Substitute must suffer as well as obey.

"Assuredly, no one can require to be guarded against the obvious sophism which would infer the identity of the imputation of righteousness, and the pardon of sin, because each is used to describe God's justification of sinners. If we were at liberty to take two assertions about the same thing, and infer that, because they *mean the same thing,* in the sense of *designating, or being applied to, the same thing,* they must *mean the same thing,* in the very different sense of *being equivalent propositions,* there are scarcely any propositions so diverse that we might not prove identical. Yet this is plainly what is done here; with the additional unfairness that, in fixing the common sense of the assertions, it is derived, not from the one which expresses most, but from that which expresses least." p. 419.

* * * * * * * * *

"After what I have said, pp. 78, 79, it cannot be necessary for me to add anything in the way of precaution against the misconception, that, in labouring at this point, I am dividing *justification* into distinct or successive acts; or, that I suppose that God can *pardon* any to whom He does not, at the same time *impute righteousness,* or *impute righteousness* to any whom He does not *pardon.* I am sure that, in the justification of sinners, these gracious acts are not only in fact, but, necessarily united; and I have so said distinctly in the place referred to, and elsewhere. By one, therefore, who had right notions of Justification, *pardon* might be used to express it. It is actually so used, not only in the Bible, but in various Protestant writers, who yet assert, in the most distinct terms, *the concomitance of the imputation of righteousness* with the *pardon of sin* in the justification of sinners. I am, of course, therefore, not labouring against any such interchange of the words, but seeking to guard against the inadequate notions of *justification* to which it is calculated to lead."

APPENDIX IV.

Note on the Doctrines of Mr. Irving.

An attempt has recently been made, first, by the publication of the Memoirs of Mr. Irving, and secondly, by the issue of a new edition of his works, to throw a halo around his name, and to hide or extenuate the evil of his doctrine. It is an attempt that can scarcely be too strongly deprecated.

The era of Mr. Irving was one in which Scriptural Protestantism, with all its foundation-truths was about to be assailed openly and covertly from various, and, not unfrequently, opposed quarters. In hundreds of minds, not actually Romanist, a disposition was beginning to appear, to assign to the Church a place which God has assigned only to Christ and to Scripture. Instead of the relation of the individual to the Church being made dependent on his relation to Christ—which is the principle of Protestantism, the relation of the individual to Christ was made subordinate to his relation to the Church—which is the principle of anti-Protestantism: and the idea was favoured of the immanence of spiritual power and authority in the Church, so as to take from Holy Scripture its place of exclusive authority. This tendency of thought was early favoured by Mr. Irving, and hence, many of his writings have derived their popularity.

How little the true doctrines of the Gospel ever took root in the mind of Mr. Irving is evidenced by the facility with which he renounced them. As early as 1828 we find him writing thus to Mrs. Irving.

"Our dear friend, Mr. Paget of Leicester, was in church all yesterday, and kindly came down to converse during part of the interval. I wish you knew him. He is truly a divine—more of a divine than all my acquaintances. . . . . . He also like Campbell and Erskine, sees Christ's death to be on account of the whole world, so as that He might be the Lord both of the election and the reprobation, and that it is the will of God to give eternal life by the Holy Ghost to whom it pleaseth Him. I first came to the conviction of that truth on that Saturday, when, at Harrow, after breakfasting with a bishop and a vicar, I sat down to prepare a meal for my people. He thinks the Calvinistic scheme confines this matter by setting forth Christ *as dying instead of, whereas there is no stead in the matter*, but on account of, for the sake of, to bring about reconciliation. He also thinks that the righteousness of Christ which is imputed to us, is not the righteousness of the ten commandments, which He kept, and which is only a fleshly righteousness, but the righteousness into which He hath entered by the resurrection—that super-celestial glory whereof we now partake, being one with Him, and living a resurrection life. This I believe; and take it to be a most important distinction indeed." *Irving's Life*, p. 242.

Here unhesitatingly was renounced the vicarious obedience and death of the great Substitute, whereby *alone* His believing people are justified: for, says Mr. Irving, "there is no stead in the matter:" and the manifested righteousness of Immanuel in loving God perfectly, and *proving* that He loved Him perfectly, even with all His heart, and with all His soul, and with all His strength—the last proof being His becoming "obedient unto death, even the death of the Cross," all this which forms the one ground of the believer's present and future blessedness, even for ever and ever, is described by Mr. Irving as "a fleshly righteousness," something too low, apparently, to have any place in Mr. Irving's scheme of salvation: and imputation, though the name be retained, is in fact, utterly rejected, for "that super-celestial glory whereof believers partake" is something imparted, not imputed. It is something that grace, after having justified fully and for ever by the imputation of the one righteousness, imparts because of the unspeakable value of that righteousness to them that are justified thereby.

The seeds of error thus scattered in Mr. Irving's mind soon germinated, fostered probably, by his acquaintance with Coleridge. Accordingly, Mr. Irving was one of the first of those who introduced the habit (since greatly extended by the Neologians) of using theological terms not only in new, but in false senses. Thus atonement does not with Mr. Irving mean what it means in Scripture, that expiatory sacrificial work which the great Substitute finished on the Cross, to appease wrath and satisfy the claims of God's governmental holiness.

Atonement is with Mr. Irving what it is with the Neologians, at-one-ment or reconciliation. To Mr. Irving's mind there was no difference between the appeasement-offering ($ιλασμος$) which was the pre-requisite and procuring cause of the reconciliation, and the reconciliation ($ἡ καταλλαγη$) which was the result. To suppose that the sufferings and death of Christ were a sacrifice offered to God " to procure God's favour," is according to Mr. Irving, a heathenish error[*]—such a supposition arises from " a most barbarous idea of God." (Irving, p 98.) Atonement and redemption, according to Mr. Irving, have no reference to God. They are merely the names for the bearing of Christ's work upon the sinner, and have no respect to the bearing on the Godhead. Mr. Irving, says Dean Goode, "explains atonement to mean merely an at-one-ment, or reconciliation of our human nature with the divine nature, which he supposes to have been effected by the second Person in the Trinity taking upon Himself human nature in its fallen and sinful state, and then constraining the human will to obey the Divine will in all things, and by this he supposes that God and man are brought into ' eternal harmony.' The atonement is not a reconciliation effected by the sacrifice of the God-man Christ Jesus upon the Cross, but an at-one-ment of all men with God from the human nature having once been united with the divine in the person of Christ, and in His person preserved from the commission of actual sin, and at last suffered to die." *Goode, Appendix p.* 326.

It is no wonder then that with thoughts like these Mr. Irving should scornfully reject the doctrines of imputation and substitution as taught in Holy Scripture. " The man," says Mr. Irving, " who will put a fiction, whether legal or theological, a make-believe, into his idea of God, I have done with ; he who will make God consider a person that which he is not, and act towards him as that which he is not, I have done with. Either Christ was in the condition of the sinner, was in that form of being towards which it is God's eternal law to act as He acted towards Christ, or He was not. If He was, then the point in issue is ceded, for that is what I am contending for. If He was not, and God treated Him as if He had been so ; if that is the meaning of

---

[*] See Irving's " Orthodox and Catholic Doctrine," p. 100, as quoted by Dean Goode in the Appendix page 320 to his valuable work entitled, "*Modern Claims to the Gifts of the Spirit &c.*" It is much to be desired that Dean Goode's excellent work should be extensively circulated at the present time. It is published by Hatchard.

their imputation and substitution, or by whatever name they call it, away with it, away with it from my theology for ever." (pp. 116, 117.)

Awful words these, for he who rejects imputation rejects the one method of God's salvation. By imputation only are we saved. Nor is there any "fiction" or "make-believe" in it. It is no fiction that Christ was God and man in one Person—the Holy One. It is no fiction that He was so recognised and loved by the Father always, even whilst He was being bruised. The recognition of His personal holiness and excellency was essential to His being what He was as the accepted substitutional Sin-bearer. It is no fiction that as the Holy One He bore the burden of His people's guilt and suffered the appointed penalties. And as the ascription of His people's guilt to the holy Substitute was no fiction, so the ascription of His righteousness to them is no fiction. All these things are realities for which the redeemed will bless God and the Lamb in the ages to come for ever and ever.

The distinctive doctrines of the Gospel, therefore, were rejected by Mr. Irving quite as much as by the Neologians, and in language very like unto theirs. His doctrines, therefore, must be regarded as heretical, even if he had never taught what he did respecting the Person of the Lord: indeed, his hatred of the doctrine of imputation seems to have been one of the causes that led him to the conclusion that Christ was in the actual condition of the sinner.

It is painful even to transcribe the passages in which Mr. Irving deliberately maintained that the humanity of the Lord Jesus was full of sin, but the interests of truth require that the real character of his statements should not be misunderstood. In the Treatise called "*The Orthodox and Catholic Doctrine of our Lord's Human Nature,*" Mr. Irving says,—"All this effect of uniting Jew and Gentile unto God, and unto one another, which is ascribed to Christ's body, to the sacrifice of His body without spot upon the cross, is derived from this very truth, that He took sinful flesh, or fallen human nature, and upheld it holy against the devil, the world, and the flesh, and the influence of all these upon the mind." (p. 8.) "If then Christ was made under the law, He must have been made by His human nature, liable to, yea, and inclined to, all those things which the law interdicted." (p. 10.) "Conceive every variety of human passion, every variety of human affection, every variety of human error, every variety of human wickedness, which hath ever been realized, inherent in the humanity, and combined against the holiness, of Him who was not only a man, but the Son of man, the heir of all the infirmities which man entaileth upon his children." (p. 17.) "If His human nature differed, by however little, from ours, in its alienation and guiltiness, then the work of reducing it into eternal harmony with God hath no bearing whatever upon our nature, with which it is not the same." (p. 88.) "Was He conscious, then, to the motions of the flesh and of the fleshly mind? In so far as any regenerate man, when under the operation of the Holy Ghost, is conscious of them. . . . . . . I hold it to be the surrender of the whole question to say, that He was not conscious of, engaged with and troubled by, every evil disposition which inhereth in the fallen manhood, which overpowereth every man that is not born of God; which overpowered not Christ, only because He was born or generated of God." (p. 111.) "Manhood after the fall broke out into sins of every name and aggravation, corrupt to the very heart's core, and from the centre of its inmost will sending out streams black as hell. This is the human nature which every man is clothed upon withal, which the Son of man was clothed upon withal, bristling thick and strong with sin like the hairs upon the porcupine. . . . . I stand forth and say, that the teeming fountain of the heart's vileness was opened on Him; and the Augean stable of human wickedness was given Him to cleanse, and the furious wild beasts of human passions were appointed Him to tame. This, this is the horrible pit and the miry clay out of which He was brought" &c. (p. 126) "I believe it to be most orthodox, and of the substance and essence of the orthodox faith, to hold that Christ could say, until His resurrection, 'Not I, but sin that tempteth me in my flesh,' just as after the resurrection He could say 'I am separate from sinners.' And, moreover, I believe that the only difference between His body of humiliation and His body of resurrection, is in this very thing, that sin inhered in the human nature, making it mortal and corruptible till that very time that He rose from the dead." (p. 127.)

If these things were true of the Holy One—if Christ had been troubled by every evil disposition that inhereth in fallen manhood—if He could have said, like the believer, "not I but sin that tempteth me in my flesh," how was not Christ personally a sinner? There were two ways in which Mr. Irving endeavoured to answer this question. First, he denied (following Rome in this) that concupiscence is sin—blotting thereby the seventh of Romans and the commandment ("Thou shalt not be concupiscent") from the Scripture, and nullifying all that God has said respecting that great constituent characteristic of the sinner's condition—"indwelling sin." "I deny," said Mr. Irving, "that it is unholiness to be tempted through the mind, provided the will yield not to the evil suggestion, provided the will consent not to the evil consciousness." *Irving's Orthodox Doctrine, p.* 153.

Observe, Mr. Irving does not say that the guilt of such unholiness is, for Christ's sake, not charged upon believers. That would have been true: for Christ has substitutionally borne and atoned for the guilt of their inward unholiness as well as of their committed transgressions. But if Christ had had these sinful propensities where was the lamb provided for *Him*? The Apostle could gaze upon the depth of the corruption within him, and yet rejoice and say, "I thank God through Jesus Christ our Lord," because in Christ, God had provided the Deliverer. But if Christ had had "that law of sin in His members," where was the Deliverer for *Him*? Where was *His* Sin-bearer? If Christ could say until His resurrection, "not I, but sin that tempteth me in my flesh," then not only would He have been unable to say, "I give my flesh for the life of the world," for it would have been a blemished sacrifice, but He would Himself have been individually amenable to death, so that to use the words of Mr. Irving, He "must have died" (p. 91). But what were the Lord's own words? "Therefore doth my Father love me, because I lay down my life, that I might take it again. No one ($οὐδεὶς$) taketh it from Me, but I lay it down of Myself. I have power to lay it down, and I have power to take it again. This commandment have I received of my Father." The life that He had as man, and which life He voluntarily laid down and took again, was as pure and as holy as the life that He had with the Father before the world was. It was the life of Immanuel.

But further: Mr. Irving also held that the human nature of the Lord was so distinct from Himself *personally*, that what pertained to it did not pertain to Him as a part of His Person. A hundred quotations might be made from the *Treatise on the Human Nature* in which the name "Christ" is appropriated not to *Jesus* as being God and Man *in one Person*, but to the Divine Word acting in and surrounded by the flesh as by a garment. The Incarnation is represented as the imprisonment, so to speak, of the Eternal Word in sinful flesh, against which He had continually to struggle, just as the Holy Ghost in believers is separate from and struggles against their evil nature. The flesh of our Lord, to use Mr. Irving's illustration, stood to Him personally, in the same relation that a miry pit does to the person who is in it, or as a garment to the person whom it clothes. Thus the true doctrine of the Incarnation is utterly denied; for the true doctrine is this that God and man were one Person in Christ. In Jesus two whole and perfect natures the Godhead and Manhood were joined together in one Person never to be divided, whereof is one Christ, very God and very Man: so that His actions were not those of God simply, or of Man simply, but of Immanuel— God and Man united together in one Person never to be divided. A garment is not one with the person whom it clothes; nor is the pit one with the person who stands in it. Mr. Irving's illustration, therefore, sufficiently shows that he rejected the true doctrine of the Incarnation. In one place he distinctly says, that it is an heretical doctrine that Christ's generation was any thing more than the implantation of the Holy Ghost life in the members of His human nature which is implanted in us by regeneration. Is this what the Scripture teaches us respecting "the Word made flesh?" Is this what it teaches us respecting Him who was as to the totality of His Person from the very moment He took flesh into union with Deity, the Lamb without blemish and without spot? If we become by regeneration that which Christ became by generation, wherein consists the difference between ourselves and Immanuel? Are we to arrogate to ourselves that name?

It is not wonderful that with views like these, Mr. Irving should deny the distinctive value of the suffering and death of Immanuel. His obedience, His suffering, His blood-shedding are precious, because of that which He was as God and Man in one Person. But what are the words of Mr. Irving: "The atonement upon this popular scheme "is made to consist in suffering, and the amount of the suffering is "cried up to infinity. Well, let these preachers, for I will not call "them divines or theologians, broker-like, cry up their article; it "will not do; it is but the sufferings of a perfectly holy man treated "by God and by men as if He were a transgressor." *Irving's Doctrine of the Human Nature, &c., pp.* 95, 96.

Compare with this the words of the Apostle. "The Word was made flesh, and dwelt among us, (and we beheld His glory, the glory as of the only begotten of the Father,) full of grace and truth." And again, "That which was from the beginning, *which we have heard, which we have seen with our eyes, which we have looked upon, and our hands have handled* of the Word of Life: for the Life was manifested, and we have seen it, and bear witness, and show unto you that eternal life, which was with the Father, and was manifested unto us, &c." Such is the testimony of the Apostle John as to the nature of the Person who suffered and shed His blood, thereby to justify His people. John saw in those sufferings something more than "the sufferings of a perfectly holy man." But when the mind of any one has once been drawn to disbelieve the great mystery of the Incarnation, and to regard the Divine and Human natures in Immanuel as separate in the same way in which the Holy Ghost is separate from the bodies of the saints in whom He dwells; and to regard sin, if bridled, as being no sin, we can easily see that a mind that has acquiesced in conclusions such as these may become the prey of any error however deadly. The flesh of Christ was as sinless, as devoid of sin or of any proclivity to sin as His Deity. When we speak of Him as "the Holy One," we use "Holy" in the same sense in which we use it of Him who dwelleth in the Heavens: and under the term Holy One, as applied to Christ, we include His flesh. We include His manhood when we say of Him that "He knew no sin"—that sin was not in Him.

I might add much more: but they who are not convinced by what has been already said, will not be influenced by any thing that could be added. The manner in which they who maintained these evil doctrines went on to claim for themselves the *miraculous* powers of the Holy Ghost, and to arrogate to themselves the authority of the "one Church of God," will never be forgotten by those who witnessed the effects of that terrible delusion. Those who wish to be instructed in its history should read Mr. Baxter's "Narrative of Facts,"* or the valuable work of Dean Goode, to which I have already referred. Acquaintance with the doctrine taught by Mr. Irving, and with the system founded thereon, and with the results of that system, would cause all who fear God and reverence His truth to tremble at the attempt now being made to hide the character of that pitfall, which is one of the most terrible and destructive that the great Adversary has ever placed in the way of pilgrims to the Heavenly City.

---

* Published by Nisbet, Berners Street.

Notes on Ephesians I. from verse XII. to end.

Verse 12.

"That we should be to the praise of His glory—we who have first hoped in Christ."

That we should be &c] These words should be connected with εκληρωθημεν—"we were appointed as an inheritance" in the verse preceding. The sure result of our being appointed as God's inheritance is, that we shall be found to be "unto the praise of His *glory*, as well as monuments of His *grace*, as soon as the hour of manifestation comes: for *then*, He shall be glorified in His saints, and admired in all them that believe."

We who have first hoped in Christ.] Him who is in truth the Messiah of Israel; whom Israel and the earth will not acknowledge until the next, that is, the millennial, age comes—Him, through God's grace, we acknowledge *now* (πριν η επιστη ὁ μελλων αιων *Theophyl.*) Hence we are described as those "who have *first* hoped in Christ," standing in contrast, as to this, with those who shall be converted in the millennial dispensation, who shall not own Him until after His glory has been revealed. Yet although neither millennial Israel nor any of the millennial saints can be numbered among those "who have *first* hoped in Christ," yet they will not on that account, be excluded from forming a part of God's inheritance in the final glory. The very expression, "God's inheritance," is derived from a passage in Deuteronomy, where it is said of Israel, "The Lord's portion are His people, Jacob is the lot of His inheritance." Deut. xxxiii. 9. This, we who believe, already are. All the spiritual and eternal blessings of Israel we already possess. Whilst Israel is cast off and called "Lo-ammi" (not my people) we are called God's "people," (1 Pet. ii. 10.) and God's "inheritance," (Eph. i. 11.) But in the millennial earth, Israel will be recognised as His inheritance in the earth, and none of those who are truly His inheritance in time shall fail of being His inheritance in eternity. Relations to God in the Spirit that commence on earth, are not transitory, but everlasting relations.

The distinction between the *heavenly* and *earthly* branch of God's inheritance shall continue during the millennium, but not afterwards. For in "the new heavens and new earth" all the redeemed of every dispensation shall form one glorified body under one Head, even Christ; and then the full glory of God's one "inheritance" will be manifested in its eternal condition.

Ελπιζω, a word denoting firm confident expectation, is often used in the Septuagint as the translation of בטח, and should always in translating be distinguished from πιστευω (האמין) and its cognates. But this is not always done in our version. See, for example, the present passage and Heb. x. 23. For some remarks on בטח, האמין, and חסה, see *Occasional Papers Vol I. No. II. p.* 171.

Verse 13.

"*In whom, moreover, ye, when ye heard the word of truth, the Gospel of your salvation, in whom, I say, ye having believed, were sealed with the Holy Spirit of promise.*"

In whom, moreover, ye, &c] In the second verse of this chapter the Apostle, addressing the Ephesians, says, "Grace to you and peace from God our Father, and from the Lord Jesus Christ," and then immediately subjoins, "Blessed be the God and Father of our Lord Jesus Christ who blessed us &c" Can we say that this word "us," as well as the word "we" in the following verses is not intended to include the Ephesians, and to associate them with the Apostle?

Sometimes, indeed, we find passages in which St. Paul speaks ministerially, and on that ground, distinguishes himself from those whom he is addressing: but in such cases the assumption of the ministerial place and the transition from it are plainly marked both by the words, and by the subject matter. See for example, 1 Cor. ii., and 2 Cor v. But here there is not the slightest indication of such a contrast. Nor would any one, I believe, have ever thought that the words "we" and "us" do not include the Ephesians except they had imagined that the verse before us must be so translated as to throw its "*ye*" into emphatic contrast with the "*us*" of the preceding verses.

The habit of thus regarding this verse, arises in great part, from a mistake as to the force of και in the first clause —εν ω και. Commonly this καί is looked upon as *emphatic* and so throwing its force upon ὑμεῖς (you) which follows: whereas instead of belonging to ὑμεῖς and emphasizing ὑμεῖς, it is used to introduce the whole clause that follows, and may be termed the *annexive* or *adjunctive* καί, to distinguish it from καί used in its ordinary *conjunctive* sense, or when it is used merely to emphasize. When simply emphatic, it always throws its force on the word or phrase that immediately follows it, and may often be expressed either by printing the word emphasized in italics, or by subjoining "too" or "also" as a kind of enclitic. But when it is used to introduce a whole appended sentence or clause (such clause containing something that is peculiarly enhansive of the preceding statements in the way of augmentation or confirmation) it is to be regarded not as a conjunction but as an adverb, (see Jelf, Gr. Gr. § 760) and should be rendered by some such word as "moreover," or "what is more," or by "also" not subjoined as an enclitic, but pointed off as a distinct word and prefixed to the clause which it introduces *

---

* The force of καί is repetition, union, emphasis it occurs not only as a conjunction, but also in its original force as an adverb, in which it has its full meaning of "too," while as a conjunction it has a weaker force, like *et* formed from ετι, *yet*. *Jelf*, § 767

The *emphatic* use of καί is very frequent in the New Testament. The following are a few examples

Rom. i 5 καὶ ὑμῖν, to *you* also, i.e. to *you* as well as to others.

Rom. i. 32. ἀλλα και συνευδοκουσι, but have even *pleasure* &c.

Acts x. 26. καγω αυτος, *I* too myself am &c.

Rom. xi. 30. ὡσπερ γαρ και ὑμεις ποτε—for even as *you* too once.

The connective force of καί is discernible in these and like instances, but its emphatic force predominates. The following are passages in which καί though not losing its connective force, and still in a measure emphatic, does *not* as in the examples just given, concentrate its force on the word that follows it, but introduces and gives prominence *to the whole clause* to which it is prefixed.

Luke xxiv 22 αλλα και γυναικες τινες εξ ἡμων, "but, what is more, certain women of our company &c."

Luke iii. 9. ηδη δε και ἡ αξινη, but now, moreover the axe &c.

Rom. viii. 34. ὁς και εστιν εν δεξια του θεου, ὁς και εντυγκανει &c. Who, also, is at the right hand of God, who, also, maketh intercession for us.

Rom. v. 2. δἰ οὑ, και, την προσαγωγην εσχηκαμεν—through whom, moreover &c.

Rom. v. 3. ου αυτο δε αλλα και καυχωμεθα &c., and not only so, but, what is more, we glory in tribulation &c.

If in the verse before us the καί in the first clause (εν ω, και, υμεις) were regarded as emphatic merely, and therefore as concentrating its force upon ὑμεις, then "you" must be looked on as standing in strong contrast with the "us" and "we" of the preceding verses. But και does not restrict its force to ὑμεις. It is used to introduce the whole succeeding clause—a clause which confirms all that had been previously stated by the great added fact, that the Ephesians had, as soon as they believed, been sealed by God with that Holy Spirit which is, says the Apostle, the earnest of *our* (our joint) inheritance. If we omit the virtually parenthetic clause, the words are connected thus — " in whom, moreover, ye having believed, were sealed &c."

But although the "ye" of this verse is included in the "us" of the preceding verses, we are not thereby precluded from speaking of the Ephesians who are denoted by the "ye," distinctly and separately. Although members of the same class cannot be set in contrast to each other as if they belonged to *opposed* classes, yet they may be treated of severally and distinctly. And this is all that the Apostle does when in this chapter and the succeeding, he passes from "us" to you, and from "you" back again to "us" His reason for thus specifying the Ephesians was this: they were Gentiles, and as such were rejected by many Jewish teachers from that full participation in the blessings of grace into which God had alike called believing Gentiles and believing Jews. Jewish teachers disturbed the souls of Gentile converts as to this. The object, therefore, of this verse is to point out to the Ephesians that God by Himself giving them His Spirit had thereby placed on them His seal, in token to them and to others, that they were fellow-partakers of the one inheritance—"*our* inheritance," as the Apostle terms it.

Few will regard as satisfactory, the usual way of translating this verse by supplying some verb after ὑμεις such as προηλπικατε, or still worse, ηλπικατε, εκληρωθητε, or εστε. The only word that could, with any show of plausibility be supplied, is προηλπικατε : but if we admit that the "us" of the preceding verses is intended to include the Ephesians, it is impossible to suppose the ellipsis of προηλπικατε : for if the preceding verses include (as they certainly do) the Ephesians as well as St. Paul, then the Ephesians are expressly numbered among those "who had *first* hoped in Christ." Consequently, it is impossible to suppose that another verse should be added to affirm, and that *emphatically*, what had been already placed beyond a question. After the Apostle had declared that the Ephesians were numbered among those who "had *first* hoped in Christ," how could he add a clause saying, "in whom ye *also* first hoped?"

The words, "who have first hoped in Christ," are evidently co-extensive with being to the praise of His glory. All who shall be to the praise of His glory *at His appearing* are numbered among those "who have *first* hoped in Christ."

Some place the clause, "when ye heard the word of truth, the Gospel of your salvation," in a parenthesis; but it is better to regard it as an instance of interrupted structure *See Winer, part III. § 62.* We may point the passage thus; $εν ᾧ, και, υμεις, ακουσαντες τον λογον της αληθειας, το ευαγγελλιον της σωτηριας υμων—εν ᾧ και πιστευσαντες$ &c. The last $και$ is emphatic. It emphasizes $πιστευσαντες$; and pointedly designates the period of their believing as the occasion and time of their being "sealed:" for when a participle and verb in the same tense are thus combined, the actions expressed by them are either cotemporaneous, or so connected that the occurrence of one implies the sure consecution of the other, like two successive links in a moving chain the presence of one of which insures the coming of the other.* "When ye believed ye were sealed" gives the force more correctly than "*after* ye believed ye were sealed." In some cases of the use of the emphatic $και$ its connective force is faintly discernible. Such cases, however, are the exceptions. In the case before us the presence of $και$ before $πιστευσαντες$ implies "when ye believed as well as heard." A certain connection with $ακουσαντες$ is indicated.

Some have objected to the connexion of $εν ᾧ πιστευσαντες$, on the ground that the Apostle generally uses $πιστευω επι$ or $εις$. But why should not the Scripture vary its expressions? In Hebrew ב is continually subjoined to האמין, בטח and חסה, and like $εν$, signifies in such connexion the fixed rest of faith or hope. In the present chapter we have $πιστοις εν$ in the first verse, and $πιστιν εν τω κυριω$ in the fifteenth. See also $πιστιν εν δικαιοσυνῃ$ &c. in 2 Peter i. 1.

Were sealed &c.] He who seals is *God.* He seals the believer by

---

* *Immediate* consecution is expressed in most of the following examples, which are all taken from Matt. ii verse 3. $ακουσας εταραχθη.$ 4. $συναγαγων επυνθανετο.$ 7. $καλεσας ηκριβωσε.$ 7. $πεμψας ειπε.$ 8. $πορευθεντες εξετασατε.$ 9. $ακουσαντες επορευθησαν.$ 10. $ιδοντες εχαρησαν.$ 11. $ελθοντες ειδον.$ 11. $πεσοντες προσεκυνησαν.$ 11. $ανοιξαντες προσηνεγκαν$ &c.

giving him the Spirit—the Spirit so given being regarded not as the sealer, but as *the seal*. It is important to observe this throughout Scripture. See 2 Cor. i. 21. "Now He that is the stablisher" (ὁ βεβαιων, observe the abstract force of the present participle*) "of us with you in Christ, is God, who, moreover (και) sealed us and gave the earnest of the Spirit in our hearts." See also Eph. iv. 30: "and grieve not the Holy Spirit of God wherewith ye were sealed (i e. by God) unto the day of redemption." God by giving to believers the Holy Ghost marks them as by a seal as belonging unto Himself: just as monarchs mark with their seal that which they claim as theirs. It is the indication of right of possession—ὡστε ειναι δηλον ὁτι Θεου εστε λαχος και κληρος. *Theoph* "Sealing" is also to be regarded as indicating our designation by God unto the coming glory. Thus we are said to be sealed "unto (εις) the day of redemption ," so that the Spirit thus given is not only a mark, so to speak, of ownership on the part of God, but is also an indication that the faithfulness of God is engaged to bring us unto the appointed glory. Yet although all believers receive from God this seal, it does not follow that they are thereby filled with peace and joy; for they may grieve that Holy Spirit whereby they are sealed. In that case, the Holy Spirit may cause the heart in which He dwells to feel that He is grieved; and then sorrow rather than joy will flow from His presence. If He be grieved, and if the putting forth of His power to comfort and to sustain be hindered, other influences may be permitted to bear down upon the soul, causing darkness, perplexity and sorrow. Ability, therefore, to recognise that which is implied by the bestowment of the Spirit as God's seal, and carefulness in so walking as not to grieve Him, are two things especially to be sought after by those who would walk in the present comfort of the Holy Ghost.

The Spirit of promise.] The Spirit is called " the Spirit *of promise*," as being one of the great subjects of promise in the Prophetic Scriptures. See, for example, the prominence given in such a passage as Joel ii. 28, to the outpouring of the Spirit on Israel and on all flesh in the yet future day of Israel's forgiveness. That promised outpouring which will yet, in a day still future, be vouchsafed to Israel, has already been granted to us who have *first* hoped in Christ. Anti-

---

* For further remarks on this, see "Occasional Papers" Vol. I. No. II. p. 96. "On force of present tense in Greek and Hebrew."

cipating Israel we have already received the *Spirit of promise.* Compare Heb. vi. 5, where the miraculous gifts of the Spirit then given to the Church are called "powers of the age to come." ($\delta v v a \mu \epsilon \iota s$ $\mu \epsilon \lambda \lambda o v \tau o s$ $a \iota \omega v o s$.)

As regards the use of the genitive $\tau \eta s$ $\epsilon \pi a \gamma \gamma \epsilon \lambda \iota a s$, it is in accordance with the ordinary use of the genitive as "the *whence*-case." It denotes that the presence of the Spirit flows from and is the result of promise. The English idiom does not always admit the same *deictic* use of the article in emphatically designating an object, as the Greek. We must be careful, therefore, not to translate with some, "spirit of *the* promise"—"word of *the* truth."

Verse 14.

"Which is the earnest of our inheritance unto the redemption of appropriation unto the praise of His glory."

Earnest.] $A \rho \rho a \beta \omega v$, in Hebrew עֲרָבוֹן, is used in the Old Testament only in one chapter, viz. Gen. xxxviii. 17, 18, 20. There it occurs three times in the sense of "pledge" ($\epsilon v \epsilon \chi v \rho o v$), not of earnest. Judah's staff &c was a pledge to Tamar that he would send her the promised kid, but it was not left with her in the way of instalment or part payment. On the contrary, that which was given her was avowedly left as a pledge that was to be redeemed. By Greek and Latin writers, however, this word was used to denote a portion of the price paid in advance by a purchaser, in token that he would in good time complete the purchase by the payment of the whole sum; that which is thus given in the way of earnest not being given back as a mere pledge would be, but retained because received in part payment. $A \rho \rho a \beta \omega v$, η $\tau a \iota s$ $\tau a \iota s$ $\omega v \iota a \iota s$ $\pi \epsilon \rho \iota$ $\tau \omega v$ $\omega v o v \mu \epsilon v \omega v$ $\delta \iota \delta o \mu \epsilon v \eta$ $\pi \rho \omega \tau \eta$ $\kappa a \tau a \beta o \lambda \eta$ $v \pi \epsilon \rho$ $a \sigma \phi a \lambda \epsilon \iota a s$. *Suidas.*

Accordingly, in the passage before us, $a \rho \rho a \beta \omega v$ is used in its proper sense of "earnest"—as the earnest, however, of something to be freely *given*, not as purchase money paid in part. God has, in sovereign grace, bestowed on us an inheritance; and the Spirit, which is part of our inheritance, is given us as an earnest of that which is in all completeness to be given us, as soon as the appointed time for "the redemption of appropriation" comes.

The relative δs (δs $\epsilon \sigma \tau \iota$) agrees with $a \rho \rho a \beta \omega v$ that follows it. The relative often agrees in gender and number with a subsequent noun, especially when that noun is intended to be made prominent, either as defining or else specifying some important relation of the noun that precedes. See Mark xv. 16, $\tau\eta s\ \alpha v\lambda\eta s\ \dot{o}\ \epsilon\sigma\tau\iota\ \pi\rho\alpha\iota\tau\omega\rho\iota o\nu$: and Gal. iii 16, $\tau\omega\ \sigma\pi\epsilon\rho\mu\alpha\tau\iota\ \sigma o\upsilon,\ \dot{o}s\ \epsilon\sigma\tau\iota\ X\rho\iota\sigma\tau os$: and Rev. v. 8, $\theta\upsilon\mu\iota\alpha\mu\alpha\tau\omega\nu,\ \alpha\ddot{\iota}\ \epsilon\iota\sigma\iota\nu\ \alpha\dot{\iota}\ \pi\rho o\sigma\epsilon\upsilon\chi\alpha\iota\ \tau\omega\nu\ \dot{\alpha}\gamma\iota\omega\nu$. See *Winer, Gr. Gr.* § *xxiv*. 3.

Redemption of appropriation.—Our redemption is in one sense perfected: for we are already purchased by God and freed from the deserved judgment by means of that precious price which has been provided in the blood of Jesus, "in whom we have redemption through His blood &c." See verse 7. The redemption by payment, therefore, is already completed. But God hath not yet put forth His glorious power to take possession of and appropriate unto Himself that which the blood of His son hath purchased. His act in thus appropriating to Himself that which is already His by purchase, is termed the redemption of appropriation (appropriation-redemption), the genitive being adjectival according to the usual Hebrew idiom. In Hebrew, when a compound idea expressed by one noun followed by another in the genitive is to be made definite, it is done by prefixing the article to the noun in the genitive; as אִישׁ מִלְחָמָה *a man of war*, Josh. xvii. 1: but אַנְשֵׁי הַמִּלְחָמָה, the men of war, i.e. the war-men. Num. xxxi. 49. *Gesenius Gr.* § 109.

The Rheimish version (following the Vulgate "*in redemptionem acquisitionis*") translates, "the redemption of acquisition." See also Stephens Thesaurus, *ad liberationem vindicationis*, scilicet, *assertionis*. See also Scott and Liddell, word $\pi\epsilon\rho\iota\pi o\iota\eta\sigma\iota s$. Compare 1 Thess. v. 9, $\epsilon\iota s\ \pi\epsilon\rho\iota\pi o\iota\eta\sigma\iota\nu\ \sigma\omega\tau\eta\rho\iota\alpha s$, unto the acquiring of salvation; and $\epsilon\iota s\ \pi\epsilon\tau\iota\pi o\iota\eta\sigma\iota\nu\ \delta o\xi\eta s$, unto the acquiring of glory. 2 Thess. ii. 14. See also 1 Pet. iii. 9, $\lambda\alpha os\ \epsilon\iota s\ \pi\epsilon\rho\iota\pi o\iota\eta\sigma\iota\nu$, a people for appropriation, i.e. a people claimed by God as His own.

$\Pi\epsilon\rho\iota\pi o\iota\epsilon\omega$, means properly *to cause to remain over and above*, and hence, *to preserve or save.* Thus Lysias, $\tau\eta\nu\ \tau\epsilon\ \pi o\lambda\iota\nu\ \pi\epsilon\rho\iota\epsilon\pi o\iota\eta\sigma\epsilon$: and Sept. $I\omega\alpha\beta\ \pi\epsilon\rho\iota\epsilon\pi o\iota\eta\sigma\epsilon\ \tau o\ \lambda o\iota\pi o\nu\ \tau\eta s\ \pi o\lambda\epsilon\omega s$, answering to the Pihel of חיה in Hebrew. $\Pi\epsilon\rho\iota\pi o\iota\epsilon o\mu\alpha\iota$, in the middle, is frequently used in the Sept. in the sense of "to preserve or secure for one's self," as in Gen. xii. 12.—$\kappa\alpha\iota\ \alpha\pi o\kappa\tau\epsilon\nu o\upsilon\sigma\iota\ \mu\epsilon,\ \sigma\epsilon\ \delta\epsilon\ \pi\epsilon\rho\iota\pi o\iota\eta\sigma o\nu\tau\alpha\iota$. Hence in 2 Chr. xiv. 13, we find $\pi\epsilon\rho\iota\pi o\iota\eta\sigma\iota s$ used in the sense of *preservation* or *survival*, $\dot{\omega}\sigma\tau\epsilon\ \mu\eta\ \epsilon\iota\nu\alpha\iota\ \epsilon\nu\ \alpha\upsilon\tau o\iota s\ \pi\epsilon\rho\iota\pi o\iota\eta\sigma\iota\nu$ (מחיה). We find it used in the same sense in Heb. x.—$\dot{\eta}\mu\epsilon\iota s\ \delta\epsilon\ o\upsilon\kappa\ \epsilon\sigma\mu\epsilon\nu\ \dot{\upsilon}\pi o\sigma\tau o\lambda\eta s\ \epsilon\iota s\ \alpha\pi\omega\lambda\epsilon\iota\alpha\nu,\ \alpha\lambda\lambda\alpha\ \pi\iota\sigma\tau\epsilon\omega s\ \epsilon\iota s\ \pi\epsilon\rho\iota\pi o\iota\eta\sigma\iota\nu\ \psi\upsilon\chi\eta s$. "but we are not of withdrawal unto perdition; but of faith unto the saving of the soul." These are the only instances, either in the New Testament or Sept. in which περιποιησις is used in the sense of "*preserving.*"

Another meaning of περιποιεομαι, immediately deducible from that just noticed, is "*to claim or take possession of* as one's own"— *to appropriate.* Hence το μη προσηκον περιποιησασθαι, "*to appropriate that which is not his.*" Synesius. And Acts xx. 28, ην περιεποιησατο δια του αιματος του ιδιου, "which He acquired or made His own by His own blood." And 1 Tim. iii. 13, βαθμον εαυτοις καλον περιποιουνται—"acquire for themselves a good degree." Hence the use of περιποιησις in 1 Thess. v. 9, and 2 Thess. ii. 14, quoted above.

No example can be produced of περιποιησις used in the sense of *possession*, i.e. as denoting *the thing possessed*. Such a use of περιποιησις is not found in the Septuagint, where indeed it is only used twice: once, in the sense of "preserving" in 2 Ch. xiv. 13 already referred to, and once in Mal. iii. 17—a passage that has, not unfrequently, been inaccurately rendered. "And they shall be mine (והיו לי) saith the Lord of Hosts, in the day which I עשה סגלה—literally, *make property*, i.e. *appropriate to myself as mine.*" Hence the Sept. renders—και εσονται μοι λεγει κυριος παντοκρατωρ εις ημεραν ην εγω ποιω εις περιποιησιν. "And they shall be mine, saith the Lord, for the day which I make for appropriation." The Sept. does not connect, as many have imagined, εσονται μοι with εις περιποιησιν, nor can the Hebrew be so taken. The connexion is עשה סגלה—ποιω εις περιποιησιν. It may also be observed that when סגלה is taken not phraseologically as when combined with עשה, but independently, it is never rendered in the Sept. by περιποιησις, but by περιουσιος or περιουσιασμος, words to which they seemed to have attached the thought of *a remaining* or *surviving possession* (from περιειμι)—*a residue,* and therefore something regarded peculiarly as one's own. This is quite a different shade of meaning from that conveyed by περιποιησις, where the thought of *acquisition* or *appropriation* predominates.

The redemption of appropriation will reach not the Church of the first-born, i.e. those who have *first*-hoped in Christ merely; but will affect Israel, the earth, creation—in a word, everything that is to be brought under the shelter of redemption.

Verse 15.

"*Therefore, I, seeing that I heard of your faith in the Lord Jesus, and love unto all the saints, cease not giving thanks for you, making mention of you in my prayers.*

Therefore] Δια τουτο. In consequence of this—that is, in consequence of God having called His people into such blessings as have been detailed. *I* (καγω)—the και being emphatic; to be expressed either by emphasis of the voice, or by rendering, "I, on my part." The effect produced on *me*, says the Apostle, by all this, is that I give thanks for you, and pray for further increase of blessing upon you. The ground of this thanksgiving and prayer was two-fold: first, the knowledge of the blessings which the Ephesians had in common with all saints; secondly, his having heard of their faith and love practically manifested. This supplied to the Apostle a ground not only for thanksgiving, but for prayer for increase of blessing. "To him that hath shall more be given." Although it be true that all who are of the family of faith are blessed, yet prayer for those who, like the Galatians and Corinthians, need to be recalled from ways of evil, cannot be of the same character as that offered for those who are advancing in paths of righteousness and truth. There may be prayer "with many tears," as well as prayer "with thanksgiving."

Your faith] Την καθ' υμας πιστιν. This is not the same as την πιστιν υμων. The former expression presents them in a corporate aspect—the faith which prevails *throughout* you as a body—in accordance the force of κατα as denoting *extension*. Compare Acts xxvi. 3—τα κατα τους Ιουδαιους εθη and Acts xxvii. 12, λιμον κατα την χωραν. See especially Acts xviii. 15, νομου καθ' υμας—"the law *which prevails throughout you as a people*," compared with τω νομω τω υμετερω addressed to the Pharisees, John viii. 17,—"the law *which ye recognise and boast in as your law.*" In the case before us καθ' υμας is of course more forcible than simply υμων. See *Jelf on κατα* § 620. *and Ellicott and Alford in locum*. Εις τους αγιους. Εις must not be rendered either here or elsewhere *towards*. It indicates not mere tendency or progress toward a point, but attainment. The point is reached.

Cease not giving thanks] Ου παυομαι ευχαριστων. The force of the present participle as indicating habitual or constantly continued action, should be noted. "The Participle denotes an action performed, or a state existing not occasioned or produced by the subject of the principal verb. Ουκ επαυοντο διδασκοντες is *teaching* (or as teachers) they ceased not; ειδον καθημενον, they *saw him as one sitting*." See Winer

Part iii. § xlv. "The participle points to a state already in existence" (Ellicott.) In Luke we find επαιτειν αισχυνομαι—"to beg I am ashamed," the person spoken of not having begun to beg: whereas if the person had already begun to beg επαιτων αισχυνομαι would have been used. See *Winer* as already quoted.

Verse 17.

"*That the God of our Lord Jesus Christ, the Father of glory, might give unto you the Spirit of wisdom and revelation in the knowledge of Him: the eyes of your heart being lightened; that ye might know what is the hope of His calling, and what the riches of the glory of His inheritance in the saints.*"

The Father of glory.] God, as the God of *glory*, hath called us, even as He called Abraham. See Acts vii. 2. "Calling," thus used, is a word of certainty. "Whom He *called*, them He also glorified" Rom. viii. 30. Our inheritance, therefore, is secure. But *to have* blessings is not the same thing as *to apprehend* them. We need, therefore, that the Spirit who dwelleth in us should develop to our souls and give to us ability to search into and comprehend the things that have been freely bestowed upon us. The blessings are given to us solely on the ground of the merits of Christ, but the power of apprehending them is from the Holy Ghost. God is spoken of in the Scripture as "giving the Spirit" when He gives any fresh developments of the power of the Spirit. Compare Luke xi. 13, with this passage. It is in this sense that believers who already have the Spirit personally dwelling in them, ask for the Holy Spirit, that is, they ask for the more abundant supply (επιχωρηγια Philippians i. 19.) thereof, in the way of development and gift.

As regards the form of expression, compare Acts vii. 2, ὁ Θεος της δοξης: also Luke xvi. 8, τον οικονομον της αδικιας: and xviii. 6, ὁ κριτης της αδικιας. In these and like instances the Genitive is expressive of characteristic quality or condition. See Winer § xxxiv. Glory characteristically attaches to the Father as an essential element in the Divine condition of being.

That He might give—ἱνα δῳη.] The optative δῳη for δοιη, not the subjunctive δῳη is here used. This is unusual: ἱνα in the New Testament being almost always followed by the subjunctive. I believe the only other exception is chap. iii. 16 in this epistle, where ἱνα δῳη again occurs in similar connexion. In Acts xxvii. 42, $\delta\iota\alpha\phi\upsilon\gamma\eta$ is the right reading, not $\delta\iota\alpha\phi\upsilon\gamma\omicron\iota$.

When the optative is used in a dependent clause, it expresses less certainty than the subjunctive. "The Subjunctive may denote an intended result *of the occurrence of which the speaker entertains no doubt whatever.* Compare Mark viii. 6, $\epsilon\delta\iota\delta\omicron\upsilon$ $\tau\omicron\iota\varsigma$ $\mu\alpha\theta\eta\tau\alpha\iota\varsigma$ $\alpha\upsilon\tau\omicron\upsilon$ $\iota\nu\alpha$ $\pi\alpha\rho\alpha\theta\omega\sigma\iota\nu$ (*that they might put before the multitude*—which they could not possibly hesitate to do). See also Acts xxv. 26—$\pi\rho\omicron\eta\gamma\alpha\gamma\omicron\nu$ $\alpha\upsilon\tau\omicron\nu$ $\epsilon\phi'$ $\upsilon\mu\omega\nu$, $\omicron\pi\omega\varsigma$ $\tau\eta\varsigma$ $\alpha\nu\alpha\kappa\rho\iota\sigma\epsilon\omega\varsigma$ $\gamma\epsilon\nu\omicron\mu\epsilon\nu\eta\varsigma$ $\sigma\chi\omega$ $\tau\iota$ $\gamma\rho\alpha\psi\omega$. The optative would express the design of effecting an uncertain result." *Winer* § xli. *part* iii. This, however, must be regarded as somewhat an over-statement as respects the New Testament.

It has been much debated whether the notion of purpose or design can be traced in all the uses of $\iota\nu\alpha$. I think it can. As respects the use of the infinitive simply, or the infinitive preceded by $\epsilon\iota\varsigma$ and the article, or the use of $\iota\nu\alpha$ or $\omicron\pi\omega\varsigma$ $\alpha\nu$, the following observations will be found, I believe, to need little qualification.

In the case of an action expressed by a verb in a dependent clause it may be our wish to direct attention primarily to the act itself, without giving any prominence to antecedent circumstances. In that case we should use the infinitive simply, as $\eta\lambda\theta\omicron\mu\epsilon\nu$ $\pi\rho\omicron\sigma\kappa\upsilon\nu\eta\sigma\alpha\iota$, we came to worship; the fact of the worshipping being that on which the attention is to be fixed. But if we wish to indicate that the action or condition expressed by the secondary verb is not only the consequence, but the *certain* consequence of the action or purpose expressed by the first verb *being carried into effect*, then we prefix $\epsilon\iota\varsigma$ $\tau\omicron$ to the infinitive as, $\lambda\epsilon\gamma\omega$ $\delta\epsilon$ $I\eta\sigma\omicron\upsilon\nu$ $X\rho\iota\sigma\tau\omicron\nu$ $\delta\iota\alpha\kappa\omicron\nu\omicron\nu$ $\gamma\epsilon\gamma\epsilon\nu\eta\sigma\theta\alpha\iota$ . . . . . $\epsilon\iota\varsigma$ $\tau\omicron$ $\beta\epsilon\beta\alpha\iota\omega\sigma\alpha\iota$ &c., "hath become a minister of the circumcision &c. to effect the confirmation &c."—$\epsilon\iota\varsigma$ indicating a condition not sought after merely, but *attained*. Or again, we may wish not to fix attention on the result (whether attained or not) but to give prominence to the thought of purpose or design on the part of the agent. In this case $\iota\nu\alpha$ with the subjunctive or optative would be used, as $\tau\alpha\upsilon\tau\alpha$ $\delta\epsilon$ $\gamma\epsilon\gamma\rho\alpha\pi\tau\alpha\iota$ $\iota\nu\alpha$ $\upsilon\mu\epsilon\iota\varsigma$ $\pi\iota\sigma\tau\epsilon\upsilon\sigma\eta\tau\epsilon$, "these things are written with the design that ye should believe." Or lastly, we may desire to direct attention especially to *the mode* in which the proposed result is to be obtained, in which case we should use $\omicron\pi\omega\varsigma$ or $\omicron\pi\omega\varsigma$ $\alpha\nu$, as; $\mu\epsilon\tau\alpha\nu\omicron\eta\sigma\alpha\tau\epsilon$ $\omicron\upsilon\nu$ $\kappa\alpha\iota$ $\epsilon\pi\iota\sigma\tau\rho\epsilon\psi\alpha\tau\epsilon$ $\epsilon\iota\varsigma$ $\tau\omicron$ $\epsilon\xi\alpha\lambda\epsilon\iota\phi\theta\eta\nu\alpha\iota$ $\upsilon\mu\omega\nu$ $\tau\alpha\varsigma$ $\alpha\mu\alpha\rho\tau\iota\alpha\varsigma$ $\omicron\pi\omega\varsigma$ $\alpha\nu$ $\epsilon\lambda\theta\omega\sigma\iota$ &c. "Repent and be converted for (i.e. to attain unto; to reach as the result—$\epsilon\iota\varsigma$ τo) the blotting out of your sins, that so (or that *in that way*, $\H{o}\pi\omega\varsigma$ $a\nu$) the times of refreshing might come," &c Thus $\H{o}\pi\omega\varsigma$ marks very decidedly that the circumstances referred to in the first clause are necessary as antecedents to the result referred to in the second; and also fixes *the attention very especially on the nature of such antecedent action as the mode by which the result is to be attained.* This is not the case with $\H{\iota}\nu a$. Even if the circumstances mentioned in the first clause should be needful to the result mentioned in the dependent clause, yet, even then, $\H{\iota}\nu a$ does not give *prominence* to that thought, nor to the mode of the action, but directs attention to the design or desire of the agent. If the sentences in which $\H{\iota}\nu a$ is used are analysed and expanded by the supply of the ellipsis, its proper force as indicating design may, I believe, in every case, be detected.

The eyes of your heart—$\tau o \upsilon\varsigma$ $o\phi\theta a\lambda\mu o\upsilon\varsigma$ $\tau\eta\varsigma$ $\kappa a\rho\delta\iota a\varsigma.$] That is, your inward eyes—the eyes of the inner man, "heart" being frequently used in Scripture to denote that which is inward as contrasted with that which is outward. Whatever the power of our vision, we see little or nothing if obscurity or darkness surround us. But when light is poured upon us plentifully, and objects are placed distinctly before us and our eye strengthened and guided, then truly we may be said *to see*. Accordingly, the especial subject of the Apostle's prayer was that God would give unto them the Spirit of *revelation* as well as of knowledge, that unseen realities might be presented as in a flood of light, clearly and vividly to the apprehensions of their souls. The meaning of $\phi\omega\tau\iota\zeta\omega$ is to lighten, i.e. to shed light on a person or thing, as in Luke xi. 36, "as when a lamp doth by its shining lighten thee"—$\H{\omega}\varsigma$ $\H{o}\tau a\nu$ $\H{o}$ $\lambda\upsilon\chi\nu o\varsigma$ $\tau\eta$ $a\sigma\tau\rho a\pi\eta$ $\phi\omega\tau\iota\zeta\eta$ $\sigma\epsilon$. Increase of heavenly light is one of the greatest blessings that the soul of a believer can seek for. It should be carefully observed that the blessing here sought was not the removal of any film from their inward eye as if they were in an unhealthful spiritual condition, but the blessing asked was *increase* of vivid light to those who already had light and walked in it.

As regards the grammatical construction $\pi\epsilon\phi\omega\tau\iota\sigma\mu\epsilon\nu o\upsilon\varsigma$ $\tau o\upsilon\varsigma$ $o\phi\theta a\lambda\mu o\upsilon\varsigma$ should not be taken as an accusative absolute. It is either an example of irregular construction [see Alford, who quotes as parallel Soph. Elect. 479, $\H{\upsilon}\pi\epsilon\sigma\tau\iota$ $\mu o\iota$ $\theta\rho a\sigma o\varsigma$ $a\delta\upsilon\pi\nu o\omega\nu$ $\kappa\lambda\upsilon o\upsilon\sigma a\nu$ $a\rho\tau\iota\omega\varsigma$ $o\nu\epsilon\iota\rho a\tau\omega\nu$ and Æsch. Choeph. 396.—$\pi\epsilon\pi a\lambda\tau a\iota$ $\delta'a\upsilon\tau\epsilon$ $\mu o\iota$ $\phi\iota\lambda o\nu$ $\kappa\epsilon a\rho$ $\tau o\nu\delta\epsilon$ $\kappa\lambda\upsilon o\upsilon\sigma a\nu$ $o\iota\kappa\tau o\nu$] or, which is better, it may be taken as an instance of ellipsis to be supplied, just as our translators have done in Acts xxvi. 3. "I think myself happy, King Agrippa, because I shall answer for myself this day before thee (επι σου) touching all the things whereof I am accused of the Jews: especially [because I know] thee to be expert (μαλιστα γνωστην οντα σε). The construction would then be—"that God might grant unto you the Spirit of wisdom &c. [thereby causing you to become] lightened as to eyes of your heart &c."

That ye may know.] Εις το ειδεναι. Attained result is expressed by these words. Lightened so as to attain unto the knowing. Εις never means "*towards*" simply. It always indicates attainment either proposed or secured.

What is the hope of His calling &c.] Some have strangely said that ελπις never indicates the "*res sperata*"—the object hoped for. But Col. i. 5 supplies a marked example—"for the hope that is laid up for you in heaven." "Calling" is here a word of certainty. "Whom He called, them . . . . . . He also glorified."

And what the riches of the glory of His inheritance in the saints.] The great fact that God hath made the Church (and by the Church I mean all the redeemed) His own inheritance, has been before referred to in the 11th verse. It is in this aspect more especially that the redeemed are viewed in this Epistle—whence the fulness of its comfort. We well know how the honour and glory of a person becomes identified, so to speak, with the condition of his inheritance. All his resources and all his energies are directed toward it for good. By its honour he is honoured: by its glory he is glorified. Such is the relation unto Himself in which God hath been pleased to set the redeemed. He has chosen for His inheritance, not angels, but the Church; and has endowed it in a manner worthy of its high destiny. Christ in all the perfectness of His person, and services, and offices, and love (for He is the husband of His Church as well as its Redeemer) is the great gift of God unto His people. In this Epistle, our thoughts are directed not only to the grace of God in giving that which He hath given, but the unspeakable greatness of the gift is brought before us, and its results in bringing us from that infinite distance in which sin had placed us, and preserving us through all circumstances until we are made in glory "the fulness of Him who filleth all in all." Hence this Epistle peculiarly sets us in the place of passive recipiency as the subjects of the formative action of His almighty and all-gracious hand who worketh all things after the counsel of His own will. His love and His power are directed towards His inheritance to bless it and to do it good, and that for ever and ever. When the time of manifestation comes "He shall be glorified in His saints, and admired in all them that believe." The *riches* of His glory will be displayed in the saints when manifested as His inheritance.

Verse 19.

"*And what the surpassing greatness of His power* (δυναμις) *unto us who believe, according to the working of the might* (κρατος) *of His strength* (ισχυς) *which He wrought in Christ when He raised Him from the dead, and caused Him to sit at His own right hand in the heavenly places, high above all rule and authority, and power, and dominion, and every name that is named, not only in this age, but also in that which is to come; and did set all things under His feet, and gave Him, (as) head over all things to the Church, which is His body, the fulness of Him that filleth all in all.*"

And what the surpassing greatness of His power &c.] Power when spoken of as to its capability—its ability to work out its purposes is δυναμις: when spoken of with reference to its *strength*, which may be passive and undisplayed (see Ellicott) it is ισχυς: its *might* evinced in action is κρατος. Throughout the New Testament δυναμις may commonly be translated, *power:* ισχυς, *strength:* κρατος, *might:* εξουσια, *authority:* this last word referring to the title on which power is exercised, or privilege claimed.

The most marvellous act of Divine power ever yet manifested, was that by which the great Substitute who had obeyed and suffered in the stead of His people, and thereby *accomplished* their justification, was afterwards raised from the dead and set at God's right hand in the heavenly places. By resurrection and ascension into glory, Christ has been avowedly constituted "Head over ALL things." However earth may blaspheme, Heaven has witnessed His exaltation, and owned Him as Lord of all. But He is not only made "Head over all things." As such, He is appointed to be Head, in another sense, of His body the Church. *Governmental* headship is that which is denoted by the expression, "Head over all things," and such headship does not involve *union* between Him who rules and those who are ruled. But the relation of the head to the body is not one of mere presidency or control: it is a relation of union in life; and such is Christ's relation to the Church. Being "Head over all things," He is also, in the other sense, Head of His body, the Church. Consequently, we are not only blessed *under* Him or *with* Him, but we are also blessed *in* Him; that is, *in union with* Him—a relation which the holy angels have not, though they are under Him as "Head over all things." Even then as Adam was, whilst in Eden, our representative and there sinned and ruined us, so Christ became in this lost earth the Representative of His believing people. Having here obeyed and suffered in their stead, and thereby completed their justification, He ascended into the heavens still to be our Representative there. He is there our "first-fruits" and our "forerunner." See 1 Cor. xv. 20, and Heb. vi. 20. This enables us, even now, speaking of that which pertains to us in the right of our Representative in the heavens to say, "old things have passed away; behold all things have become new." God is pleased, even now, to view and to treat us as belonging to that "new creation" of which Christ is the beginning and the Head. See Rev. iii. 14.

Again, seeing that Christ is not only our Representative, but that He is united to us no less closely than the head is united to the body, this marks the mode of our participation in His glory as something no less wonderful than the fact of the participation itself. We are not only to be glorified with Him, but glorified as His body; thus being "the fulness of Him who filleth all in all."

Moreover, as a consequence of this union with Him in His present glory, a power, different indeed in development, but analogous in character to that which raised Him from the dead, works even now in believers. It is this that is referred to in the words before us—"the surpassing greatness of His power unto (not *toward* merely) us who believe." It is again referred to in the concluding verses of the third chapter. "Now unto Him that is able to do exceeding abundantly above all that we ask or think, *according to the power that worketh in us*, unto Him be glory in the Church by Christ Jesus throughout all ages, world without end. Amen." This power (though its operation may be greatly obstructed and its presence be little, if at all, recognised) does, nevertheless, work in all God's believing people. It worketh even in the feeblest of us who believe, accompanying us through all circumstances, whether of life or of death, until the hour when, suddenly put forth in all its fulness, it shall change us altogether into the glorious likeness of our risen Lord, and supply us with practical ability to walk with Him on our high places. And if even the Ephesians needed the prayer of the Apostle that they might be caused to apprehend the working and character of this glorious power that had reached them, how much more must believers need to be so prayed for now. It is well for us that we have an Advocate with the Father who ever liveth to make intercession for us, for our apprehensions are limited and our faith weak. Feebly do we recognise either the fact that we have such a Priest officially to represent us and care for our interests in the Courts of heaven, or the further fact that we are ourselves *representatively*, though not actually, in the heavens, in virtue of our Priest being also our new covenant Head with whom we are one—He being the head—we the members; so that "as He is, so are we" in the judicial estimate of God, and in the estimate of faith. Feebly do we recognise these things: yet least of all perhaps, do we estimate the present operation in us of that glorious power whereby we might be "strengthened to all patience and long-suffering with joyfulness." It was to this power doubtless, that the Apostle referred when he said,—"that I might know the power of His resurrection and the fellowship of His sufferings." Yet, notwithstanding the feebleness and imperfectness of our apprehensions, these blessings are not taken away from us; for grace has given them, not in the title of our names or of our strength, but in the title of the name of Immanuel.

Unto us who believe.] Εις ἡμας, not as in our version, "to us-ward," but "unto us." See remarks on εις in preceding note. The power spoken of *has reached* us, and works in us.

It is exceedingly important to mark the limitation indicated by the words "who believe." The attention of many in the mere *professing* Church has been recently directed to the subject of Christ's heavenly Headship. They had before in a sense universalized regeneration by ascribing it to all the baptized: they have now actually universalized union with Christ by teaching that when He assumed humanity into union with His Divine Person, He did thereby unite all men unto Himself. If this had been so, all men would most certainly be saved: for all who are "in Christ" are sure heirs of glory.

But it is all a fiction. The Son of God by taking man's nature did not thereby become the Representative of *all* men, nor did He unite *all* men unto Himself. He became the Representative not of those who believe *not*, but of them that believe: and such only have union with Him—a union that is not in the flesh, but in the Spirit. "As many as received Him, to them gave He power (εξουσιαν, *authority* or *title*) to become the children of God, even to them that believe on His name: who were born, not of blood, nor of the will of the flesh, nor of the will of man, but of God." John i. 12. The mere possession of a common nature does not constitute union. Two vines growing side by side have a common nature, for they are both vines; but there is no union between them unless the one be so graffed into the other that there is the flow of the same sap, and so community of life. There is no abstract common nature such as the Realists dreamed of, forming a point of union to all the individuals of a like species. Every system formed upon this thought is folly and falsehood. Christ by the mere fact of taking man's nature, united no one unto Himself. He came to be the "new thing" in the earth—Immanuel, God manifest in the flesh. He came therefore as One whose personal condition was isolated, singular, and unlike that of all others But when any through faith, became livingly united to Him, a oneness was then established between Him and them, which continues for evermore.

It must be remembered, therefore, that none are to be included within the scope of such a passage as this, except those who are actually reached by the power and grace spoken of. Although all God's elect people are chosen in Christ, and will in due time be called into participation of the blessings here described, yet the glorious power here mentioned does not reach them, nor work in them until they have believed and received the Holy Ghost. Till then they are not "quickened" nor "seated in heavenly places in Christ;" on the contrary, they remain "dead in trespasses and sins." Accordingly, St. Paul speaks of those who "were in Christ before him" (Rom. xvi. 7), and yet Paul and they were all chosen in Christ together before the foundation of the world. The family of faith from Abel downwards, has always had its living representatives in the earth; and it is of such living representatives that the expressions by which Scripture defines their condition at any given period of their history, are to be understood; remembering always that whatever everlasting blessings are given in Christ are as truly possessed by that portion of the family of faith that lived before the period of their full development at Pentecost as by those who have lived subsequently; for they are all given, not on the ground of anything connected with our own personal condition, but altogether in the title of the name of Christ From a description, therefore, of the eternal blessings of the redeemed at any given period of their history, we learn also what pertains to all those who have gone before and entered into their rest, as well as those that will pertain to all who shall, at any future period, be born into the family of faith.

The Church which is His body.] We must be exceedingly careful not to limit the words of such a passage as this to "the Church *of the first-born ones*," that is, those who being "Christ's at His coming," shall rise in the *first* resurrection. They when they enter into their glory, are only "first-fruits"—"first-born ones." Their very glory will be a pledge that all who shall afterwards (i.e. during the millennium) be born into the family of faith shall inherit like glory. All the redeemed, finally, shall "reign in life through one Jesus Christ" (Rom. v. 17) and shall alike bear the image of the Heavenly One, being changed into His risen likeness. Which of the blessings mentioned in the concluding part of the fifth of Romans and in 1 Cor. xv. (and there are no higher blessings, for they involve union with and likeness to Christ in heavenly life and glory)—which of these blessings are not true of all the redeemed of every dispensation? All the redeemed were chosen in Christ before the foundation of the world—all, subsequently at the time when they believe receive life in Him—all are made members of His mystical body—all are children of that heavenly City which is the mother of us all. Exclusion from that one body, or from that heavenly City is perdition. See Rev. xxii. 19.

The attempt made by some to divide the redeemed, and to exclude from the Church and the Church's eternal glory the saints of the Old Testament, as well as those who shall be converted during the millennial age, cannot be too earnestly condemned. It is a doctrine so false that it could only be maintained by supposing that there are two ways and two ends of salvation—in fact two Gospels and two Christs. The Scripture teaches us that all who are of faith, in whatsoever dispensation they may live, are redeemed—that they are redeemed by, and quickened in, one Christ—and that having Christ they "have all things." Destroy this relation of all the redeemed to Christ, and you destroy Christianity as taught in the Holy Scripture.*

The limits of the present paper would be exceeded if we were to discuss this subject fully. At present I content myself with the following general statements, some of which, indeed, have been already made.

I. That "the Church" in its eternal sense includes all the redeemed of every dispensation.

II. That although "the Church of the first-born-ones" is complete

---

* See a Tract entitled "Old Testament Saints not excluded from the Church of God," as advertised at end.

when the Lord returns at the commencement of the millennium, yet the Church as a whole is not complete until the close of the millennium.

III. That the Church being " chosen in Christ," and having " the promise of life in Him before the world was," has necessarily a oneness of everlasting blessing which nothing can destroy. Its members whilst on earth may be in a condition of pupilage (which they were whilst under the Law, see Gal. iv. 1.) or in the more advanced condition they now hold under the Gospel, but this temporary and dispensational difference in no way affects their eternal standing in Christ.

IV. That the Church's eternal blessings and glories were gradually revealed: but that when once made known, they were made known as the portion not only of those to whom the knowledge was first communicated, but as the portion of all of the one family of faith who had preceded, or who should follow after, those to whom the knowledge was so communicated.

V. That whilst we have to remember that the being quickened in Christ and seated in heavenly places in Him, is an accomplished fact true of the feeblest believer (because dependent not on the power of his apprehension of it through the Spirit, but on the fact of the resurrection of his Lord into glory), yet we have likewise to remember that the resurrection of our Head, whilst it brings us representatively into Heaven and opens Heaven to our faith, yet leaves us personally below, to find in earth the sphere of our conflicts and service.

VI. That the blessed fact of being "quickened in Christ" and " alive unto God in Him," does not imply that we are to be practically dead to *every thing* below. On the contrary, whilst seeking to be dead unto sin, and unto the world *morally* (for we have died unto both in Christ) we are to seek to live to every thing in the earth that is according to God; for there are in the earth things good as well as evil—there are the people of God, His interests, His truth, and in living to such things and in discharging aright the humblest duties required of us by God, we live unto God. We are not therefore to say with the Jesuit, " Mortuus sum. I am a dead man. Touch not, taste not, handle not;" nor are we to say I am alive only to God in Heaven; but we are to seek so to live to Him in the earth that He may not only be *in* us and *with* us in the sense in which He is *in* and *with* all His believing people, but that He may also be *with* us in the sense of approving fellowship as sanctioning our habits and ways. " If a man love me, he will keep my words: and my Father will love him and we will come unto him and make our abode with him." This is the greatest of all present blessings in the earth. We are not therefore to seek to ignore the earth as the sphere of our present service, because we are representatively in Heaven, and because by faith we enter Heaven and go within the veil to comfort ourselves and to strengthen ourselves for conflicts below.

Lastly, the truth of heavenly union with Christ, which is made so prominent in the Epistle to the Ephesians, does not supersede or render of secondary value the equally precious truth revealed in such an Epistle as that to the Hebrews. On the contrary, he whose soul most enters into the truths of the Epistle to the Ephesians will most prize the truths that characterise the Hebrews: for he who most appreciates his heavenly union with Christ, and seeks in consequence to live as a heavenly person here, will most feel his need of that blood and mediation and intercession of which the Epistle to the Hebrews treats. By the height and dignity of our calling we have to measure the evil of failure or shortcoming in it: and what meets the sense of such failure except those everlasting mercies which the Epistle to the Hebrews so peculiarly unfolds?

Notes on Psalm LXVIII.

To Him that presideth. A Psalm of David—a song.

Verses 1, 2, 3.

1 Let God arise, let His enemies be scattered;
  And let them that hate Him flee from before His face.

2 As the driving away of smoke, so do Thou drive them away;
  As the melting of wax before the fire,
  So let the wicked perish from before the face of God.

3 But let the righteous be glad, let them exult before God,
  Yea, let them rejoice with exceeding joy.

Let God arise &c.] This Psalm belongs to that yet future hour when "the transgressors having come to the full," God shall at last rend the veil from the heart of Israel; forgive them, deliver them from their enemies; re-gather those of them that are scattered; lead part of them in triumph through the wilderness; establish His glory on Zion, His holy mountain; and re-occupy His sanctuary in Jerusalem.

In these and like parts of Scripture the Prophet, carried onward in prophetic vision into the distant future, describes briefly and rapidly the objects that are successively presented to his view. Hence the abruptness of many of the utterances, and the quickness of transition. The scope of the Psalm is comprehensive. Commencing from the period when God will arise to deliver Israel, it concludes with a reference to the final establishment of His glory in Zion, and His worship as the God of the whole earth in Jerusalem.

The last deed of daring that human wickedness will, *in this dispensation*, attempt, is, the formation of a mighty confederacy against Israel, with the view of utterly extinguishing them and blotting out their name. "Come, and let us cut them off from being a nation; that the name of Israel may be no more in remembrance." See the whole of Psalm lxxxiii. How nearly Israel will be crushed may be seen from Joel ii. But "the Lord shall judge His people, and repent Himself for His servants, when He seeth that their power is gone, and there is none shut up or left." See Deut. xxxii. 36. So also Psalm cxxiv. "If it had not been the Lord who was on our side, now may Israel say; if it had not been the Lord who was on our side, when men rose up against us: then they had swallowed us up quick when their wrath was kindled against us. Then the waters had overwhelmed us, the stream had gone over our soul: then the proud waters had gone over our soul. Blessed be the Lord who hath not given us as a prey to their teeth." These words need no comment. They evidently belong to the time when God will place Himself "on the side" of Israel, when He will "render vengeance to His adversaries," and will be "merciful to His land and to His people." The ancient cry of Israel when the Ark of the Covenant moved at their head was, "Arise, Jehovah, and let thine enemies be scattered, and let them that hate thee flee before thee." Num. x. 35. This cry will once more be heard at the period to which the commencing verse of the Psalm we are now considering belongs; for then He whom the Ark typified—the Messiah of Israel, will have placed Himself at their head, so that "he that is feeble among them at that day shall be as David; and the house of David shall be as God, as the angel of the Lord before them." Never more "from that day and onwards," will these words of triumph, "Let God arise &c.," be taken from the lips of Israel. The occasions on which they will be uttered and responded to will be various, for the enemies of Israel after Israel have been taken under the protection of their heavenly King, will be many. Even after the destruction of the mighty hosts that Antichrist will lead from Armageddon into the valley of Jehoshaphat (see Joel iii.), many foes of Israel will remain; just as of old Amalek and Moab, Ammon and many others, remained after the overthrow of Pharoah in the Red Sea. Yet, however numerous the foes that may resist or assail *forgiven* Israel, they shall never be permitted to triumph over them even for a moment. After Israel have been caused "to look on Him whom they have pierced," they shall ever be known as the people whom Jehovah protects, and whom Jehovah blesses. The *last* great confederacy against Israel will be in the next dispensation, at the close of the Millennium, when Satan, loosed out of his prison, shall again deceive the nations, and gather them together from the four quarters of the earth against "the citadel ($\tau\eta\nu$ $\pi\alpha\rho\epsilon\mu\beta o\lambda\eta\nu$) of the saints" on Zion,* and against Jerusalem "the beloved city." See Rev. xx. 9. An earlier, and somewhat similar gathering of the same nations against Israel, is described in Ezekiel xxxviii.; but *this* takes place not at the close, but at the commencement of the Millennium, and before the full development of Israel's millennial blessing is attained. The gathering described in Ezekiel is, therefore, to be carefully distinguished from that referred to in Rev. xx. Both utterly fail. Israel, without an effort on their part, are defended and triumph, for "God is with them."

As the driving away of smoke &c.] These words will find their first and great fulfilment in the destruction of those mighty hosts which, gathered at Armageddon (Rev. xvi. 16), will thence march on Jerusalem (Is. x. 28), and entering the valley of Jehoshaphat (Joel iii. 9) will there be trodden as in the winepress. See Joel iii. 13 and Rev. xiv. 20. The suddenness and completeness of their destruction is often referred to in Scripture "As a snail that melteth, let every one of them pass away: like the untimely birth of a woman, that they may not see the sun. Before your pots can feel the thorns, He shall take them away as with a whirlwind, both living and in His wrath." Ps. lviii. 8. Luther comments on the force of these two emblems, smoke and wax. "The smoke disappears before the wind; the wax before the fire. It is most contemptuous to compare to smoke and wax such mighty enemies who think that they can combat heaven and earth."

But let the righteous rejoice &c.] The servants of God shall no longer have to say as now that "he who departeth from evil maketh himself a prey"—that "Truth falleth in the streets, and equity cannot enter." On the contrary, righteousness, blessed and prospered from on high, shall then flourish in the earth. Compare the conclusion of the song of Deborah, whose victory foreshadowed this future triumph of Israel's King "So let all thine enemies perish, O Jehovah, but let them that love Him be as the sun when he goeth forth in his might." Judges v. 31.

---

* See notes on Psalm lxxxiv. in succeeding paper.

Verse 4.

4 Sing unto God, sing psalms unto His name;
   Cast up a highway for Him who rideth in the deserts*
In the power of Jah His name, and exult before Him.

Who rideth in the deserts &c.] The desert and the wilderness, especially those deserts and wildernesses that begirt the Land of Immanuel, will be peculiarly the sphere where the mighty power of the Jehovah of Israel will be displayed, when the Lord sets to His hand the second time to recover Israel; of whom, however, only a remnant shall be spared. See Is. x. 21, 22. Of those of Israel left in their Land " a third part" only will be spared. Zech. xiii. 8, 9. Others scattered in distant lands will be slowly gathered "one by one." Is xxvii. 12 Others will be brought by repentant Gentile nations as an offering to Jehovah. See Is. xviii. 7 and Zeph. iii. 10, translating the latter passage thus: "From beyond the rivers of Cush (the Nile and Euphrates) they (the nations) shall bring as an offering to me, my suppliants the daughter of my dispersed."† But a fourth division of Israel will be brought by the Lord into the wilderness, as of old, there to be disciplined, proved, and finally led (the Lord being at their head) triumphantly to Zion. "Arise, O Jehovah, into thy rest; thou and the ark of thy strength. Let thy priests be clothed with righteousness; and let thy saints shout for joy. . . . . For Jehovah hath chosen Zion; He hath desired it for His habitation. This is my rest for ever. here will I dwell; for I have desired it." Ps. cxxxii. 8.

This second progress of Israel through the wilderness to the Land of their rest and glory—from Sinai to Zion, is one of the chief subjects of the Psalm before us, and is referred to in many other parts of Scripture. " I will bring you out from among the peoples, and will gather you out of the countries wherein ye are scattered, with a mighty hand, and with a stretched out arm, and with fury poured out. And I will bring you into the wilderness of the peoples, and there will I plead with you face to face. Like as I pleaded with your

---

* בערבות—This word, derived probably from ערב, *to be arid, sterile*, is continually applied to the plains or steppes that abound in and around Palestine, and is sometimes translated "plains," sometimes "deserts." Compare Is lx. 3 "In *the desert* make straight a highway for our God." See also Isaiah lvii. 13. ("Cast ye up, cast ye up the way" סלו סלו, סלו) as referred to in Notes on Ps. lxxxiv. in succeeding paper.

† See note on this verse in Occasional Papers No. I. p. 59.

fathers in the wilderness of the land of Egypt, so will I plead with you, saith the Lord God. And I will cause you to pass under the rod, and I will bring you into the bond of the covenant." Ez. xx. 34-37 "Behold, I will allure her, and bring her into the wilderness, and speak comfortably unto her. And I will give her her vineyards from thence, and the valley of Achor for a door of hope. and she shall sing there, as in the days of her youth, and as in the day when she came up out of the land of Egypt." Hosea ii. 14. "According to the days of thy coming out of the land of Egypt will I shew unto him marvellous things. The nations shall see and be confounded at all their might: they shall lay their hand upon their mouth, their ears shall be deaf. They shall lick the dust like a serpent, they shall move out of their holes like worms of the earth: they shall be afraid of the Lord our God, and shall fear because of thee." Micah vii. 15-17. "The wilderness and the solitary place shall be glad for them (Israel); and the desert shall rejoice, and blossom as the rose . . . . In the wilderness shall waters break out, and streams in the desert." Is. xxxv. 1. "And the Lord shall utterly destroy the tongue of the Egyptian sea (the Gulf of Suez); and with his mighty wind shall he shake his hand over the river (Nile), and shall smite it in the seven streams, and make men go over dryshod. And there shall be an highway for the remnant of his people, which shall be left, from Assyria; like as it was to Israel in the day that he came up out of the land of Egypt." Is. xi. 15 "I will open rivers in high places, and fountains in the midst of the valleys: I will make the wilderness a pool of water, and the dry land springs of water. I will plant in the wilderness the cedar, the shittah tree, and the myrtle, and the oil tree; I will set in the desert the fir tree and the pine, and the box tree together: that they may see, and know, and consider, and understand together, that the hand of the Lord hath done this, and the Holy One of Israel hath created it." Is. xli 18. Such is the character of that coming hour to which the Psalm before us belongs. Marvellous was the march of Israel through the wilderness of old, but more marvellous and more blessed will be that which is yet to be. "Ye shall not go out with haste, nor go by flight: for Jehovah will go before you, and the God of Israel will be your rereward." Is. lii. 12. This Psalm is one of the evidences that Israel will then have "seen, and known, and considered, and understood together" what God hath wrought. They will be ready to extol Him "that rideth forward in the deserts in Jah His name," *i.e.* in the strength and potency of

His own great name, and will say, " Cast ye up a highway &c.;" that is, let His course be established, and prospered, and triumph

Verses 5, 6.

5 A father of orphans, and a judge of widows
  Is God in his holy habitation
6 God is he that causeth the solitary to dwell in a home;
  That causeth the prisoners to come forth into prosperity,
  Only the rebellious dwell in a land of drought.

A father of orphans &c.] In the midst of the great and awful displays of almighty power that will introduce the millennium, and cause " the earth to tremble and be still," the goodness and graciousness of God will not be forgotten. Forgiven Israel will in a peculiar manner prove His *lovingkindness,* for they will greatly need it. Orphanhood, widowhood, solitariness, destitution, oppression—in a word, every form of calamity and of sorrow will, before the hour of their deliverance comes, have stamped upon Israel an aspect of woe the like to which has never been seen " from the beginning of the creation that God created, unto that time ; neither shall be." Having loved and followed after strangers, from them they shall receive their portion. Under Antichrist—" the idol shepherd," that is to be raised up for them in the Land of Israel, (see Zech. xi. 16.) they will be " trampled down like the mire of the streets." Is. x. 6. " The Lord also was as an enemy : he hath swallowed up Israel, he hath swallowed up all her palaces : he hath destroyed his strong holds, and hath increased in the daughter of Judah mourning and lamentation." See Book of Lamentations throughout. But when the time arrives for the Psalm before us to be accomplished, the hour will have come for Zion to be comforted. " As one whom his mother comforteth, so will I comfort you, and ye shall be comforted in Jerusalem." Israel will have gone " through fire and through water;" but they will be " brought out into a wealthy place." Ps. lxvi. 12. " The people shall dwell in Zion at Jerusalem : thou shalt weep no more : he will be very gracious unto thee at the voice of thy cry : when he shall hear it, he will answer thee." Is. xxx. 19. Nor will the mercies and lovingkindnesses of the Jehovah of Israel be restricted to Israel. In Zion a feast of fat things shall be made for " all nations." Is. xxv. 6. Even Edom, deep as it shall be made to drink the dregs of the cup of the Lord's fury, yet even in Edom a remnant shall be spared. " Leave thy fatherless children, I will preserve them alive; and let thy widows trust in ME," are words addressed to Edom. Jer. xlix. 11. Well therefore may it be said in that day, "A father of orphans, and a judge of widows is God in his holy habitation." The results of His being this will be manifested throughout the whole earth.

Verses 7, 8.

7 O God at Thy going forth before Thy people,
At Thy marching in the desert; Selah.

8 The earth trembled, yea the heavens dropped, at the presence of God;
This Sinai, at the presence of God, the God of Israel.

O God, at thy going forth &c.] I do not regard this passage as referring (as certain other passages, such as Deut. xxxiii. 2, do) to the past manifestation of Divine glory at Sinai, but as describing that future hour when God will again lead Israel into and through the wilderness (see the many passages just quoted) and when the glory of Him who once manifested Himself on Sinai will re-enter Sinai's wilderness, and through it pass to Zion. The march of Him, whom the Ark of the Covenant typified, through the wilderness and through enemies from Sinai to Zion, and the establishment of His glory there, and the results thereof, is the great subject of the Psalm before us. Then the typical acts of David and of Solomon, when the one brought up the Ark to the Citadel of Zion (see 1 Chron. xv. and xvi.), and the other to the Temple (see 2 Chron. v.) will receive their full accomplishment, and it shall be once more said amidst the rejoicing of Heaven and of earth, "Arise, O Jehovah into thy resting place, thou and the ark of thy strength;" and then again shall Israel "bow themselves, and worship, and praise," saying, in a manner in which they have never yet said, "Praise Jehovah, for He is good, for His mercy endureth for ever"

The verse we are considering, places us in the wilderness. We stand as with Sinai before us. Hence the words, "this Sinai," or "yon Sinai." We see Sinai tremble and the earth likewise at the presence of One who chooses not Sinai for the place of His rest, nor Bashan, nor Lebanon, but Zion. The last chapter of Habakkuk may be regarded as extending over and comprehending the period described in the verses before us. "God came from Teman, and the Holy One from Mount Paran. Selah. His glory covered the heavens, and the earth was full of his praise. . . . . . . He stood, and measured the earth: he beheld, and drove asunder the nations; and the everlasting mountains were scattered, the perpetual hills did bow: his ways are everlasting." Habakkuk, however, directs our minds chiefly to the effect of the manifestation of the glory on the nations and the earth generally, on whom it will bear terrifically and destructively; whereas the Psalm describes its relation to forgiven Israel, which will be one of protection, strength, and blessing. Israel will behold Sinai, and Bashan, and the nations, and the whole earth trembling at the presence of a glory which will be the glory of their God and King, moving at their head until it finds its resting-place on Zion. It will be the hour when the cherubic power which once watched over Israel, but which was grieved away by their iniquities (see Ez. xi. 22.) will return in everlasting blessing (see Ez. xliii.)—the risen saints being entrusted with its exercise. See "Thoughts on the Apocalypse" as advertised at end.

Verses 9, 10.

9 A shower of freenesses thou wilt dispense, O God;
Thine inheritance (and it was weary) thou hast established.

10 Thy congregation have taken up their dwelling place therein;
Thou wilt establish [it] in thy goodness for the afflicted, O God.

A shower of freenesses &c.] A shower of blessings, or gifts, freely given. "Pluviam munificentiarum aut liberalitatum." God will then in the abounding riches of His goodness pour forth showers of abounding blessings on His forgiven people. The Land of Israel—Immanuel's Land, found by Him worn out and wearied with affliction will be by Him established. His congregation, formed of those who will be preserved, quickened and sustained in life by Him, will take up their abode therein, and find a quiet habitation and sure dwelling places. It will be the compensating gift of His goodness to those who will just before have said, "Have mercy upon us, O Lord, have mercy upon us: for we are exceedingly filled with contempt. Our soul is exceedingly filled with the scorning of those who are at ease, and with the contempt of the proud." See Psalms cxxiii. and cxxiv.

Verse 11.

11 The Lord (Adonai) will give the word,
The women who bear the tidings are a mighty host.

The Lord will give &c.] That is, the Lord will cause the tidings of

Zion's rescue and blessing to be proclaimed throughout all the earth. Compare Is. lxii. 11. "Behold, Jehovah hath proclaimed unto the end of the world, Say ye to the daughter of Zion, Behold, thy salvation is come (בא); behold, his reward is with him, and his work before him." And Is. xiv. 32, "What shall one then answer the messengers of *the nation?*"—that is, the messengers sent by those of Israel who are in distant parts of the earth, to enquire respecting the result of the great day of visitation to their Land. The reply shall be, "That Jehovah hath founded Zion, and the poor of His people shall trust in it." In the verse before us the daughters of Jerusalem, like Miriam of old (Exodus xv. 20.) are described as going forth to aid in the proclamation of the joyful tidings. They are again referred to in the twenty-fifth verse—"Among them were the damsels playing with the timbrels."

Verses 12, 13.

12 Kings of armies shall flee, shall flee;
And she that tarried at home shall divide the spoil.

13 Though ye shall have lain down among the furnace-ranges,
Yet (shall ye be as) the wings of a dove
Covered with silver
And her feathers with brightness of fine gold.

Kings of armies &c.] Here we revert (and this is usual in prophecy) to circumstances that precede the deliverance described in the previous verses. The Prophet speaks as if beholding before him the mighty hosts that are to gather against Jerusalem, and then pronounces the sentence of their overthrow. "They shall flee, they shall flee," and Israel, even though helpless and inexertive, shall triumph and divide the spoil. Compare 1 Sam xxx. 21-24.

Among the furnace-ranges.] Or as some render it "cattle-ranges:" in either case the emblem of a filthy and defiled place. In such degradation and defilement Israel shall be found; yet however defiled, her defilement and dishonour shall pass away, and she shall become like a dove covered with silver, and her feathers with brightness of the purest gold.

Verse 14.

14 When the Almighty scattereth kings in it [the Land]
It shall be as snow in Zalmon.

It shall be as snow &c.] Snow seen in contrast with a dark mountain seems bright with whiteness. Such shall be the aspect of Israel's Land when cleansed and recognised as the Land of Immanuel The discomfiture and flight of the kings gathered against Israel, are again and again referred to in the Psalms See especially Ps. xlviii. 4.

Verses 15, 16.

15 A mighty mountain is the mountain of Bashan,
   A mountain of heights is the mountain of Bashan.

16 Why are ye on the watch ye mountains of heights
   [Behold] the mountain desired of God to inhabit;
   Yea, Jehovah shall dwell there for ever.

A mighty mountain &c.] Literally, a mountain of God; an expression indicative of exceeding greatness. See Joel iii. 3, where Nineveh is called "an exceeding great city," literally, "a city great unto God." Compare ἀστειος τω θεω Acts vii 20 The frequent allusions to the fir trees of Bashan, the oaks of Bashan, the bulls of Bashan, sufficiently mark the vigour, sturdiness, and insolence of strength that Bashan symbolises Bashan, therefore, stands in Scripture as one of the chief emblems of that proud Gentile power which dominates over the earth during the time of Israel's abasement and looks down contemptuously on Zion. It is in fact a vast mountain range of basaltic formation, standing in very marked contrast with the comparatively insignificant hills of central Palestine. Yet Zion, the mountain of the God of Israel, is to be exalted, the Gentile Bashan to be abased.

Why are ye on the watch &c.] It is difficult to determine the precise meaning of רצד which is only used in this place. The Sept. renders it by ὑπολαμβανετε—Aquila, εριζετε—Symmachus, περισπουδαζετε—Jerome, *contenditis*—Horsley, "Why are ye upon the watch, ye high hills? What would ye contend for?" Gesenius, "to observe insidiously." The word does not appear to denote contention or rivalry (the time for *that* will have passed) but rather anxious and expectant observancy of the result of the Divine actings in awarding to each their portion. All will be conscious that the time is come to abase that which had been high, and to lift up that which had been low.

This is the mountain or see the mountain desired of God &c.] Compare Ps. cxxxii. 13. "For Jehovah hath chosen Zion; He hath desired it for His habitation. This is my rest for ever: here will I dwell; for I have desired it." See also Ps. lxxxvii. 2, 5

Verse 17.

17 The chariots of God are twice ten thousand,
Thousands on thousands repeated;
The Lord is among them—Sinai is in the holy place.

The Lord [Adonai] is among them &c] Some translate this verse, "The Lord among them") i.e. in the midst of the chariots of His strength) hath come from Sinai into the sanctuary. But this is a paraphrase, not a translation. It is better to render the clause strictly, and to retain the abruptness. The glory once manifested at Sinai is seen in vision to move through the wilderness to Zion, the mountain of holiness and grace. Sinai, therefore, is regarded as moving to Zion. It is the same glory, the same holiness, but it removes from Sinai, and finds its dwelling place on Zion. Believers, by faith, know it there already; but Israel and the earth generally, have persisted in despising the grace of Zion: they stand before the thunders and lightnings of Sinai (see Rev. xi. 19), which will finally break forth upon them in all their devouring power, when none shall be spared, except a remnant. When the time comes for this Psalm to be fulfilled, Israel will well understand what it means for God's relation to them to be changed from Sinai to Zion.

Verse 18.

18 Thou didst ascend unto the height;
Thou didst lead captive captivity;
Thou didst receive gifts to be in man,
Yea, even the rebellious shall be for Jah, God, to dwell in.

Thou didst ascend &c.] This verse looks back to a period far anterior to that to which the preceding verses refer. The Messiah and God of Israel, long previous to that yet future display of His glory on Zion which the preceding verses describe, had also (even at a time when Israel acknowledged Him not) effected that wondrous work which the verse before us sets forth. He had ascended up to the height even high above all Heavens (and in order to do this He must first have descended) and when He so ascended, He burst the bars of Hades, and took with Him the souls of His departed saints into the Paradise of God, and so captive led captivity; and He likewise received from His Father gifts that were to find the place of their collocation and settlement, not in Israel merely, but in MAN (באדם), so that not only in Israel, but among the distant Gentiles, men found in the place of rebellion and revolt were sought after and made the "temples of God"—persons "for Jehovah to dwell in." All this had been accomplished at the ascension of the Messiah of Israel, whilst Israel's eyes were yet blinded; and thus the Apostle explains this verse in the fourth of the Ephesians.

It was fitting that in the midst of a Psalm devoted for the most part to the day of Israel's gladness, reference should be made to that previous triumph of their King over sin and death to which their deliverance, and triumph, and glory will be due. Unless He had first descended, died and risen, wrath would have been their portion. Nor would one of the great constituent parts of that glory which will then greet their eyes on Zion have been present, if the Lord their Redeemer had not in the way described led captivity captive, and gathered out from among the rebellious, whether Jew, or whether Gentile, those who shall in that coming day surround Him, bright in unearthly light, and next after Christ, give to Zion its chief characteristic glory.

Unto the height.] The word translated "the height" or "the high place" (המרום) sometimes denotes the seat of God's earthly government, whence He will rule Israel and the earth, when the hour of Israel's forgiveness shall have come. It is thus used in Ps. vii. where God is entreated to return to the high-place of Israel, as to a place which He had left. "Arise, O Jehovah, in thine anger, lift up thyself because of the rage of mine oppressors: and awake for me the judgment which thou hast commanded. So shall the congregation of the peoples compass thee about. for their sakes therefore RETURN THOU to the high-place." See also Ps. xciii. where God is described as having returned to the high-place of Israel and there reigning.

In the verse before us, however, a different sense attaches to the word המרום, for there is another "high-place" higher than "the high-place" of Israel. In the quotation of this passage in Eph. iv. the Apostle interprets this word as meaning *here*, that place of exalted glory into which Christ hath already ascended, high above all heavens —a place of exaltation far higher than that high-place of Israel to which in due time He will return and ALSO occupy, without resigning the place of His glory above the Heavens.

We must therefore translate the connected words, not as in our version, "thou *hast* ascended," as if they referred to an event just accomplished, but "thou *didst* ascend," in the aoristic sense — the action referred to being one that had long passed. In the preceding verses the Prophet had spoken as if standing in the presence of that glory which will be revealed on Zion, when the Lord surrounded by heavenly hosts shall be there; after He shall have returned to the high-place of Israel. After describing this glory as present, the Psalmist refers to another event (to him future, to *us* past) and addressing Him whose glory is seen on Zion, speaks of that first and higher exaltation into which the Holy One of Israel entered when He brake the bands of death and ascended up high above all Heavens, taking with Him into the Paradise of God the souls of the redeemed, for whom He burst the gate of Hades; when also He received from the Father and dispensed to His people on earth (whether Jew or whether Gentile) those gifts of ministry whereby His people are built up in the Truth. And as the ascension of the rejected Messiah of Israel into His heavenly glory was thus marked by His leading "captivity captive," and receiving gifts for men; so His return to the high-place of Israel shall be marked by His recapturing captive Israel, and by His dispensing those gifts which shall be the result of the outpouring of the Spirit in the latter day. In both cases it is a day of like grace; forgiving, reclaiming, and blessing the rebellious, so as for Jehovah to dwell among them.

Thou didst receive gifts for man &c.] "Man" is here used in a collective sense, denoting men generally, and indicating that the gifts spoken of were not received for Israel only, but for men—Gentiles as well as Jews—another reason why the Apostle should quote this verse as corroborative of his teaching to the Ephesians.

"Gifts *for* men" is the best rendering of מתנות באדם—gifts that are *for* and to be *in* men. See Gesenius on the force of ב, as including the signification of אל *to or for*, but also "signifying the reaching the end and remaining at it." When a person receives gifts *for others*, he must receive with a view to *giving*, so that there is nothing expressed in the words of the Apostle "*gave gifts*" (ἔδωκε δόματα ἀνθρώποις) that is not necessarily included in the words, "received gifts for man." The Apostles in quoting from the Old Testament, often develop meanings which are necessarily involved in the passages quoted, though they may not be formally expressed in words. All the comments of the Apostles on Old Testament texts, whether in the way of interpretation or of application, are of course authoritative, because they wrote by inspiration.

Verses 19, 20, 21.

19 Blessed be the Lord,
   Day by day [with blessings] he loadeth us
   The God of our salvation.

20 God is to us the God of salvation,
   And to Jehovah, the Lord, belong the goings to death

21 But God will wound the head of his enemies,
   The hairy scalp that goeth on still in its guiltiness.

God is to us &c.] The relation of God to reconciled Israel is forcibly contrasted in these verses with His relation to obdurate enemies. The commencement of the Millennium, like the commencement of Solomon's reign, will be marked by judgment on adversaries. Indeed, the very object for which the Lord assumes His millennial power, is that He may subdue all enemies. "He must reign till He hath put all enemies under his feet." The Millennium, therefore, is not a perfect nor the final dispensation. It leads on to the dispensation of the fulness of times where all will be perfect and according to God. "We according to His promise look for new heavens and a new earth wherein dwelleth righteousness." This will be as true in the Millennium as now.

The goings unto [or that have relation unto] *death*—למות תוצאות Phillips and others have observed that the English version of these words "issues from death," cannot be sustained by the Hebrew; for ל has never the force of *from*. The clause, however, must not be understood as if antithetical to the first clause of the same verse and speaking of judgments on the enemies of Israel. The antithesis evidently does not begin until the next verse, and is introduced by the word "*but*" or "*only*" (אך). Israel had been brought by oppressive affliction and judgment close to the very gates of death: but unto God pertained the control of the "goings unto death," as of all things, and He delivered them.

Verses 22, 23.

22 The Lord said,
   From Bashan I will bring again,
   I will bring again from the depth of the sea

23 That thou mayst plunge thy foot in blood;
   As to the tongue of thy dogs, from the enemies shall be its portion.

From Bashan &c.] The future triumphant march of Israel from

Assyria, and from Egypt, is described in these verses, when they will be used as "the battle-axe and weapons of war" of Jehovah, against His and their enemies. Compare Is. xi. 11 to end. "They shall fly upon the shoulders of the Philistines toward the west; they shall spoil them of the east together: they shall lay their hand upon Edom and Moab, and the children of Ammon shall obey them." See also Micah v. 8, and ii. 12. Israel being thus used *first* for judgment on the nations, moves, as it were, through a sea of blood. The word I have translated "plunge," means properly, to agitate, shake, or move rapidly.

Verses 24, 25, 26.

24 They have seen thy goings O God,
The goings of my God, my King, in the sanctuary.

25 The singers went before,
The players on instruments after;
In the midst were the virgins, playing on timbrels.

26 In the congregations, bless ye God the Lord,
Ye who are of the fountain of Israel.

The goings of my God, my King, in the sanctuary] The scene described in these verses was foreshadowed in 2 Chron. v. 6, where the Ark was brought by Solomon into *the Temple:* just as the establishment of the Divine glory on Zion referred to in the previous part of this Psalm was foreshadowed by David bringing the Ark to *the Citadel* of David on Zion—the latter being the place of strength and governmental power—the former, i.e. the Temple, the place of worship and instruction in Truth. When the glory of the Lord chooseth Zion for its resting place (see verse 16) Bashan and the proud Gentile mountains tremble and are still: when His goings are seen as He entereth His sanctuary, Israel His people rejoice, and, in congregated worship, bless Him.

Verse 27.

27 There is Benjamin, the little one, their subduer;
The princes of Judah their minister of judgment,
The princes of Zebulun, and the princes of Naphtali.

Their subduer.] From רדה, applied generally to power that encounters resistance and is put forth in order to subdue enemies. This character of power against God's enemies will be especially exercised by *Benjamin*—the least of the tribes, and therefore the more suited to show forth the glorious power of Him from whom its strength cometh. There is some difficulty in determining the translation of רגמה applied to Judah. It is no doubt derived from רגם to stone, to destroy by stoning *as a judicial penalty.* Hence רגמה means, "obrutio, lapidatio, interitus." As here used, I understand it to ascribe to Judah the power of inflicting righteous *judicial* penalties, just as to Benjamin is ascribed the power of conquest and subjugation on behalf of Israel. Both characters of power need to be exercised against that mighty strength of evil which David longed to subdue, but could not. The earth will teem with evil when the reign of the Messiah of Israel begins. See the dying words of David respecting the sons of Belial. There must be power to subdue, and power to rule also. Both will be found in Israel.

Verses 28, 29.

28 Thy God hath commanded thy strength:
Strengthen, O God, that which thou hast wrought for us.

29 Because of thy temple which is over Jerusalem,
Shall kings bring a gift unto Thee.

Thy God hath commanded &c.] Israel will be very sensible then whence their strength cometh. They will have learned to say, "Lord, thou wilt ordain peace for us; for thou also hast wrought all our works for us." (לנו) See Is xxvi. 12—a chapter which may be read throughout as harmonizing with this Psalm.

Because of thy Temple &c] Διὰ τον ναον σου. *Symmachus.* The prefix מ is often used, as it is here, to indicate the source whence influence or operative power emanates. From the Temple of Jehovah shall go forth the influence that shall constrain the subjection of the earth and all its kings. There is no reason, therefore, for altering, as some do, the position of these words and subjoining them to the previous clause. The word translated gift, or present, (שׁי) is used twice elsewhere, but always in the singular, viz., Ps lxxvi. 11. "Bring a gift unto Him that ought to be feared;" and Ps. xviii. 7. "At that time shall be brought a present to Jehovah of Hosts" &c. This word seems to indicate not so much a multiplicity or continuance of offerings as a gift specifically presented in token of submission to the One great Ruler of earth. The words על־ירושלים may be understood to denote the relation of the Temple to Jerusalem as exalted above it and protective of it: or the verse may be translated, "Because of Thy Temple—up to Jerusalem shall kings bring a gift unto Thee."

Verse 30.

30 Rebuke the beast of the reed,
The herd of bulls with the calves of the nations,
[Behold each one] submitting itself with pieces of silver:
He hath scattered the nations that in wars delight.

Rebuke &c.] גער not necessarily meaning rebuke unto destruction, but unto correction. See Gen. xxxvii. 10 and Ruth ii. 16. The nations rebuked are described as submitting themselves one by one. "The beast of the reed" evidently denotes Egypt or its head. Egypt is throughout the prophets referred to as being visited with judgments of peculiar severity at that period. As the language of this passage is clearly figurative, it is best to translate אבירים *bulls*, a meaning which it bears in Is. xxxiv. 7, and Jer. xlvi. 20. "Egypt is like a very fair heifer, but destruction cometh; it cometh out of the north. Also her hired men in the midst of her are like *calves of the stall*." See also Jer xxxi. 18. "*A calf* unaccustomed to the yoke." Some alter the received reading, and change בְּרַצֵּי into ברצי as if from רָצָה to delight in, and translate—"Trampling down them that delight in silver," and so referring מתרפס (Hithp. part) to God. The meaning would be satisfactory, but there is not sufficient authority for the change of reading.

Verse 31.

31 Princes shall come out of Egypt;
Cush shall stretch out his hands unto God.

Out of Egypt.] Egypt, though it is to be terribly smitten, shall finally be healed. "The Lord shall smite Egypt; he shall smite and heal it; and they shall return unto the Lord, and he shall be entreated of them, and shall heal them. In that day there shall be a highway out of Egypt to Assyria, and the Assyrian shall come into Egypt, and the Egyptian into Assyria, and the Egyptians shall serve with the Assyrians. In that day shall Israel be the third with Egypt and with Assyria, even a blessing in the midst of the land: whom the Lord of hosts shall bless, saying, Blessed be Egypt my people, and Assyria the work of my hands, and Israel mine inheritance." Is. xix. 22. The meaning of הַשְׁמַנִּים *Chashmannin* is uncertain. It is supposed by many to be identical with מִשְׁמַנִּים, *fat ones, great men, princes*, as used in Ps. lxviii. 31. Others take it to be a proper name and to denote the inhabitants of the Egyptian province *Aschmunim*. Whichever interpretation be taken the general meaning of the verse is not affected. *Cush* is here the African Cush or Ethiopia; a general name for Africa and its, at present, unpenetrated regions. "Cush shall make his hands run, or hasten to God," is the literal translation.

Verses 32, 33, 34.

32 Ye kingdoms of the earth, sing ye unto God,
   Sing psalms unto the Lord,

33 To Him who rideth on the heaven of heavens which are of old:
   Behold, He uttereth forth His voice, a voice of strength;

34 Ascribe ye strength to God;
   Over Israel is His excellency (excellent majesty)
   And His strength is in the skies.

Ye kingdoms of the earth, sing ye &c.] The former clause had given the result of the previously described judgments on the nations, in that they were brought to submit themselves and own the God of Israel. Here they are called on to rejoice before Him and to worship. His excellent majesty as regards manifestation in the earth will be peculiarly "over Israel," but the home of His glory is in the Heavens. "O Lord our Lord, how excellent is thy name in all the earth! who hast set thy glory *above the heavens*." Ps. viii. In the former part of the Psalm, whilst executing judgment on the nations, He is described as riding *in the deserts* in the power of Jah, His name (see verse 4): here He is described as riding in the Heaven of Heavens, the home of the excellency of His power being there and now recognised and submitted to, as there.

Verse 35.

35 Terrible art thou O God out of thy sanctuaries,
   The God of Israel:
   He it is that giveth strength and power unto THE people.
   Blessed be God.

Terrible art thou O God &c.] The awe of Divine power and glory must be ever felt by man whilst he remains in the flesh. It is only to those "changed into His likeness" that awe gives place to full communion. So it will be to all the redeemed in the new heavens and earth. In the millennial earth, however, there will be some, not in Israel but among the nations who will render a feigned obedience: (See Ps. xviii.) and at the very close there will be a great apostasy, and the terrors of God out of His holy places will be defied —though for the last time. Whilst the possibility of such sin remains it is needful that terror should accompany manifestations of Divine glory. "Out of thy *sanctuaries*," is an expression that includes the heavenly as well as the earthly seats of His glory. Compare Ps. lxxxiv.; and see remarks on it in succeeding paper.

Unto the people] העם, or THE nation, הגוי, are titles which Israel are most jealous in appropriating to themselves. Hence the verse from the application of which they shrink almost more than any other in the Old Testament is Is. xlix. 7,—": to Him whom THE NATION abhorreth." They see that "Him" must refer to the Messiah of Israel, and they will not allow that "THE nation" is a title that can belong to any except Israel. Here then is a verse that clearly predicts their rejection of their Messiah. But when the time comes for this Psalm to be fulfilled, the veil will be taken from their heart, and they shall be owned "THE PEOPLE whom Jehovah hath blessed." "God shall bless THEM, and then all the ends of the earth shall fear Him." "The Lord hasten it, in His time."

Notes on Psalm LXXXIV.

Verse 1.

1 How beloved (i.e. how dear to me) are thy Tabernacles,
    O Jehovah of hosts.

This Psalm has been commonly taken as belonging to an Israelite coming from a far distant land to Jerusalem, there to keep the appointed feasts.* So far as respects the returning Israelite, the thought is doubtless true; but it is a *prophetic* Psalm, not belonging to the present or any past dispensation, but to the coming age—ἡ οἰκουμένη ἡ μέλλουσα. It is a millennial Psalm and is to be read as the utterance of a spared and forgiven Israelite, who having heard in some far distant place of exile that the Lord "had founded Zion" (Is. xiv. 32.), hastens back to the Land of his fathers, and as he draws nigh to Jerusalem and beholds its glory, thus expresses his sense of that which God had accomplished for his people.

We must carefully bear in mind that the millennium is to be a period in which the glory of God will be *manifested*. Jacob's vision, when he saw the Lord standing above the ladder whose foot rested on the earth, but whose top reached unto Heaven (the vision to which our Lord referred when He said, "Verily, verily, I say unto you† ye shall see heaven opened and the angels of God ascending and descending upon the Son of Man") shall in the millennium receive its antitypical accomplishment. A ladder is the symbol of *connexion* between two places whose distinctness is preserved. In the millennium, earth will remain earth, and heaven will remain heaven; but there will be communication between heaven and earth, and that communication will

---

* "Describitur flagrantissimum pii hominis desiderium veniendi in sacrum cœtum, et felicitas eorum, qui cultui divino vacare possunt."—*Rosenmuller.*

† It will be observed that in quoting this passage I omit the word ἀπαρτι, *henceforth*, wrongly rendered, *hereafter* in our version—that word being an interpolation. See *Tregelles in locum.*

be visible. The foot of the ladder (to adopt the emblem of the vision) may be said to rest on the height of Zion which will be miraculously exalted high above all the hills that will begirt Jerusalem (see Is. ii, and Ps. cxxv.) and is called "the mountain of the house of Jehovah" (see Is. ii. 3, and Micah iv. i.) because it will be the place of Divine authority and governmental power, whence the interests of Truth, represented by the House or Temple of Jehovah, will be watched over and protected. Jerusalem always had in Zion its strong-hold or citadel—מצודה. Thus we read in 2 Sam. v. 8, David took *the stronghold* of Zion . . . . . . and David dwelt in *the fort*: and again in 1 Chron. xi. 5, David took *the castle* of Zion—the same word מצודה, being used in these three places. In the Acts, the same fortress on Zion is referred to six times (Acts xxi. 34 and 37: xxii. 24: xxiii. 10, 16 and 32,) as *the castle*—$παρεμβολη$: and the Revelation in describing the close of the millennial period again refers to it as $ἡ παρεμβολη των ἁγιων$—"the camp or citadel of the saints." Zion, therefore, as being the citadel of the "beloved city," is continually spoken of in the Scripture as one of the resting-places of the Divine glory. See Is. xxiv. 23. It is called, "the place of the name of the Lord of Hosts," Is. xviii. 7: "the mountain of his holiness," Ps xlviii. 1: "the joy of the whole earth," Ps. xlviii. 2: "the perfection of beauty," Ps. l. 2. In Ps. lxviii. 16, it is described as the mountain which God has chosen for His habitation, and therefore looked on with anxious wonder by Bashan, and other like mountains that had been the seats of ungodly Gentile power.

> "A mighty Mountain is the Mountain of Bashan,
> "A Mountain of heights is the Mountain of Bashan,
> "Why are ye on the watch ye Mountains of heights?
> [Behold] the Mountain [Zion] desired of God to inhabit,
> "Yea, Jehovah will dwell there for ever.
> "The chariots of God are twice-told myriads,
> "Thousands and thousands repeated,
> "The Lord is among them &c."

In the Revelation also Zion is referred to as one of the places in which the glory of the redeemed and of the Lamb is to be displayed in connexion with the earth's future government, and also in Hebrews xii.* "Ye have not drawn nigh to a place by fire enveloped

---

* It is important to observe, that, although $ορει$ (mountain) is implied in this passage, yet it is not expressed, much less interposed between $ψηλαφωμενῳ$ and

[literally, *handled*, grasped] and consumed, nor unto blackness and darkness &c., but ye are come unto Mount Zion &c.:" and then follows the recital of certain glories with which Zion in the coming day of her glory shall be connected—glories manifestly *future*, for Zion is at present desolate (see Lamentations), and the Heavenly City as yet existeth not. It is only in the anticipation of faith that we can say that " we are come to Mount Zion, AND to the city of the living God, the heavenly Jerusalem, AND to myriads of angels, a general assembly AND to the Church of the first-born ones enrolled in heaven " &c. Mount Zion, having such glories as these *connected with it*, is to be the earthly centre of that economy to which we belong—the economy of the New Covenant.

The Temple also at Jerusalem is to be another seat or resting-place of Divine manifested glory. Thus in Ezekiel xliii. 1, we read; " After, he brought me to the gate, even the gate that looketh toward the east: and, behold, the glory of the God of Israel came from the way of the east· and his voice was like a noise of many waters: and

---

και κεκαυμενῳ—the true reading being—ου γαρ προσεληλυθατε ψηλαφωμενῳ και κεκαυμενῳ πυρι—" for ye have not drawn nigh [as ye did at Sinai] to that which is grasped and consumed by fire." Ψηλαφοω means to *handle*, to *grasp*, as fire when it seizes on an object. Or if we take another meaning of ψηλαφοω, viz., *to grope after*, as when any one feels after a thing hidden in darkness, we may render, " Ye have not drawn nigh unto that that is groped after [because of being enveloped in darkness] and that is burned with fire " &c. So *Wetstein*—ψηλαφωμενῳ ορει, " est mons tenebris et fumo obductus qui oculis conspici non poterat, potuisset autem contrectari: at ne hoc quidem concedebatur nisi Mosi soli." This meaning of ψηλαφοω agrees with its use in the Septuagint, where it is used as the translation of מִשֵּׁשׁ in Pihel—*to feel in the darkness, to grope*. Deut xxviii. 29. See *Gesenius*. It is also used in the Sept. as the translation of גִשֵׁשׁ in Piel, which has the same meaning as in Is. lix 10. " They *grope for* the wall as blind men." Whichever of these meanings of ψηλαφοω be taken, it is certainly not to be translated as if it were synonymous with θιγγανω *to touch*, which is used immediately after; nor can the participle ψηλαφωμενος be translated as if it were the verbal ψηλαφητος. There is therefore nothing in this verse when rightly translated that so ascribes tangibility to Sinai, as by implication to ascribe intangibility to Zion. Zion is, and will be in the millennium, a tangible mountain quite as much as Sinai. It will be strictly an earthly mountain, though on its height heavenly glory will rest as it did for a season on Sinai of old. The omission of the word ορει (*mountain*) in describing Sinai, and its application to Zion only, seems intended to give more vividness to the thought that the stability and authority indicated by that word pertains not to Sinai and its economy, but that it is the heritage of Zion alone.

the earth shined with his glory. . . . . . And the glory of Jehovah came into the house by the way of the gate whose prospect is toward the east. So the spirit took me up, and brought me into the inner court; and, behold, the glory of Jehovah filled the house. . . . . . And he said unto me, Son of man, the place of my throne, and the place of the soles of my feet, where I will dwell (אשכן) in the midst of the children of Israel for ever" &c. But whilst there will be these resting-places of the Divine glory in the earth, its home will be above the heavens. High above Zion (visible indeed to the earth, but far away and separate from it) will be the heavenly City, new Jerusalem; called in the Hebrews ΕΠουρανια, answering to על־השמים in Ps. viii. indicating that its location is to be *above* the created heavens. Again, beyond the heavenly City will be the Heaven of heavens—the dwelling place of God—this answering to the Holy of Holies in the typical Tabernacle, whilst the heavenly City will be the antitype to the Holy Place, and the earthly Jerusalem to the external Court where Israel worshipped.

Thus then we read of four tabernacles or dwelling-places (משכנות) of Divine glory, viz., the Temple; Mount Zion; the heavenly City; and Heaven: the two first being at Jerusalem, but all being *connected with* it: whence Jerusalem is called in Ps. xlvi. 4—" the holy place of *the Tabernacles* of the Most High:"—משכני עליון It is as contemplating this glory that the speaker in this Psalm says, " How beloved are thy Tabernacles, O Jehovah of Hosts."

It should be observed that ידיד always signifies "beloved," and never "amiable." *Hengstenbergh.* See Deut xxxiii. 12. "The beloved of the Lord shall dwell" &c This word expresses the general character of the Psalm as showing that the saints of God will not then esteem for a light thing the blessings which God has given, but will appreciate them in a manner worthy of their excellency. Want of appreciation of the privileges and blessings bestowed by God on His people has been a marked characteristic even of true Christianity in our dispensation. but it will be otherwise when Israel shall be graffed back into their own olive tree.

Verse 2.

2 My soul hath longed, yea, even pined for the Courts of Jehovah,
My heart and my flesh crieth out for the living God.

The words used in the first clause of this verse are expressive of the strongest and most vehement desire. The first verb כָּסַף *to long vehemently*, signifies strictly *to become pale*, either with desire, or terror, or shame; whence כֶּסֶף, *silver*, because of its pale colour. It is here used in *Niphal* in a transitive sense, as in Gen. xxxi. 30. "Thou sore *longedst* after thy father's house." See also its use in Zeph. ii. 1, where הגוי לא נכסף had better be translated, "O nation not *ashamed*," and not, "O nation not desired." See Gesenius.*

The second word כָּלָה *to pine* or *waste away* from grief or earnest desire, is continually applied to the "soul," or "spirit," or "eyes," or "reins" as *pining* or *languishing*. See Lam. ii. 12, Ps. lxxxiv. 3, Ps. cxliii. 7.

In the millennial age the experiences of the spared in Israel will stand in marvellous contrast with all that they will have previously known. They will suddenly come out of the very depth of the night of darkness into the joy and brightness of the millennial morning—"the morning without clouds." When the day of glory breaks, a large part of the spared remnant of Israel will be found in distant lands, for they will have been scattered to the four winds of heaven. There, in the earth's uttermost parts, where they and their fathers will have known many a year of bitterness and woe, will the tidings reach them that "Jehovah hath founded Zion, and that the poor of His people shall trust in it." Thus they shall return to Jerusalem; many of them slowly and gra-

---

* See also his remarks on the first clause of Zeph. ii. 1. He takes קָשַׁשׁ in Hithpoel in a metaphorical sense as meaning "*to gather one self*" in the sense of reflection—"*to collect one's thoughts together*." In this case it would be a call to Israel to reflection and self-examination before they drew near unto God. Much of the difficulty in understanding the prophets arises from not remembering that there frequently occur abrupt parentheses and exclamations which interrupt the construction. I should translate the whole passage thus: "Consider and gather yourselves [unto me] O nation not ashamed, before the decree bringeth forth (like chaff the day hath passed); before that there cometh on you the fury of the wrath of Jehovah, before that there cometh on you the day of the wrath of Jehovah. Seek ye Jehovah, all ye meek of the earth &c." I understand "the decree" to refer to the decree of Antichrist abolishing the worship of Jehovah in Israel and establishing his own. Before it "bringeth forth," i.e. produceth its results in bringing on the day of the wrath of Jehovah "consider (קָשַׁשׁ in Hithpoel) and gather (קֹשׁוּ in Kal) yourselves unto me." After the decree of evil had been mentioned there is a parenthetical exclamation speaking of the day *of evil* as a thing past—something that was, but is not;—like chaff the day (of evil) has passed its fleeting transitory character being thus indicated.

dually—some being gathered "one by one." See Is. xxvii. 12. This Psalm may be regarded as the utterance of one *late* returning, and thus expressing his apprehension of that which God had wrought for His people. It is the expression of one whose soul after having long experienced darkness, captivity, oppression and woe, beholds for the first time the blessedness and glory of the Courts of the Jehovah of Israel—longs after and faints for them, and is about to have those longings satisfied with full fruition: for he will find himself permitted and commanded to enter those Courts of praise. See Ps. cxxxv. 1. "Praise ye Jehovah. Praise ye the name of Jehovah; praise Him, O ye servants of Jehovah Ye that stand in the house of Jehovah, in the courts of the house of our God. . . . . . For Jehovah hath chosen Jacob unto Himself, and Israel for His peculiar treasure." This nearness of Israel to God the speaker in this Psalm is about fully to prove—a nearness involving the possession of outward as well as inward blessings; for the time when the servants of the Truth are esteemed as "the filth of the world and the off-scouring of all things" will have passed; nor will God any longer appoint tribulation as the portion of His people. The discrepancy which is at present found between the inward blessings and outward circumstances of the redeemed will then cease. "The ransomed of the Lord shall return and come to Zion with songs and everlasting joy upon their heads, and sorrow and sighing shall flee away." Is. xxxv. 10. Hence the expression in this Psalm—"my heart and *my flesh* crieth out for the living God" The outer as well as the inner man will then be expectant of, and will receive, plenitude of blessing from Jehovah.

The word translated "cry out," רנן, is used either of the cry of joy —its most frequent meaning, or of the cry of anguish, as of parents bereft of their children, see Lam ii 19, or of earnest remonstrance as Proverbs i 20. It is a word expressive of great depth of feeling. Here it denotes the cry of intense desire.

Verse 3.

3 Yea the sparrow hath found a house,
And the swallow a nest for herself,
Where she hath set her young
Even thine altars, O Jehovah of Hosts
My King and my God.

This is an interesting verse as showing that the least things of creation will then have found an abiding shelter under redemption, which the altar represents. At present it is far otherwise. Creation groans in the bondage of corruption. Neither the beasts of the field, nor the birds of the air, nor the fishes of the deep are at rest. They are pursued by fear or by hunger, by pain or by death. The sparrow and the swallow quail before the storm, or before the hawk, or the destroying hand of man. Creature preys upon creature: terror and destruction reign: and there is nothing that can be said to repose in peacefulness. But when the time comes for this Psalm to be fulfilled, the sparrow and the swallow, together with all other of God's earthly creatures, shall rest under the shelter of applied redemption: and God's servants in the earth whose "flesh" also will have rest, will know the added joy of beholding creation enjoying its sabbath under redemption. Then the song which John in the vision heard *anticipatively* sung, will find its accomplishment in "every creature that is in heaven, and on the earth, and under the earth, and such as are in the sea, and all that are in them, saying, Blessing, and honour, and glory, and power, be unto him that sitteth upon the throne, and unto the Lamb for ever and ever." Rev. v.

My King.] Although Israel and the earth have rejected Jesus, yet believers at present recognise Him as *their* King, for they own His legislation, and conform, or should conform, to the order of that *spiritual* Kingdom which He hath already established in the earth, in anticipation of that coming hour when He will assert His title not only as "Head of the Church," but as "Head over all things"—"King of kings, and Lord of lords;" before whom "all kings shall fall down;" whom "all nations shall serve." Ps. lxxii. The Father, because of His being rejected, hath said unto Him, "Sit thou at my right hand until I shall have set ('εως αν θω) thy foes a footstool for thy feet." Mark xii. 36. When that footstool has been constituted He shall be brought before the Ancient of days (see Dan. vii.) and solemnly invested with the sovereignty of earth. This is the period referred to in the Revelation when it is said, that there were heard great voices in heaven saying, "The sovereignty of the world (ἡ βασιλεια του κοσμου) has become the sovereignty of our Lord and of His Christ" Again, "We give thee thanks O Lord God Almighty, that is, and that was, because *thou hast taken to thee* thy great power and hast reigned." It is of this future period that we are to understand those ascriptions of *Kingship* to Christ by Israel and the nations that are so common in the prophetic Psalms. They belong to a period when the power of Christ will be so definitely applied to the government of earth as for all the arrangements of human life to be effectually ordered thereby. He will not be then a rejected King, but a King "inaugurated" on Zion—recognised—acknowledged and obeyed.

Verse 4.

4 O the happiness of the dwellers in thy House,
They will be still praising thee. Selah.

O the happiness of] אשרים, *prosperities, happinesses* is to be distinguished from ברכים, *blessings.* When God *blesses,* then happiness results See Occasional Papers No. II p. 147

The resurrection-glory of the "Church of the first-born ones who are enrolled in heaven" (Heb. xii. 23), or as they are prospectively termed in Daniel, "the saints of the high places," (קודשי עליונין) will be a very prominent subject of contemplation to millennial Israel. They will see in the risen saints as "first-fruits from the earth" (Rev. xiv.) a pattern and pledge of that unearthly glory which they themselves will finally inherit in the *New* Heavens and Earth. The millennial saints, as being in earthly bodies, will have for their present dwelling place, *earth;* whereas the risen saints being in spiritual bodies, will have for their home, *heaven*—the dwelling place of God. The verse before us I understand as applying to the risen saints as being "*dwellers* in His Courts." Compare Rev. iii. 12. "Him that overcometh will I make a pillar in the temple of my God and *he shall no more go out.*" No duties, no employments, no needs such as the saints of God are conversant with during their sojourn in this fallen earth, shall any longer affect these "dwellers in His Courts," so as to interrupt the perpetual employment of their energies in things that *immediately* and *directly* concern the interests of God and His Kingdom.

Verses 5, 6.

5 O the happiness of man!
Strength is unto him in Thee:
The highways are in their hearts—
6 Passing through the valley of Baca they make it a well:
Moreover with blessings the early rain covereth it.

O the happiness of man] "Man" is here used in a collective sense, and denotes the redeemed who will be yet dwellers on earth: so that there is a contrast between this verse and the preceding—the preceding verse referring to those who have their dwelling place above. We might perhaps have expected in such a verse as this to have found the happiness of *Israel* and not of *Man* emphasized. But it is not so. The blessings subsequently described are not restricted to Israel but include Man within their scope All amongst *men* who find their strength in the Jehovah of Israel are included.

In interpreting this and like passages, when in the original the clauses are independent and not united by connecting particles, it has been, for the most part, the habit of interpreters to link the clauses together by particles arbitrarily supplied. But the supply of such links take from these passages their true vividness, which is preserved by their being read as exclamations of one whose eye glances with wondering admiration at various objects presented in quick succession to his regard, and who rapidly and abruptly expresses his apprehensions. There are many examples of this in prophetic Scripture

Strength is unto him in Thee.] That is, strength is now become his in Thee. He is possessed of it now. It is not only strength proposed, but strength possessed. Israel had been slow in apprehending where their strength was. But now not only Israel, but *man* had learned the lesson, and found their strength in Jehovah.

The highways are in their hearts.] The former clause is evidently most comprehensive in its scope. The thoughts of the speaker are directed towards the condition of men generally as having at last found their strength in Jehovah. It may be questioned whether this clause is co-extensive with the former or of more restricted reference; whether the pronoun "*their*" is to be referred to man in the previous clause; or whether the mind of the speaker suddenly passes on to a fresh subject of contemplation, and speaks of some *amongst* men whom he sees employed for the blessing of man—persons whose hearts and energies are devoted to the facilitating the approach of their fellow-men to Jehovah—who are enabled to open fountains of water in dry places, and who in recognition of their service are permitted like Moses and the elders of Israel at Sinai, to ascend to the height of Zion, and there to appear in the presence of God. The latter is the interpretation I adopt. I regard the speaker as concentrating his view on a body of faithful labourers in the midst of Israel and of men, and as describing their employments and their honour.

It must be remembered that one of the chief characteristics of the millennial age will be the multiplication of what may be called symbolic facts—facts blessed in themselves, but chiefly blessed because of that which they are appointed to signify. Thus to behold the wolf and the lamb dwelling in peace together will be a fact that is in itself blessed; but that which it symbolizes will be yet more blessed, for it denotes that universality of peace, outward and inward, which will prevail wheresoever the sceptre of Jesus shall be owned. The like may be said of the waters described in Ezekiel as going forth from the sanctuary in the Holy City, and healing the waters of the seas. See Ezek. xlvii. and Zech. xiv. 8, and Joel iii. 18. No doubt this will be a fact, but a *symbolic* fact. It will indicate that flow of spiritual blessing that shall go forth from Jerusalem as the place which shall then be the appointed centre of light and truth to all peoples. Another symbolic fact in the millennial age will be the preparation of *highways*, with a view to the earth being subdued and brought under control so as for a right direction to be given to its energies, especially by connecting it with Jerusalem as the great centre of Divine instruction and government in the earth. "Many peoples shall go and say, Come ye, and let us go up to the mountain of the Lord, to the house of the God of Jacob; and he will teach us of his ways, and we will walk in his paths: for out of Zion shall go forth the law, and the word of the Lord from Jerusalem." We are all familiar with the moral force of such expressions as "safe paths," "wise paths," "happy paths," and the like. When the path is right all is well. "A way cast up" is in Scripture the symbol of a care graciously exercised towards the wayfaring stranger whereby he is enabled to proceed in the right direction as well as safely—dangers, ruggedness, and stumbling-blocks being removed. Thus we read in Proverbs xv. 19: "the way of the righteous is made plain," or more literally as given in the margin, "*raised up as a causey*" And in Jeremiah "to walk in a way not cast up" is regarded as identical with walking in a way that causeth stumbling. "Because my people hath forgotten me, they have burned incense to vanity, and they have caused them to stumble in their ways from the ancient paths, to walk in paths, *in a way not cast up &c.*" Jer. xviii. 15. Thus too Job in describing the bearing down upon him of *afflictive* power from the hand of God says, "His troops come together, and *raise up their way* against me." Job xix. 12. And again, "upon my right hand rise the youth: they push away my feet, they *raise up against me the ways* of their destruction, they mar my path &c." From these passages we can well understand the symbolic force of those Scriptures which speak of highways being prepared or "cast up," in order that the power of light, truth, and blessing that is to be concentrated in Jerusalem may be accessible to the whole earth, and made to penetrate all nations; so that they may cease to walk in "paths causing to stumble," and may find instead, paths that lead to and associate with blessing. Thus in Is. lvii. 13, we read. "He that putteth his trust in me shall possess the land, and shall inherit my holy mountain; and shall say, Cast ye up, cast ye up the way, (סֹלּוּ סֹלּוּ) make clear the path, take up the stumbling-block out of the way of my people," עַמִּי i.e. Israel. See also Isaiah lxii. 10. "Go through, go through the gates; prepare ye the way of the people; (הָעָם, Israel) cast ye up, cast ye up the highway; gather out the stones; lift up a standard to the peoples." (הָעַמִּים). Also xlix. 9. "That thou mayest say to the prisoners, Go forth; to them that are in darkness, Shew yourselves. They shall feed in the ways, and their pastures shall be in all high places. They shall not hunger nor thirst; neither shall the heat nor sun smite them: for he that hath mercy on them shall lead them, even by the springs of water shall he guide them. *And I will make all my mountains a way and my highways shall be raised up.* (מְסִלֹּתַי יְרֻמוּן). Behold these shall come from far: and lo these from the north and from the west and these from the land of Sinim" (i.e. the north-eastern parts of Asia). See also Is xxxv. 8. "And a highway shall be there, and a way, and it shall be called The way of holiness; the unclean shall not pass over it; but it shall be for those: the wayfaring men, though fools, shall not err therein. No lion shall be there, nor any ravenous beast shall go up thereon, it shall not be found there; but the redeemed shall walk there: and the ransomed of the Lord shall return, and come to Zion with songs and everlasting joy upon their heads: they shall obtain joy and gladness, and sorrow and sighing shall flee away."

We can well understand, therefore, how it will be one of the honours and privileges of those who appreciate the blessings of Zion, to go forth from their place of rest and strength in order to facilitate the approach of others thereunto, and to remove all hindrances that obstruct either access to, or the diffusion of, the blessings that God will have prepared for all peoples. See Is. xxv. 6. That the energies of many will be employed in preparing *outward* means for access to Zion and for dissemination of its blessings will be, no doubt, a fact, but a *symbolic* fact. It will indicate the appointment by God of abundant spiritual labourers, who, like Paul in his day, shall seek to make straight and easy paths for the feet of them who fear the Lord. Of all who so labour it may well be said, that "the highways are in their hearts"—i.e. that the delight of their souls is in preparing safe, peaceful, and happy ways for the steps of God's people. They not only themselves understand the ways of God, but the joy of their hearts is in bringing others to the knowledge of them; that they too might walk in them and find them ways "of pleasantness and peace."

Passing through [or when traversers of] the valley of Baca they make it a well.] Whether we take the valley of Baca* to mean a valley of tears, or of dark shady trees, it is evidently regarded as a place of sorrow and of *drought;* for if *drought* were not intended there would be no force in the contrast of "springs" or "wells of water" and "rain." The emblem of a dry and thirsty land turned into watersprings is frequently found in Scripture, especially in connexion with the blessings of Israel in the millennial day. "Behold, I will do a new thing; now it shall spring forth; shall ye not know it? I will even make a way in the wilderness, and rivers in the desert. The beast of the field shall honour me, the dragons and the owls: because I give waters in the wilderness and rivers in the desert to give drink to my people, my chosen." Is. xliii. 19. See also Is. xlix. already quoted, and many like passages.

The opening up springs in dry places is in an especial sense emblematical of the ministry of those who are employed, under God, to unfold the consolations of grace in the midst of circumstances of weakness and sorrow. Such was the ministration of Paul—such will be the ministrations of others, by and by, when the dawn of the millennial day shall break on a groaning world, and on a "poor and

---

* *Gesenius* says, "בָּכָא, *weeping, lamentation,*—עֵמֶק הַבָּכָא, *the valley of weeping or lamentation,* name of a valley in Palestine, so called from some reason connected with its name; probably, gloomy and sterile." *Hengstenbergh* remarks, "The old translators with wonderful agreement, give to בכא the sense of *weeping:* and even the Massorah remarks that the א at the end stands instead of ה (בכה meaning to weep). Others on the ground that the form with the א never occurs, consider Baca as the name of a tree which is mentioned in 2 Sam. v 23, 24, (and the parallel passage in Chron.) according to the old translators, *a mulberry tree,* according to Celsus in his sacred botany, a tree something like the balsam shrub. If we adopt this view, we must consider that the reason why the valley of the Baca tree is mentioned, is that the tree has its name from weeping, so that in reality the sense is the same as in the former view—*in the valley of the tear-shrubs.*"

afflicted" remnant (see Zeph. iii. 12) left in the midst of Israel. The diffusion of light and blessing in the millennium will be gradual; and instrumental ministry will be abundantly employed. While man remains in the flesh he will never be independent of those consolations which grace has provided for weakness and sin.

Moreover with blessings the early rain covereth it.] This seems the preferable rendering of this verse.* See *Gesenius*, word עָטָה. This subjoined clause describes the immediate ministration of the hand of God in pouring out blessings from above in addition to those ministrations in which His servants are employed below. To penetrate the dry and hardened ground, and dig for the well in the desert, is *their* employment. Thus we read of the Princes of Israel in the wilderness, digging, at the command of the Lawgiver, with their pilgrim staves, and forthwith sprang up the well and Israel rejoiced and sang, saying, "Spring up, O well, sing ye unto it." See Numbers, xxi. 17. Whenever the servants of God stand with the staff of their pilgrimage in their hand (a condition very contrasted with that of sitting down to eat and drink and rising up to play) and so occupy the place to which obedience to the command of their Lawgiver leads,—when they seek as Princes in Israel to cheer and lead on others through the

---

* "If we were to translate בְּרָכוֹת *pools*, as if it were the plural of בְּרֵכָה, the pointing would be different, viz בְּרֵכוֹת, as in the only case where it occurs in the plural, Cant. v. 4. But בְּרָכָה is *blessing*." De Burgh.

The root of מוֹרֶה, *early or autumnal rain* is יָרָה, the primary signification of which is, *he cast*. Hence it is used in the sense of *scatter*, and thence *to moisten* as by scattering water. Hence מוֹרֶה and יוֹרֶה are used of the *former rain* which falls in Palestine in autumn, preparing the earth to receive the seed. See *Gesenius* on יוֹרֶה In this sense it is used in Joel ii. 23, which I should render thus—"Therefore ye children of Zion be glad and rejoice in Jehovah your God, for He hath given to you the early rain of righteousness (הַמּוֹרֶה לִצְדָקָה)—the rain that is to produce righteousness) and hath shed upon you rain, the early rain and the latter rain (מַלְקוֹשׁ) from לָקֵשׁ, *to be ripe*, used of the later or spring rain which falls in Palestine in the months of March and April before the harvest—see *Gesenius*) *first*," that is before shedding it on other peoples. The reasons given by Hengstenbergh and others for understanding מוֹרֶה, in the sense of "*teacher*" are altogether unsatisfactory. Compare Hosea x. 12 "Sow to yourselves in righteousness, reap in mercy break up the fallow ground: for it is time to seek the Lord, till He come and rain righteousness upon you"—יוֹרֶה צֶדֶק לָכֶם.

wilderness into the rest, they will always find that they have a measure of ability to dig for and to find the wells of God's strengthening and refreshing Truth. God's servants may, through His grace which desires to put honour upon them, be employed in digging for the well in the dry and thirsty valley; but "rain" we dig not for: it is God's gift, coming from above, apart from any instrumentality of ours. In another millennial Psalm we read—"Rain of freenesses (נדבות גשם—that is blessing given in the freeness and fulness in which the willingness of love delights to give it) thou wilt dispense, O God. Thine inheritance, when it was weary, thou hast established." Ps. lxviii. 10.

They go from company to company or *from band to band*—de turmâ ad turmam,* מחיל אל־חיל.] This word חיל is used continually of strength of resources whether of wealth, or of armies, or of defences, such as walls or bulwarks. Here it evidently means hosts or cohorts set in manifold positions of strength, and doubtless refers to those various divisions of the "hosts" or "mighty ones" of the God of Israel, which will be distributed in various positions of strength on the sides of Zion, or on the mountains connected with Zion: for Zion will then be miraculously exalted above all the mountains that will begirt *it* as well as Jerusalem. In the height of Zion will be the glory of the Lord, as on Sinai of old; but there will be various and successive out-posts all occupied by those appointed guardians whose province it will be to watch over Jerusalem and Israel—the whole constituting (the height of Zion included) that which is called in Rev. xx. 9 ἡ παρεμβολη των ἁγιων, "*the encampment or citadel of the saints,*" which is distinguished from Jerusalem itself, which is called "the beloved City." Both will be encompassed in that last great apostasy which is, at the close of the millennium, to conclude the history of this Adamic earth. I understand the word חיל to refer more to the glorious companies that occupy these various positions of strength, than to the positions themselves. Compare Ps. xlviii. 12, which is also millennial. "Walk about Zion and go round about her; tell the towers thereof: mark well her bulwarks (חילה) consider her palaces" &c. See also Ps. cxxii. 7, and the note on first verse of this Psalm in present paper.

---

* "De copiis ad copias—a turmâ ad turmam, turmis penè continuis, modò cum postremis, modò cum secundis, mox cum primis. Sic חיל pro copiis multis, 2 Reg. vi. 15. Ideo exercitus, et copiæ etiam δυναμεις in Novo Test. dicuntur." *Cocceius.*

Each shall appear before God in Zion.] That is, each of those so occupied shall be honoured by being allowed to pass through the series of glorious companies that begirt the Mountain of God, and so to reach the height of Zion and there appear in the presence of the God of Israel. Compare Exodus xxiv. 9. "Then went up Moses, and Aaron, Nadab, and Abihu, and seventy of the elders of Israel: and they saw the God of Israel: and there was under His feet as it were a paved work of a sapphire stone, and as it were the body of heaven in his clearness. And upon the nobles of the children of Israel he laid not his hand: also they saw God, and did eat and drink." In both cases, the thus appearing before God is mentioned as a distinctive honour.

Verses 8, 9, 10, 11, 12.

8 O Jehovah, God of hosts, hear my prayer:
Give ear, O God of Jacob. Selah.

9 Do thou [who art] our shield, behold, O God,
And look upon the face of Thine Anointed.

10 For a day in thy Courts is better than a thousand;
I had rather be at the threshold in the House of my God,
Than dwell in the tents of wickedness.

11 For a sun and a shield is Jehovah, God.
Grace and glory will Jehovah give:
He will not withhold good in respect of them who walk uprightly.

12 O Jehovah of hosts,
Happy is man confiding in Thee!

These words of the returning stranger sufficiently indicate the general condition of Israel after "the Spirit of grace and supplication" has been poured upon them. They will recognise Jehovah as a sun and as a shield, and as the giver of every good and perfect gift—all coming to them through the Anointed. They will walk in paths of integrity and uprightness, and will lead others unto like blessings; so that at last there shall be manifested in the earth the happiness of MAN trusting in God; "*man*" being here again used collectively.

Israel when again graffed back into their own olive tree, are the first who will, as a body, continue to maintain unswervingly the testimonies of God. They will uphold His testimonies and not permit the banner of Truth, as their Gentile predecessors have done, to be trampled in the dust. The present ignorance and arrogancy of Gentile Christians, and the manner in which they magnify themselves above Israel and take from them the privileges and glories which God's faithfulness has given them, is one of the most melancholy evidences of the delusion with which the great enemy of souls has been permitted to darken and deceive.

There can be little question that the seventh verse of this Psalm was present to the mind of St. Paul when he wrote the concluding part of 2 Cor. iii. After adverting to the yet future hour when the veil shall be taken from the now blinded heart of Israel, he speaks in the last verse of the chapter of the transforming effect that the recognition by faith of Christ's glory has, even at present, on the soul; whereby in all who stedfastly by faith behold it, an inwardly transforming change is wrought, progressing from one degree of glory to another; analogous to that advance from one position of glory to another which shall, by and by, in the day of manifestation be granted to those who are here described as passing "from company to company," and so appearing before God in Zion.

There was no one who estimated more than the Apostle Paul the present condition of the earth as groaning under the power of Satan, and how its deliverance must be delayed until Jerusalem "convert and be healed." He was well able to contrast the character of this present age, ruled as it is by spirits of darkness, with the coming day of light, when "truth shall spring out of the earth, and righteousness look down from heaven." But he also knew that the resurrection of Christ into glory had commenced "the acceptable day and the day of salvation," and that the millennial day would, as to this, only *manifest* that which faith could already recognise and rejoice in. Hence, taught by the Holy Ghost, he was in the habit of comforting his own soul and the souls of others by applications of millennial passages. Although the time was not yet come for the heralds of the Gospel to go forth and to be welcomed, as by and by they will be, so as for their feet to be pronounced beautiful on the mountains, yet he knew that the ministration of the rejected and despised Gospel was as honourable and precious in the sight of God as when it shall be sent forth to triumph. He knew that there abounded throughout the earth valleys of Baca, in which as truly *now*, as in the coming age, wells to refresh the weary pilgrim might be opened. He looked upon himself as one of the openers of these wells, and rejoiced in the service; the more because he knew that if it should not be the hour for the full out-pouring of "the rain" of blessing from on high wells in the earth were the more needed. He knew also that although he could not prepare ways for the approach of men to Zion's manifested glory, yet that he could and did "cast up ways" for them whereby they might draw nigh to God and to His governance, and to the light of His truth: and although he could not go from "company to company," so as actually to ascend into the height of Zion's glory, yet his view by faith of Christ's glory, both present and to come, caused him, in the apprehensions of his soul, so to advance from one degree of glory to another, that the experiences of his soul were not less blessed (perhaps more blessed) than that of those who shall, when the time for the accomplishment of this Psalm comes, ascend into the height of Zion and there appear before God, and behold His manifested glory. Millennial Scriptures, therefore, though future in interpretation, have *applications* which faith, rightly instructed, will know how to use for present encouragement, and guidance, and joy of faith.

Postscript.—Note on "Ecce Homo."

BEFORE concluding this number, I wish to repeat the sentiment I have already expressed in my remarks on the recent Judgment respecting the "Essays and Reviews,"* viz., that that Judgment, whilst unrevoked, constitutes a national sin of the deepest dye,—in that it permits the governmentally authorised Teachers of this country to ascribe falsehood to the God of Holiness and Truth, and to declare His Word, which He has said that He honors above all His name, to be, in great part, a lie. Furthermore, the worship of the sacramental bread and of images with other of the abominations of Popery, is known to be introduced into hundreds of Churches, throughout the country, and yet no effectual steps are taken to put down these iniquities On the contrary, they are cherished and encouraged. Statesman vies with statesman in manifesting the readiness with which they sacrifice Truth to expediency: and even our present Government signalise their accession to power by an humble request to Cardinal Manning to declare what further concessions, in the management of the Reformatories &c. of England, would be acceptable to Rome. Truth has been found to be like a sword in a household; it is hated therefore, and the prevalent desire of society seems to be to rid themselves of it.

Can we wonder that under such circumstances the judgments of God should be multiplied in our land? Our flocks are now smitten as well as our herds; and that awful pestilence which never visited our shores until England renounced her national protest against Romish idolatry, is now sweeping away thousands in this city. There may be indeed, through God's great mercy, intermission in the infliction of His judgments, but I dare not hope for their final cessation unless prayer for their removal be connected with specific confession of the great national sin that has been committed in the recognition of Idolatry on the one hand, and of Neology on the other. Idolatry

---

* See page 65.

and Deism are both violations of a *natural* relation, in which man as man stands to God. I cannot therefore but fear that judgment will follow upon judgment, until obduracy shall so harden itself against chastisement as for God to say, as He once did of Israel, that it is useless to chasten any more. Then will ensue that awful hour of judicial blindness which will bring on the great day of final visitation.

It would seem that the condition of society in this country is hopelessly diseased. Is there one of the great organs of public opinion (as they are called) that does not favor either Ritualistic Sacerdotalism or else Latitudinarian Scepticism?* Think too of the reception that has of late been accorded to such a book as "*Ecce Homo.*" That book has been justly characterised by a well-known Christian nobleman, as one "*vomited from the jaws of Hell.*" Truly, it is a book that comes from the pit—a shaft shot from the quiver of Satan, who no doubt rejoices in it the more, because his own personal existence and agency are by it evidently ignored. I cannot see that one distinctive doctrine of Christianity is acknowledged by the author of that awful book. It is true that he has not avowed all that he holds; but unless we are dull as the ass's colt, we can easily discern what he does *not* hold. The writer asks that we should receive his statements as embryo statements, hereafter to be more fully developed. But whether embryo or not, they are manifestly incompatible with the doctrines of Christianity as revealed in Holy Scripture—and that is the question with which we are concerned. There is scarcely a sentiment in the book that might not have been advanced by a Jew or by a Mahomedan: for there are many Jews and many Mahomedans who

---

* The wide circulation too of such publications as "Good Words" (in which Stanley, Kingsley, and other such, are allowed to write) also of "The Christian World" and "The Cotemporary Review," are sad indications of the indifference of the public mind to the growth of Scepticism. Reviews of "Good Words" and of Dean Stanley's writings appeared in "The Record" newspaper, and have since been published separately and may be obtained at the office of "The Record." These reviews should be extensively circulated by all who love the Truth. Remarks on "The Christian World" may be found in an excellent Tract entitled "Broad Churchism,—The Rev. C. H. Spurgeon and The Christian World a Letter from One of the Old School." It is published by Houlston and Wright. Mr. Spurgeon after reading this letter, being convinced as to the real character of the doctrine of "The Christian World," withdrew, with a candour and uprightness that do him honour, the commendation that he had inadvertently bestowed on it.

would allow that Jesus was a great Reformer, and who would moreover, do what this writer has not done, treat the Old Testament with respect and reverence. There are many Jews whose hearts would shrink from language such as this:

"Between the rude clans that had listened to Moses in the Arabian desert and the Jews who in the reign of Tiberius visited the temple courts there was a great gulf. The 'hardheartedness' of the primitive nation had given way under the gradual influence of law and peace and trade and literature! ! ! [Very different this from the teaching of our God and Saviour. See Matt. xxiii. 32 to end.] Laws which in the earlier time the best men had probably found it hard to keep could now serve only as a curb upon the worst. . . . . . . No one who had felt, however feebly, the Christian enthusiasm could fail to find even in Deuteronomy and Isaiah, something narrow, antiquated, and insufficient for his needs." *"Ecce Homo"* p. 184.

So again in page 26.

"A thousand years had passed since the age of David. A new world had come into being. The cities through which Christ walked, the Jerusalem at which he kept the annual feasts, were filled with men compared with whom the contemporaries of David might be called barbarous—men whose characters had been moulded during many centuries by law, by trade and foreign intercourse, by wealth and art, by literature and prophecy. . . . . . Meanwhile the Christ himself meditating upon his mission in the desert, saw difficulties such as other men had no suspicion of. He saw that he must lead a life altogether different from that of David, *that the pictures drawn by the prophets of an ideal Jewish King were coloured by the manners of the times in which they had lived; that those pictures bore indeed a certain resemblance to the truth, but that the work before him was far more complicated and more delicate than the wisest prophet had suspected.*"

The italics are mine. I repeat that there are thousands of Jews who would refuse to write thus of God's holy Prophets—for they believe that what the Prophets wrote was neither "ideal" nor "coloured," nor the fruit of man's wisdom—but that they wrote words dictated by the Holy Ghost.

The author of this book evidently believes that Jesus was a mere man.* His highest notion of Him seems to be that He was one in whom the "enthusiasm of humanity" pre-eminently worked. He throws contempt upon that Gospel and that Apostle whose peculiar

---

* Thus in page 254 he says—"A Whitfield, a Bernard, a Paul,—not to say a Christ—have certainly shown that the most confirmed vice is not beyond the reach of regenerating influences. *Inspired men* like these appearing at intervals have wrought what may be called moral miracles."

province it was to describe Jesus as the Living One (ὁ ζων)—the Eternal Son—the ὁ ων in the bosom of the Father. Thus he writes of the Gospel of John:

"The peculiar mannerism, if the expression may be used, of the Fourth Gospel, has caused it to be suspected of being at least a freely idealised portraiture of Christ. In this book, therefore, it is not referred to, except in confirmation of statements made in the other Gospels, and once or twice where its testimony seemed in itself probable and free from the suspected peculiarities." *Preface to Fifth Edition, p. xii.*

The meaning of this is that the Author, like the Essayists, accepts the testimony of the New Testament so far as it accords with his own opinions, and no further. It is not to him, the testimony of the Holy Ghost, revealing, on the authority of God, things about which we have no right nor any power to form independent conceptions of our own—among which things, the nature of the Person of the Eternal Son stands pre-eminent: for " no one knoweth the Son but the Father." Nothing therefore can exceed the unholy audaciousness of the book throughout, reminding us forcibly of the words that

"fools rush in
Where angels fear to tread."

The doctrine of the Trinity—of the Incarnation—and the Propitiatory Sacrifice of the Cross are evidently to the Author, falsehoods. See for example his comment upon the blessed words uttered by John the Baptist: " Behold the Lamb of God that taketh away the sin of the world!"

"When we remember that the Baptist's mind was doubtless full of imagery drawn from the Old Testament, and that the conception of a lamb of God makes the subject of one of the most striking of the Psalms, we shall perceive what he meant to convey by this phrase. The Psalmist describes himself as one of Jehovah's flock, safe under his care, absolved from all anxieties by the sense of his protection, and gaining from this confidence of safety the leisure to enjoy without satiety all the simple pleasures which make up life, the freshness of the meadow, the coolness of the stream. It is the most complete picture of happiness that ever was or can be drawn. It represents that state of mind for which all alike sigh, and the want of which makes life a failure to most; it represents that *Heaven* which is everywhere if we could but enter it, and yet almost nowhere because so few of us can. The two or three who win it may be called victors in life's conflict; to them belongs the *regnum et diadema tutum*. They may pass obscure lives in humble dwellings, or like Fra Angelico in a narrow monastic cell, but they are vexed with no flap of unclean wings about the ceiling. From some such humble dwelling Christ came to receive the Prophet's baptism. The Baptist was no lamb of God. He was a wrestler with life, one to whom peace of mind does not come easily, but only after a long struggle His restlessness had driven him into the desert [the Scripture says God sent him into the desert, there to prepare the way of Christ] where he had contended for years with thoughts he could not master, and from whence he had uttered his startling alarum to the nation. He was among the dogs rather than among the lambs of the Shepherd. He recognised the superiority of him whose confidence had never been disturbed, whose steadfast peace no agitations of life had ever ruffled. He did obeisance to the royalty of inward happiness. One who was to earn the name of Saviour of mankind had need of this gift more than of any other. He who was to reconcile God and man needed to be first at peace himself. The door of heaven, so to speak, can be opened only from within Such then was the impression of Christ's character which the Baptist formed." pp. 6, 7.

These words are sufficient to stamp the character of the whole book in the judgment of any one who has the slightest apprehension of the glory of the Person of his God and Saviour, or of the one only way of salvation found in "the fountain opened for sin and for all uncleanness" in the atoning blood of the Son of God—"led as a lamb to the slaughter" It is very evident that any one who can write thus, no more accepts the doctrines of Scripture respecting Christ than did Julian the Apostate, or any other like rejecter of Jesus—the only difference being that Julian assails openly, whilst the writer of "Ecce Homo" betrays with a kiss. According to this author, when St. Paul says that he gloried only "in the Cross," it was a glorying in "the greatness and self-sacrifice" there exhibited.

"Men saw him (Jesus) arrested and put to death with torture, refusing steadfastly to use in his own behalf the power he conceived he held for the benefit of others. It was the combination of greatness and self-sacrifice which won their hearts, the mighty powers held under a mighty control, the unspeakable condescension, the *Cross* of *Christ.* By this and by nothing else, the enthusiasm of a Paul was kindled. The statement rests upon no hypothesis or conjecture, his Epistles bear testimony to it throughout. The trait in Christ which filled his whole mind was his condescension. The charm of that condescension lay in its being voluntary. The cross of Christ, of which Paul so often speaks as the only thing he found worth glorying in, as that in comparison with which everything in the world was as *dung*, was the voluntary submission to death of one who had the power to escape death." Page 48.

So too when he speaks of the words—"Except ye eat the flesh and drink the blood of the Son of Man, ye have no life in you," he comments thus:

"As to the metaphor itself, if it seems at first violent and unnatural, we are to observe that on the subject of the personal devotion required by Christ from his followers, his language was often of this vehement kind, and that his first followers in describing their relation to him in like manner overleap the bounds of ordinary figurative language. Christ, in a passage to which allusion has already been made, demanded of his followers that they should *hate* their father and mother for his sake, and St. Paul in many passages declares that Christ is his life and his very self. It is precisely this intense personal devotion, this habitual feeding on the character of Christ, so that the essential nature of the Master seems to pass into and become the essential nature of the servant—loyalty carried to the point of self-annihilation—that is expressed by the words, eating the flesh and drinking the blood of Christ." p. 176.

Of the Supper of the Lord he writes as follows:

"A common meal is the most natural and universal way of expressing, maintaining, and as it were ratifying relations of friendship. The spirit of antiquity regarded the meals of human beings as having the nature of sacred rites. If therefore it sounds degrading to compare the Christian Communion to a club-dinner, this is not owing to any essential difference between the two things, but to the fact that the moderns connect less dignified associations with meals than the ancients did, and that most clubs have a far less serious object than the Christian Society. The Christian Communion *is* a club-dinner; but the club is the New Jerusalem; God and Christ are members of it; death makes no vacancy in its lists, but at its banquet-table the perfected spirits of just men, with an innumerable company of angels, sit down beside those who have not yet surrendered their bodies to the grave." p. 173.

It is most painful to transcribe words like these. Irreverence marks the whole book throughout. It is very evident that the Author has never had within his bosom one true solemn thought either of sin, or of God, or of redemption. Indeed it is very manifest that he repudiates the thought of redemption: else how could he talk of angels who have never sinned and need no redemption, sitting down at the Table which is specifically appointed to show forth redemption? The irreverence of the passage is quite equalled by its absurdity, for the Lord's Table is designed for the Church militant whilst they have yet to "judge themselves," because of the sin within and around them, and therefore is not that around which the "spirits of the just" are gathered; nor are the spirits of the just, although freed from all sin and corruption, as yet made perfect in resurrection. Every page of this book shows that the Author repudiates the fifty-third of Isaiah, the sixth of John, the fifth of the Romans, the tenth of the Hebrews,—in a word, every part of Scripture that enforces the great truth that "without shedding of blood is no remission." He scorns the one way of salvation through the sufferings of a vicarious wrath-bearer; and therefore, if he repent not, he will remain to be numbered among the adversaries who will meet the wrath of the living God because they have despised redemption.

Nor can it be said that the writer admits even the personal sinlessness of Jesus. He does not own Him as " the Lamb without blemish and without spot;" for he could not, in that case have written of the Holy One that He " was seized with an intolerable sense of shame," and that " in his burning embarrassment and confusion he stooped down so as to hide his face and began writing with his finger on the ground." (p 104.) Could " shame," " embarrassment," and " confusion," (no matter what the supposed cause)—could such things, on any ground whatsoever be attributed to Immanuel ? Could they be attributed to any one who was not personally a sinner ? Was He, who was the searcher of hearts and knew well what was in man, so ignorant of man's condition as to be surprized into " shame," " confusion," and " embarrassment," by a sudden development of man's evil ? But I forbear to comment. I content myself with subjoining the passage. Let it speak for itself.*

Nor is the Author really satisfied with the results of the Legislation of Christ. He thinks we now stand on a higher grade than that on which Christ's own disciples and Apostles stood that in us " the

---

* He was standing, it would seem, in the centre of a circle, when the crime was narrated, how the adultery had been detected *in the very act*. The shame of the deed itself, and the brazen hardness of the prosecutors, the legality that had no justice and did not pretend to have mercy, the religious malice that could make its advantage out of the fall and ruin and ignominious death of a fellow creature— all this was eagerly and rudely thrust before his mind at once. The effect upon him was such as might have been produced upon many since, but perhaps upon scarcely any man that ever lived before. He was seized with an intolerable sense of shame. He could not meet the eye of the crowd, or of the accusers, and perhaps at that moment least of all of the woman. Standing as he did in the midst of an eager multitude that did not in the least appreciate his feelings, he could not escape. In his burning embarrassment and confusion he stooped down so as to hide his face, and began writing with his finger on the ground. His tormentors continued their clamour, until he raised his head for a moment and said, ' He that is without sin among you let him first cast a stone at her,' and then instantly returned to his former attitude. They had a glimpse perhaps of the glowing blush upon his face, and awoke suddenly with astonishment to a new sense of their condition and their conduct. The older men naturally felt it first and slunk away, the younger followed their example. The crowd dissolved and left Christ alone with the woman. Not till then could he bear to stand upright: and when he had lifted himself up, consistently with his principle, he dismissed the woman, as having no commission to interfere with the office of the civil judge." p. 104.

enthusiasm of humanity" has more worked, and caused us to develop a higher and a better way. These are his words:—

"No man who loves his kind can in these days rest content with waiting as a servant upon human misery, when it is in so many cases possible to anticipate and avert it. Prevention is better than cure, and it is now clear to all that a large part of human suffering is preventible by improved social arrangements Charity will now, if it be genuine, fix upon this enterprise as greater, more widely and permanently beneficial, and therefore more Christian than the other . . . . The truth is, that though the morality of Christ is theoretically perfect and not subject, as the Mosaic morality was, to a further development, the practical morality of the first Christians [who, be it observed, were the Apostles of our God and Saviour, and those whom they taught and guided] has in a great degree been rendered obsolete by the later experience of mankind, which has taught us to hope more and undertake more for the happiness of our fellow-creatures. The command to care for the sick and suffering remains as divine as ever and as necessary as ever to be obeyed, but it has become, like the Decalogue, an elementary part of morality, early learnt, and not sufficient to satisfy the Christian enthusiasm. As the early Christians learnt that it was not enough to do no harm and that they were bound to give meat to the hungry and clothing to the naked, we have learnt that a still further obligation lies upon us to prevent, if possible, the pains of hunger and nakedness from being ever felt. This last duty was as far beyond the conception of the earliest Christians as the second was beyond the conception* of those for whom Moses legislated." p. 196.

But I will not multiply these quotations. I am not sure that I have done right in quoting so much as I have already done from a book whose sentiments and expressions are so marked by irreverence and impiety. They who are not convinced of the evil character of the book from the extracts already given will be, I fear, convinced by nothing. Lord Shaftesbury may well marvel that some even of the Evangelical Ministers of our Land, profess themselves unable to detect the poison We may indeed stand aghast at such a confession. It must be taken, I suppose, as a proof that the "strong delusion" of which Scripture warns us, is spreading more widely and more potently than we are accustomed to think.

If such books as "Ecce Homo" are welcomed in our Land, it is no wonder that the degradation of Holy Scripture involved in the

---

* The early Christians apprehended that great truth of which the writer of "Ecce Homo" has no conception, that the whole world lieth in wickedness; morally distant from and rebellious against God, and therefore that it cannot know relief from suffering, until the times of restitution shall come, and the morning without clouds arise upon a groaning, but delivered earth.

Judgment pronounced by the Committee of the Privy Council, should be acquiesced in and approved. All these modes of thought belong to the same school. Coleridge, Bunsen, Stanley, the Essayists, Jowitt, and the Author of "Ecce Homo," all concur in making an inward principle or power, supposed to be inherent in man, the rule of his conduct, and denounce the thought of subjection to any *external*, especially any *written* Rule. In other words, they take from Holy Scripture the place assigned to it by God, and substitute for it the will of man's unregenerate heart. Whether they term this supposed inherent power, "the inner consciousness," or "the inward universal Light," or the "verifying faculty," or the "enthusiasm of humanity," it all comes to the same thing. There is substituted for that one Test of truth which God has given us in His written Word, the guidance of man's wilful, erring, rebellious heart.* *There,* "the mind of the flesh," $\phi\rho o\nu\eta\mu\alpha\ \sigma\alpha\rho\kappa o\varsigma$,—"that which is not subject to the Law of God, neither indeed can be," *rules*—leading in paths of everlasting death. It is able to lead into no other: nor can any be raised above its power except by casting themselves on the love and grace of God, as revealed in the atoning blood of the Lamb by Him provided. There, and there only, are found reconciliation, peace, and deliverance from the wrath to come. The gift of reconciliation is accompanied by the gift of life—heavenly life in Christ glorified. The "new man" created in us here, is the result of life being thus given in our new risen Head; and in order that that "new man" may be succoured, strengthened and sustained, the Holy Ghost is sent abidingly to dwell in all believers. Yet even the Holy Ghost, though He be God, acts in conformity with His own ordinances He guides

---

* Thus on page 202 we find the Author of "Ecce Homo" attributing to the "Enthusiasm of Humanity" the same place that the Essayists assign to their "verifying faculty." His words are these —"The most devoted Christians . . . . think they must needs be most Christian when they stick most closely to the New Testament, and that what is utterly absent from the New Testament cannot possibly be an important part of Christianity. A great mistake, arising from a wide-spread paralysis of true Christian feeling in the modern Church! The New Testament is not the Christian law; the precepts of Apostles, the special commands of Christ, are not the Christian law. To make them such is to throw the Church back into that legal system from which Christ would have set it free. The Christian law is the spirit of Christ, that Enthusiasm of Humanity which he declared to be the source from which all right action flows. What it dictates, and that alone, is law for the Christian."

not independently of the written Word, but by means thereof: appointing that every thought, every doctrine, should be tested thereby. Thus, and thus alone, is secured liberty from the tyranny of man, who is ever ready to impose the yoke of his own opinions on his fellow.

All who give heed to the message of reconciliation preached through the atoning blood of Jesus and cast themselves on the efficacy of that one finished sacrifice, receive of these blessings. But they who scorn this one way which God's grace and love have opened, will be left to eat the fruit of their own devices. They will be numbered among the despisers who will "wonder and perish."

"Ecce Homo" sufficiently shows us what is the nature of the conclusions to which "the Enthusiasm of Humanity," or "the verifying faculty" leads. It leads to the unholy, presumptuous, and forbidden attempt to form for ourselves, apart from revelation, an estimate of Christ. That attempt is in itself sin It leads to the forming an estimate of Christ which is altogether destructive of the great distinctive characteristic of Immanuel; for it speaks of Him as if He was of earth merely. It allows not that He was from above—that He was God manifest in the flesh. It sees not in the Babe born at Bethlehem One whose "goings forth were of old from everlasting." It leads too to a total rejection of all that Scripture reveals respecting the condition in which sin has placed us for it teaches that we are able to be so attracted by the presentation of perfect holiness as to love and delight in it; whereas it only needs that perfect holiness should be presented to us in its fulness, and we instantly show that we have not only no power to love or delight in or hold communion with it, but that we have in us enmity against and hatred of it. Hence our guilt—hence our need of that refuge which is provided for us, not in the living holiness, but in the expiatory death of the Holy One. Christ in death—Christ made a sacrifice—Christ stricken judicially, is a sinner's hope. But it is a hope that "Ecce Homo" repudiates and abhors. Nor is the personal existence of the Tempter recognised. In a word, the light that the revelation of God has shed on the past, the present, and the future, is utterly set aside, and other light substituted in its room. Can such substituted light have any other origin than the pit? No. It comes from the pit and to the pit it leads.

The following Extract is from an excellent Speech of Lord Shaftesbury at the Annual Meeting of "the Pastoral Aid Society," in May, 1866.

"The other day a great Dissenting minister put to me in conversation this question, 'From which do you think there is the greatest danger, the progress of ritualism or the progress of neology?' I replied, 'To the Church of England as an Established Church I apprehend there is the greatest danger from ritualism, but as regards the Church of Christ and the cause of religion in the Church of England I apprehend there is the greatest danger from neology.' Neology is now growing up in such a way that even from a large proportion of the pulpits of the Church of England we no longer hear, as we used to hear, sound doctrinal, dogmatic, practical teaching. Many of our ministers if you remonstrate with them on this will tell you that they feel it and regret it, but that their congregations would not bear now what was borne formerly. This is, I believe, true, and a more awful fact, a more dangerous state of mind or of moral existence I cannot conceive to exist in any nation under heaven. See how men are deluded, how they are misled by those who should be their guides. I confess I was perfectly aghast the other day when speaking to a clergyman and asking him his opinion of that most pestilential book ever vomited, I think, from the jaws of hell, I mean *Ecce Homo*—when I asked him what was his opinion of that book, he deliberately told me—he being a great professor of Evangelical religion—that that book had excited his deepest admiration, and that he did not hesitate to say that it had conferred great benefit upon his own soul. Why, if we are to have this miserable and uncertain teaching, if the guides to whom we look for light and help can approve such works as that, how can we expect that the mass of the people, the mass even of the educated middle classes who are supposed to think for themselves, will not be led to wander out of the right way? Look at the policy on which the neological party proceed. They are praising a sensuous religion. They hope to get rid of doctrines by sentiments. They hope to get rid of creeds by feelings. Take up the writings of the most gifted and fascinating among them, and you will find them conceding almost all that you desire. You will find that they concede to you the incarnation and divinity of our Lord, and almost everything that you could wish in the history of our Lord and the history of our religion. But when you come to the great fundamental work, when you come to the great turning-point of our religion, without which there is nothing in it worth having, when you come to the atonement which was made on the cross, when you speak of the atoning blood of our blessed Lord, there they stop short, and they refuse it to you altogether While this Society has determined to 'know nothing but Jesus Christ, and Him crucified,' the Neologists and all who belong to that school will tell you that you may claim everything else but *that* you must not claim. Now this is the way that we are going on. Through a false and foolish policy many persons are surrendering a little to ritualism on the one side, and to neology on the other, saying, 'We cannot be altogether behind the generation in which we live; we cannot be entirely opposed to the society in which we move' A great many persons of good intentions, but, I am sorry to say, weak minds, fall in with that miserable idolatry which has now begun to pervade educated society —the idolatry of humanitarianism and intellect. Men must have something to adore, and many persons, having ceased to adore Christ, will adore man instead. They will fall on their knees and worship intellect; nay, they will even worship themselves, their own ignorance, their own vices, their own abominations, rather than worship that God who has revealed Himself in his blessed Word. This is what is creeping over the laity in the present day with regard to dogmatic statements of truth. Let me allude for a moment to those two Bills which have been recently brought into the House of Commons for the regulation of the Universities. The promoters of those Bills would be offended if you charged them with a desire to extinguish religion; but when you tell them that their object is to shut out the dogmatic and specific teaching of religion, they will not deny the imputation, but will tell you they think that young men ought to be educated in the Universities only in the general principles of religion,—which may mean everything or nothing, —and that doctrinal and dogmatic teaching should be reserved for their homes, for their fathers and their mothers. That is the way that we are going on; that is the way that delusions are being imposed upon us; that is the way the young are being flattered in their intellectual pride, and made to think that they are wiser than their ancestors, and wiser than those who first taught them."

May God, in His mercy, grant that many hearts may be opened to give heed to these words of truth, before it is too late.

Old Truths.

OLD TRUTHS, by Rev. JOHN COX. The Third number of the Third Year's issue of this Periodical is now published. The first eight numbers, neatly bound in one volume, with an Index, may be had of the Editor and Publishers, or may be obtained through any Bookseller, price 5s. The aim of the Editor has been to set forth Prophetic Truths, based upon a literal interpretation of Scripture, as well as the good "Old Truths" taught by the Reformers and Puritans. The four numbers for 1866 will be published and sent, post free, on the First of March, June, September, and December, to any person who may forward a subscription of Two Shillings to the Editor, JOHN COX, Ipswich.

Works by BENJAMIN WILLS NEWTON

ROMANS VII CONSIDERED. Demy 12mo., cloth boards, 1s. 6d., neat Wrapper, 1s.

NOTES EXPOSITORY OF THE GREEK OF THE FIRST CHAPTER OF the Romans, with Remarks on the Force of certain Synonyms, &c. Crown 8vo., cloth, 2s. 6d.

THE FIRST AND SECOND CHAPTERS OF THE EPISTLE TO THE Romans Considered, with Remarks on certain Doctrines recently promulgated by the Savilian Professor of Geometry, and the Regius Professor of Greek in the University of Oxford. 1s. 6d.

NO CONDEMNATION TO THEM WHO ARE IN CHRIST JESUS. A Tract Compiled from Notes of a Lecture. 12mo., price 2d.

JUSTIFICATION. Being the Substance of a Discourse recently delivered in London. 12mo., 2d.

ETERNAL RECONCILIATION. 12mo., price 2d.

REGENERATION IN ITS CONNEXION WITH THE CROSS. 12mo, price 2d.

GREAT PROTESTANT TRUTHS, being two of the "Leicestershire Lectures":
Priesthood and Sacrifice Essential to Worship. Price 2d.
The True Unity of the Church of God in Time and Eternity. Price 2d.

DOCTRINES OF POPERY AS DETERMINED BY THE COUNCIL OF Trent Considered. No. I. On Holy Scripture and Tradition, price 8d. No. II. On Original Sin, price 4d.

THE BLOOD THAT SAVETH. Four for 1d., or 2s. per 100. Large Type Edition, 8 pp., ½d.

ACCEPTANCE WITH GOD. Four for 1d., or 2s. per 100.

DOCTRINE OF SCRIPTURE RESPECTING BAPTISM, Part I, price 6d. Part II, price 8d. Bound in one, cloth, 1s. 6d.

CHRIST, OUR SUFFERING SURETY. Hebrews ii. 10, and v. 7. Price 6d.

ANCIENT TRUTHS RESPECTING THE DEITY AND TRUE HUMANITY of the Lord Jesus. Price 3d.

NOTE ON 1 PETER ii. 24. Price 2d.

THOUGHTS ON THE APOCALYPSE. Second Edition, revised, demy 8vo., cloth, 8s. 6d.

THOUGHTS ON PARTS OF LEVITICUS. CONTENTS: The Burnt Offering—The Meat Offering—The Peace Offering—The Sin Offering—The Trespass Offering. Cloth, 3s. 6d.
    Vol. I. PART I THE CONSECRATION OF THE PRIESTS 10d.
           II THINGS CLEAN AND UNCLEAN 6d.
           III THE LEPROSY. 4d.

DAVID, KING OF ISRAEL. 12mo., cloth boards. Price 2s.

THE RECHABITES. Jeremiah xxxv. A Tract compiled from Notes of a Lecture. 12mo., 2d.

AIDS TO PROPHETIC ENQUIRY.

AIDS TO PROPHETIC ENQUIRY. First Series. Second Edition, 12mo., cloth lettered, price 3s. 6d.

BABYLON. ITS REVIVAL AND FINAL DESOLATION, being the Second Series of *Aids to Prophetic Enquiry.* Second Edition, 12mo., cloth lettered, price 3s.

PROSPECTS OF THE TEN KINGDOMS OF THE ROMAN EMPIRE Considered, being the Third Series of *Aids to Prophetic Enquiry.* 12mo., cloth lettered, 4s.

OCCASIONAL PAPERS ON SCRIPTURAL SUBJECTS. No. I. Price 2s.
  I. On Justification through the Blood and Righteousness of a Substitute
  II. On Song of Solomon, Chap. i, from verse 5 to 11 inclusive
  III. On Ephesians iii. 15
  IV. On the Omission of the Greek Article before Definite Words
  V. On the Duty of giving heed to the Predictions of Scripture respecting Events that intervene between the Departure and Return of the Lord
  VI. On Isaiah xviii.—Introductory Observations.
  VII. Notes on Isaiah xviii.
  VIII. Examination of a Work entitled "Christ's Second Coming—Will it be Pre-Millennial?" By Rev. David Brown, D.D.
  IX. Abraham's History in Genesis xii.
  X. Notes on the words λογιζομαι, ελλογεω, λογιζομαι ΕΙΣ
  XI. Falsification of the meaning of "Justify" at the Council of Trent
  XII. Notes on 2 Peter, i.

OCCASIONAL PAPERS ON SCRIPTURAL SUBJECTS. No. II. Price 2s. 6d.
  I. On Sanctification by the Blood of Jesus
  II. Sanctification through the Spirit
  III. On the Song of Solomon, from Chapter ii. 8, to verse 17 inclusive
  IV. Abraham and Lot, Genesis XIII.
  V. The Second Advent of our Lord not Secret but in manifested glory
  VI. Examination of a Work entitled "Christ's Second Coming—Will it be Pre-Millennial?" By Rev. David Brown, D.D.
  VII. Israel in the Days of Haggai and Zechariah
  VIII. Note on the Prophecy of Haggai
  IX. On the Force of the Present Tense in Greek and Hebrew
  X. Notes on 1 Corinthians Chapter i.
  XI. Notes on Zechariah xiv.
  XII. On the First Psalm
  XIII. Notes on First Psalm
  XIV. On the Second Psalm.
  XV. Notes on Second Psalm

OCCASIONAL PAPERS ON SCRIPTURAL SUBJECTS. No. III. Price 3s. 6d.
  I. Jesus washing His Disciples' Feet
  II. Jacob's History in Genesis xxviii.
  III. On the Song of Solomon, from verse 7 to 16 of Chapter iv.
  IV. Examination of a Work entitled "Christ's Second Coming—Will it be Pre-Millennial?" By Rev. David Brown, D.D.
  V. Note on Dr. Brown's Interpretation of 2 Thes. ii. 8.
  VI. Note on Matthew xxiv. 34
  VII. Remarks on "Mosaic Cosmogony," being the Fifth of "Essays and Reviews"
  VIII. Note on the Locality of Hades
  IX. European Prospects
  X. Note on the Spread of Neology in England
  XI. Uses of ευλογεω in the New Testament, especially with reference to 1 Corinthians x. 16
  XII. Notes on the Greek of Ephesians i., from verse 1 to verse 11 inclusive

THE SECOND ADVENT OF OUR LORD NOT SECRET BUT IN Manifested Glory. Price 2d.

DUTY OF GIVING HEED TO THE PREDICTIONS OF SCRIPTURE respecting Events that are to precede the Return of our Lord. Price 2d.

ON JUSTIFICATION THROUGH THE BLOOD AND RIGHTEOUSNESS OF a Substitute. Price 2d.

ON SANCTIFICATION BY THE BLOOD OF JESUS. Price 1½d.

THE ANTICHRIST FUTURE. A Tract written with relation to certain Lectures recently delivered at the Town Hall, Worthing. 2d.

THE 1260 DAYS OF ANTICHRIST'S REIGN FUTURE. A Second Tract with relation to Lectures recently delivered at Worthing. 3d.

THE PROPHECY OF THE LORD JESUS, AS CONTAINED IN MATT. xxiv. xxv. A Lecture with Notes and Appendix. Price 8d.

ON THE PROPHECIES RESPECTING THE JEWS AND JERUSALEM, in the form of a Catechism. 2nd Edition, revised, 12mo., 1½d.

JERUSALEM, ITS FUTURE HISTORY. 2nd Edition, price 4d.

PROPHETIC PSALMS IN THEIR RELATION TO ISRAEL, BRIEFLY Considered. Price 6d.

ISRAEL'S PROSPECTS IN THE MILLENNIUM. Being the Substance of a Lecture. Price 4d.

EUROPE AND THE EAST:—
    Part I. FINAL PREDOMINANCE OF RUSSIA INCONSISTENT WITH THE DECLARATIONS OF SCRIPTURE. Price 6d.
    II. ENGLAND'S FUTURE COURSE IN THE EAST. Price 6d.

IN A DISPENSATION OF FAILURE, CATHOLICITY THE SURE TOKEN of Apostasy. Price 2d.

THOUGHTS ON THE HISTORY OF PROFESSING CHRISTIANITY, AS given in the Parables of Matt. xiii. 12mo., price 4d.

THE DAY OF THE LORD. A Lecture on Zechariah xiv. 2d.

ORDER OF EVENTS CONNECTED WITH THE APPEARING OF CHRIST and His Millennial Reign. 12mo., price 6d.

SCRIPTURAL PROOF OF THE DOCTRINE OF THE FIRST RESURRECTION. 12mo., price 4d.

CONVERSATION ON REVELATION XVII. 12mo., 2d.

WHAT IS THE EPHAH OF ZECHARIAH V.? or the Exhibition of 1851 Considered. Second Edition. Price 3d.

THE WORLD TO COME. Price 1½d.

AN EXAMINATION OF THE PROPHETIC SYSTEM OF MR. ELLIOTT and Dr. Cumming. Price 4d.

A LETTER TO THE MINISTER OF SILVER STREET CHAPEL, TAUNTON, in reply to his Lecture against the Premillennial Advent of the Lord. Third Edition. 3d.

LONDON: HOULSTON AND WRIGHT, 65, PATERNOSTER ROW.

CPSIA information can be obtained at www.ICGtesting.com
Printed in the USA
LVOW070122151012
302798LV00017B/55/P